Now That I've Told You All That

WOULD YOU?

Marry a Man Like Me?

Or at Least Give Me a Second Date?

LAWRENCE,
NOW YOU'LL KNOW HOW YOU
INFLUENCED MY LIFE.
Thanks!

BY

Winston G. Williams

Now That I've Told You All That
Would You?
Marry a Man Like Me?
Or at Least Give Me a Second Date?

Silver Box Publishing
P.O. Box 685061
Austin, Texas 78768

First Printing 2005

ISBN 0-9749621-0-4

Printed in the United States of America
at Morgan Printing in Austin, Texas

DEDICATION

This book is dedicated first to my father. In taking this journey, I appreciate what you did for us as a family more than I ever have. You may not know it, but I feel like our relationship has become more of what I always wanted it to be. Not because you changed, but because I finally grew up. And to my mother; I didn't realize how rich our relationship was until I finished the book, and now our conversations help me understand more about life. To my brother Darrell, thank you for your continued support and advice. Our seven o'clock Sunday morning talks have been invaluable. And yes, I owe you a lot of therapy fees. One day I'll pay up. To Leonard, what can I say man? I wish I could bottle up your friendship and sell it. But I'll settle for being rich just from having you as a friend. You are a great example of what a true friend is. James, you brought me through. You challenged me, understood me, and just let me be me. Sorry for the choices I made. I'll probably never be able to make it up to you on this side of heaven, but I'll consider you a great friend for the rest of my life. To Dina, you have proven yourself. Thank you for allowing me to test this concept on you. I know it was difficult for both of us, but your willingness to be adventurous helped me continue on this journey. To Anoa, thank you for pushing the project forward. You have incredible vision. I couldn't have gotten this far without you. To each of my friends, you have no idea how valuable you are to me because I tend to keep my feelings bottled up inside. But know that you are important to me.

While writing this book, I presented a scenario to several people. I told them that if I brought the woman I wanted to spend the rest of my life with to each of them, I would want them to tell her the truth of who they know me to be. To those of you who responded to my request, Darryll, Darrell, Kiata, Linda, Nicole, Robert, (another) Robert, Robin, Ron, and Windsor, I thank each of you. I have included some of your responses in this book.

And finally, to God, I don't know what You are doing in my life and I've always told You I didn't want to take this path. But You insisted, so here I am. Thank You? Well . . . we'll see.

DISCLAIMER

This is a (almost totally) true story, told as I experienced and perceived it. Most of the names were changed to protect the innocent. The guilty? That's on them. I initially wrote this book so that I could understand myself before I got married and started having children. Later I decided to share it and the concept with others. The stories and recollections are not meant to hurt anyone. They just capture and convey part of my journey through life.

PROLOGUE

I pulled into my driveway, emotionally and physically tired. I didn't press the garage door opener. I barely had enough strength to turn the steering wheel. I sat in the car knowing I couldn't stay there all night. I needed to find the energy to go into my house. The files I brought home from work sat in the passenger seat and seemed to whisper my name but I blocked them out. No work would be done tonight. I dragged myself out of the car and to the front door. I remembered it was cleaning day. I loved the smell of my house after the cleaning crew came. I loved the way the carpet looked after they vacuumed and how the ceramic tile shined. On cleaning days, I didn't mind paying the mortgage.

I peered through the oval-shaped glass of my front door and noticed the cleaning crew had done as I requested. They left the entryway light on to let me know they had come and gone. I could see the shine of the tile. It gave me strength. I opened the door, entered my house and took off my burgundy monk-strap Ferragamo shoes. I felt the cold tile beneath my feet. The phone rang.

I hurried to the kitchen, threw my keys on the counter and answered before the third ring. Habit. "Hello." I wanted to hit myself for not screening the call.

"Winston?" It was my friend Sharon.

"Hey, what's up?" My words trailed off into silence. I didn't want to talk to Sharon, especially after what had just happened.

"You know what's up." Sharon wanted to get the conversation to its destination without any pleasantries. "I just got off the phone with Zanovia."

Where could I run? Where could I hide from this conversation? I was silent.

Sharon is a talker. She will talk to a lamppost if necessary. "The girl is crying her eyes out. Now what did you do?"

I hopped up onto the kitchen counter and buried my chin in my chest. There was nowhere to run. Nowhere to hide. I had to have this conversation with the person who helped get Zanovia and me together.

"Negro, you hear me talking to you!" Sharon loved me, I knew that, but I had been through several of her friends and she was just about through with me. I needed to say something. I lay on the kitchen counter, feet and all, and stared at the ceiling before I spoke.

"Sharon, you have every right to be upset with me." A weak introduction, but I was being honest.

"But I thought you guys were getting along. This was the best relationship you've ever had. Winston, you know I love you, but you have to make me understand." I could tell she was holding back her anger. She was caught in the middle.

The ceiling wasn't enough to distract me from this conversation. I needed something to do while I talked to Sharon. I stood up, breathing heavily, not speaking. Sharon waited, which must have been killing her. I looked over the kitchen counter into the family room that didn't have a family. Just me. "Sharon, it's just so messed up," I said as I walked around the counter and into the family room. I looked for the television remote. "Zanovia and I had a conversation tonight. There are a lot of things going on in my life right now. I asked her to wait for me and she said she wouldn't." I found the remote and turned on the television pressing the mute button as soon as the power came on. I didn't want Sharon to feel disrespected.

"But what the hell you need to wait on?" Sharon's anger started to seep out.

I flipped channels wondering if I should tell Sharon more. Maybe I owed it to her, but I thought she understood the golden rule of matchmaking: *if you make the introduction, walk away and take no responsibility for what happens.* That's always been the rule, but few people could stick to it. That's why I liked meeting women on my own. The Weather Channel.

I stopped changing channels. It looked like it was about to storm. "Sharon, I wanted to marry Zanovia." I was being honest.

"And?" she asked.

"I prayed to God." Still being honest.

"And?" Her pressure retreated.

"He said no." The truth.

"Now Winston you know that ain't right." The anger she had been holding in was gone.

"But Sharon, it's the truth. I heard Him say 'no' just as plain as I can hear your voice." The honesty felt good. I continued. "But I decided not to listen to Him. I decided to ask her anyway and that's when all hell broke loose."

I heard Sharon exhale, not because of what I had said, but because she was smoking. "Winston, I know you and God have this strange relationship that I don't even understand, but it ain't fair for you to fall back on that now. Something else is going on."

Wind. Clouds. Rain. Storms. Where am I on the map? There, right down there in the heart of Texas. Austin. What's the weather going to be like around here? "Sharon look, I'm telling you the truth. That's what happened. I needed Zanovia to wait until I figured out why God told me not to marry her and she said she wouldn't wait." Even though God had told me 'no,' there was more to the story and Sharon was no fool.

"Well, I'm not gonna try and get in between you and God, but I will say this. In all the relationships you've been through, *you* are the common denominator," Sharon said without anger but with conviction. "And I'm gonna leave it alone. But you think about that."

"I'll think about it. Holla at ya later." I hung up. She was right. I was the common denominator. Standing in front of my television set with the phone in one hand and the remote in the other, those words kicked me in the seat of my navy blue slacks. So hard my tie flipped up and smacked my forehead. So hard my socked feet lifted off the ceramic tile. Those words sent me on a path of self-discovery that I had been reluctant to travel. That was August 6, 1997.

I Have to Go Back
I Have No Choice
But God, I Really Don't Want To

CHAPTER ONE

Dear God. How did I get here?

I found myself sitting at the corner of Commerce and whatever the name of that street is. Strange. I grew up in this li'l ole town and I don't even know the name of the cross street. That's typical of how my brain works. Being places and not even knowing where I am, no matter how often I've been in the very same place. Details. Sometimes I don't notice the details of where I am. But now I have to make a change. Details. What is the name of that street? I look for a street sign, but it isn't there. I don't want to make the left turn. That turn will take me to the very place I never wanted to go. That turn will put me on the street with the forgotten name and lead me to the place I never wanted to return to.

It is October 11, 1999. The trees are still green in autumn. Not like when I was a child. Back then we had seasons. Not anymore. One season blends into the next. The trees should be turning brilliant colors, even here in Texas, but they are not. The leaves should be blowing in the season's whirlwinds, but they are not. My car is facing south on Commerce Street. To my left, on the southeast corner, is my grandparents' house. Vacant and run down. But still standing. Just like they were before they died. There's not a stop sign here, but I sit in my car waiting as though other cars have to go before it's my turn. I let the car inch forward just a little. I feel the gravel from the street without a name crunch against the pavement of Commerce Street. Just like when I was a child, not much of this side of town is paved. Details. Commerce Street is paved. The street without a name isn't. I've grown accustomed to pavement.

Why am I here? How did I get back here? I had to come back, there was no other choice. I had no other place to go but here. Back home. I left Marlin, Texas, over eighteen years ago, bright-eyed and never wanting to return; at least not to live. To visit, but not to live. But here I am again. My thoughts are repeating themselves. I just can't believe I'm back here and all I've worked for is gone.

Where do storms come from? Why do they come without warning? How are ferocious tornadoes formed? Why are they so devastating? That's what happened to me. A terrible storm. It came without warning, or maybe I didn't want to notice the weather report. Either way, it caught me by surprise. My beautiful house, gone. The life I created, gone. I had built both from the ground up. I had designed both, as difficult a task as it was, all by myself.

I want to cry but I won't. This is where I am, this is what I have to do, and this is what I have to go through. But my God! I don't want to be here! Help me!

At least I still have my car. A little black 1993 Honda Prelude. It isn't much. A lot of miles on it and dings here and there. But it's mine and it has brought me back to the only home I have now. Finally, I press down on the clutch, put the car in gear, turn the wheel, make the turn. The potholes in the gravel street are familiar. But it seems like this is the first time I have traveled over them. The first time I really feel them. I somberly pass my grandparents' house, blocking the fun memories from my mind. I'll have plenty of time to remember them since I'll be living here now. I'll keep the good memories for when I really need them. I see the chain-link fence, which runs alongside the peeling, white painted house. I am moving slow enough to see the old Ford truck through the overgrown trees, shrubs, and weeds; it's still in the unpainted wooden shed where it has slept for the last twenty-five years. It's probably worth some money. Maybe I could sell it to make some money to get out of this place. Out of this predicament I am in. No. Stay here. Deal with this.

I press down on the clutch, give the car a little gas, and climb the upward slope leading to the railroad track. Just like I was taught, I look both ways. But this time to the left first. I don't want to look to the right. But I do. Nothing is coming in either direction. Why haven't they put those automatic arms up at this railroad crossing since so many people have died on these tracks? Not my problem. People still live here and put up with it, so let them deal with it. Why am I going so slowly? I'm not in a parade. I see the vacant houses along the sides of the street. To the right is Momma Dude's house. To the left is Miz Whatshername's house. What *was* her name? All I can remember is that at Christmastime we loved to pass her house every night after working in our father's restaurant. We called her house Jazz Town of Bethlehem. She had every color of light imaginable strung outside of her unpainted, wood-frame house. That woman put lights in the trees, in the shrubs, on the roof, and on the dirt ground in front of her porch. She even wrapped the trees with foil. Remembering, I laugh out loud. At the end of the street with the forgotten name, I stop at the sign. Only two more quick turns and I'll be on my old street. No need to prolong it. Just do it. I press the buttons to let the windows down. I want to see if I can smell my father's feet. My sister Linda used to say Daddy's feet stank so bad you could smell them as soon as you hit our street. I knew it wasn't true, but since I'm going back in time, why not have a little fun? Turn right. Now left. Here it is. Harter Street. Still unpaved. And no smell of Daddy's feet. Maybe because my parents don't live on this street anymore. It looks so much smaller than when I was a child. Or am I just that much bigger?

Most of the houses are still here. All wood-frame houses with porches; some made of wood, some of concrete. The first house on the northeast corner is the one my father bought, rented out and later sold. He did all of that after I left for college. The two lots across the street now have a basketball goal with a big dirt court. There's the owner, Howard Hamblin, leaving his front yard on a bicycle. Wonder where he's going? Howard is a tall, muscular guy with golden skin. He seems to have turned into a good man. His picture was in the local newspaper a few years ago because he used his own money and labor to build a recreation field for kids. His older brother Marcus was my classmate all through school. I haven't seen Marcus since high school graduation. I heard he hadn't turned out so well. Howard married Betty, a girl several years older than himself and moved into the house across the street from Betty's mother. He must have a good sense of family and community.

The lot next to my father's old house is still vacant. Has been for many years. There used to be a house there. But one night while me, Harrell and Darrell, were walking to work, we spotted fire coming from the house. As we watched the blaze, the sirens blared in the distance, racing to douse the fire. You would think, because we were kids, we would be most enthralled by the fire and the commotion of the big red trucks and men with hoses spewing white water on the spectacular orange and yellow flames. But what captivated our attention were the thousands of rats covering the roof. We heard them squeal as they burned, jumping on top of one another. *Willard* and *Ben* were two of our favorite movies. As the fire destroyed the house, we kept watching to see if Ben was somewhere in the thick grayness of the rats, masterminding the whole thing. I laugh again, this time a little louder.

My parade of one drags on, except no one is watching. I see children I don't know but I recognize. They are tiny replicas of their parents, people I grew up with. Some of the houses are still home to folks, although Mr. Ed's family has vacated the premises. Was that his real name? What about Fat Albert from up the street? What was *his* real name? Why can't I remember the names? I remember the faces though.

A stop sign? On this little street? Who thought a stop sign here was important? I can't believe somebody would put a stop sign here but no crossing guard at the railroad crossing where people have been killed. Oh well, that's not my concern. That's not why I'm here.

And there, next to the stop sign, a brick house? That lot should be empty. It had been empty since I was a kid. But. . . I'm not eight years old anymore. But where is Miz Jones's house? There *she* is, coming out of the front door of a brick house. Another brick house? And right behind her is James D. I hope he doesn't still live at home. He has to be at least fifty years old. But what if he does still live with his mother? What does that mean? Maybe it means he loves and is committed to his mother. It could be just that simple.

The houses on the right side of the street were the homes of the Daniels, the Dobsons and the Millers. The Millers were a great family. The mother and all the kids had big smiles and dimples. My mother used to let me go to their house and play with David. He was in my class. Mr. Miller was a schoolteacher. He passed away years ago. There were a bunch of cars on our street the day of his funeral. Mr. and Mrs. Miller had a lot of kids, just like my parents. There were at least two sets of twins born in that family before Mr. Miller passed away. I can't remember all of the kids' names but I do remember two things. One, the house always smelled like pee, and two, I never could get used to Mrs. Miller breast-feeding right in front of me. I let out a gut-busting laugh. But what I see next stops it short.

There it is coming into plain view. The lot next to Miz Jones's new house is now vacant. Miz Price's house used to be there. Now that it's gone, our old house can be seen more easily. Today, I am the only one looking for it.

There's my father's old parking spot. On the left. Parallel to the dirt street. You just have to pull the car off the road to be in it. The chinaberry tree and the maple tree are cool shady spots during hot summers. That's where I'll park my car. Right in Daddy's spot. As I get out of my car, I see the last two houses on this block across the street in front of me. Miz Leola's and Miz McGruder's houses. Miz Leola still lives in her house, but I don't know about Miz McGruder. Both yards are still very well kept, just like the old days. I half expect Miz Leola to come outside with her broom to see if I had made it home from school, just like she did back in the day. Before I look at my own childhood home, I take a better look at Miz Bernice's house. Needs paint. One of her sons, Richard, still lives there; maybe I'll see if he plans to paint soon. On the corner next to Miz Bernice's house is an empty lot that my brother-in-law owns. Maybe if I fix up our old house, Richard paints his house and my brother-in-law builds a house on his lot, we could revitalize this street and then maybe even the whole town. Maybe we could. . . . I'm staring at my brother-in-law's empty lot, building houses in my head when I remind myself that is not why I'm here. Just leave things the way they are. Empty and old.

When I was little, there used to be a house on that lot. I don't remember the family's name, but I do remember they were Mexicans. That's what we called them back then. Now I know better. Hispanic. The daughter was a tall, beautiful, long-haired girl named Tanzes. I was much younger than she, in awe and afraid of her at the same time. She was good with a whip. Once, I remember her taking that whip to two dogs that were "stuck" butt-to-butt. Tanzes took what seemed to be a hundred ballerina-like steps raising the whip above her head and making it dance with her. Then with razor-sharp precision, she cracked the whip and caught them right where the parts were stuck together. I can still hear the dogs screaming as the whip parted them. I only grunt at that memory.

Folding my arms and leaning against my car, I look at the pink house with blue trim around the windows. So much to remember. Eighteen years of life in that beautiful, odd-colored house.

I need some beer.

Chapter Two

I return the same way I came the first time, but with a six-pack of cold Corona and a new bottle opener. No reminiscing this time, though. Just thinking about my stay. The sun starts to slip from the sky into evening. I won't take the beer inside because that's Momma's rule and I will abide. I park in Daddy's spot again and walk up the cement walkway that parts the yard and the two trees on either side. The maple tree to my right and the evergreen tree to my left. I remember when Daddy's brother, Uncle Aubrey the tree man, brought both of these trees on a huge flatbed trailer. Both of these trees seem to have grown out of control. Much like me. The thick Saint Augustine grass is gone and only dirt remains on either side of the sidewalk. This can't be the same sidewalk I used to run up and down like there was no end to it. Fewer steps are required to walk the length of the sidewalk. A ninety-degree turn left, a few steps, and another ninety-degree turn to the right. Two steps up to the cement porch with blue iron rails and curly designs in them. I'm home. Again.

I carefully place the beer on the porch and open the screen door to look through the diamond-shaped window of the wooden door. No life inside. No emerald green carpet, and no matching gold sofa and chairs. My piano is gone too. I let the screen door close and open a matching screen and door with diamond-shaped window to my left. This one opens onto the old room that was handed down from my parents to my sisters and then to me. Same thing. No carpet, no bed, no life. This is too painful. Before I enter, I need to set the tone for my stay here. Maybe I should approach it like a business venture. I learned in the business world to begin with the end in mind. And on my journey back to this place, I realized I was brought back here to start again. To do it right this time. Storms don't just come out of nowhere. And if that's true, maybe they *do* come for a reason. But why? That's what I need to find out.

The front porch was always a good place to sit. Whether it was when I was five years old, sitting with my mother in the springtime, eating breakfast and waiting for the bus to take me to kindergarten. Or ten years old sitting with my family in the summertime eating watermelon and spitting the seeds on the ground to see if any of them would sprout over the next few weeks. Or when I was thirteen playing with my dog King in the autumn, trying to avoid homework. Or at seventeen talking on the phone with Lowanda in the winter when it was too cold to take Sunday walks. And now is a good time, at thirty-six years old, with a six-pack of Corona, to contemplate what brought me here and what the hell I'm going to do next.

Realization
The Dream Was Just That,
a Dream

CHAPTER THREE

On the drive back to my childhood home, I realized the life I had created and all the things I had dreamed of and built up were for a reason. And now most, if not all, of what I had attained and obtained, is gone. I am left with only me. Maybe I use the word painful too much, but that is what this is. Painful. It hurts to admit that I. . . that *I*. . . did all of that to. . . to obtain a woman. A *woman*. The woman who would be my friend, my wife, the mother of our four children, and the sharer of my home, my bed, and my life. I believed that I needed to look good on paper and have all the assets in order to find that woman. I believed if I took care of certain things before I got married, like money and career and got past failed ventures and foolishness, my marriage would have a better chance of succeeding. Unlike men who tried to do those things after they got married.

I *thought* I was making progress. But it was all blown away. And now, at my age, I have to start all over again. There, I've said it. This is actually therapeutic! The beer is good and cold but it won't be for long if I don't put it on ice, but I forgot to buy some. Sure would be nice to have a cigarette too, while I sit outside and go through this process. What am I thinking? Beer? Cigarettes? On my mother's front porch? I can't go inside, but I can't stay outside either. What if Miz Leola sees me trying to act grown and tells my parents like she did the last time?

It is so strange that at my age I still care what people think of me. The slightest slip-up and I will fall from grace. Sometimes I feel like yelling down from this pedestal for someone to call the rescue team to come and get me off of this thing before I jump. Tell the firemen to crank up the truck and send up the little bucket and get me down from here! I want to live down there. With people who can go through life screwing up one thing after another and just say "oh well," and keep moving right along to the next mess. Arrrrrrrgggggghhhhh! I frustrate myself so much. Why can't I be like them?

CHAPTER FOUR

I return the same way I came the first time but with a cooler and ice for my beer, a pack of Marlboro Light 100s, and new lighter to go with my new bottle opener. And I will sit here on the front porch of my mother and father's house in the bright sunset. And I will drink my beer and smoke my cigarettes and contemplate. I will look straight ahead and wait for Miz Leola, love her as I do, to come and meet my eyes. And if she decides to tell? So what.

Miz Leola, one of the people in Marlin's supposed village, shouldn't have had to stand watch over me. I was a good kid, got good grades and was self-motivated. Besides, what I did do was so innocent. Admittedly, my parents' reaction wasn't that bad. But that was the fact, I couldn't move without them knowing about it.

My parents had eight children; five boys and three girls. I was the youngest and the only child left at home my junior and senior years in high school. My brother used to ask my parents if they had lost their minds because I had so much freedom. I could drive the car out of town on dates. Come home after midnight on the weekends I didn't have to work. I saved my money to go to California in the summer to buy my school clothes. I was never in trouble, never gave my parents any reason to restrict me.

But I had never been left alone in the house by myself overnight. I think television shows and movies that depict teens having parties while the parents are away are ridiculous. The way I was raised, that would never happen. I knew I couldn't get away with it. Number one, you can never get rid of all the evidence because somebody is going to smoke and throw cigarette butts everywhere, and two, somebody else is going to put trash where you would never find it but your parents sure would. So, I just don't get those movies. Anyway, my father won a trip through his insurance company and my parents decided to go. They would be gone for a couple of days during the school week and I would be alone until they returned. They thought about sending me to my grandparents' house while they were gone, but I convinced them that was just plain stupid. Of course, I didn't say "stupid" to them. So they left me at home. It was about time. After all, I was a senior in high school.

They left the keys to the 1977 canary yellow Ford LTD with the brown top, complete with the CB antenna. It was 1981 and CBs had run their course. I was supposed to go to school and return home right afterwards. They never instructed me not to have any friends in the car. I had been driving since I was about eight. I was the only one of the last six kids my father had taught to drive. They were all too scared of him. I guess my brothers, the two oldest, passed down their bad experiences. But my father knew I was responsible with a car. He taught me that I needed to either learn how to fix a car or make enough money to pay to have it fixed. I learned that lesson the hard way the summer before my senior year.

That summer night I had a few friends in the car. We were way out on a dirt road late at night in the boonies, trying to find a party. We smelled smoke. Typical high school experience. I stopped the car, got out, and popped the hood. Flames leapt out from under the hood and nearly grabbed us. My friends and I scrambled around, falling down on the gravel road throwing rocks and dirt on the engine to put out the fire. It didn't work. Then I snatched the keys from the ignition hoping the car wouldn't explode with me in it. I stumbled to the trunk to try and find something, anything to put out the fire. The first thing I put my hands on was a bottle of Clorox bleach. I had almost reached the fire when the pounding in my chest brought me to my senses and told me using Clorox would be a big mistake. I ran back to the trunk to find something else.

My good old resourceful mother, who had been self-employed since before I was born, was a Stanley Products dealer. She also sold Tupperware, Avon, Lucky Heart cosmetics and spiritual supplies, and Shaklee vitamins.

She hosted parties, took orders and delivered product to her customers. You name it, she sold it. But on this night, it was Stanley's Degreaser that saved my butt and the LTD from burning up. I poured the thick liquid over the fire and out it went. We all laughed so hard. Here was my parents' car that my mother used for part of our livelihood about to burn up and we thought it was funny. After we walked over a mile, in thick blackness, to find a phone to call my father, and after his first comment was "how is my car?" and not "are you hurt?" and after he came to pick us up and proceeded to blame the fire on me because I had added brake fluid without anyone showing me how to do it (because I was trying to prove myself to him) . . . after all of that, I decided I would always make enough money to have a car fixed, rather than learn to fix it myself. To this day, I know very little about cars except how to start them. So as far as I was concerned, the short time alone at home while my parents were on their trip would be uneventful.

They left on a Wednesday morning. I took the car to school and came right home afterwards. I knew they must have devised some method of keeping track of me and I had to figure it out. Not that I was going to do anything wrong, I just wanted to know what they knew. Whenever my older brothers and sisters asked to borrow the car, my father wanted to know where they were going and what they were going to do. Then he would calculate how long it should take and the direction from which they should return. He could wake from a dead sleep and know if they were late. And if he heard the car drive up, he would go out to look at the tire tracks in the dirt to see the direction from which they came. Family legend has it that one time he let my oldest sister use the car for her prom. Her date, who later became her husband, didn't have a car so my sister was instructed to drive herself and her date to the prom. When my father saw them riding through downtown, the date was driving. My father made them stop, put my sister in the middle, and all three of them drove to the prom.

I didn't like that kind of drama. So I had to figure out how my parents were going to watch me from their vacation spot. When I got home, a mere fifteen or twenty minutes after school let out, Miz Leola was out sweeping her front porch. It was a huge cement porch, high off the ground spanning the entire front of her house and was covered with luscious plants.

I bid her good day like always. She was short, small-boned and wore black horn-rimmed glasses on a chain that sometimes hung around her neck like jewelry. Her movements were always quick and short. She smiled and threw up her hand with a greeting, never missing a sweep of the broom. I went into the house and did whatever I did. But when I came outside near dusk, hours after I had arrived home, Ms. Leola was still sweeping the porch. The next day when I came home from school she was raking the yard. We exchanged our daily greetings and at that point I knew how my parents knew what they knew. No problem, all would be fine. My parents would be home the next day, Friday, and Miz Leola, the village reporter, would give my parents the good news.

For lunch on Friday I decided to go off campus to the Dairy Queen with some friends. The Dairy Queen had been our junior high school hang-out and my friend Lowanda had gotten a job there in high school. Sometimes she gave me free food. That Friday, we all had a great time. Just good, clean fun. I figured I would return home as usual, on time; my parents would be waiting and I would be the good son. When I arrived home, Miz Leola was washing her car. We said our "heys" and I went inside to welcome my parents home. We were glad to see each other and I asked how their trip had been. But before they answered *my* question, my father had a question for *me*. He wanted to know why I was driving through downtown during my lunch hour. I said, "What?" not to try and deny it but in amazement that they hadn't been home an hour and already knew.

I had learned not to lie to my father years ago after he questioned me about taking a Tootsie Roll from the candy jar at his restaurant, Williams Snack Center. I was about ten years old and had asked him if I could have a Tootsie Roll and he had said no. I figured he wouldn't know if I had one or not, so I took one anyway and went outside, ate it and returned to my little part-time job. God only knows how he knew, but he did, and he beat me outside in broad daylight near the railroad tracks behind the Snack Center. That day, when I was ten, he taught me not to lie. So on this day, I simply explained that some friends and I had gone to lunch at the Dairy Queen. I had followed the rules and returned home each day after school, especially since I knew Miz Leola was the watchman. Inside I felt I wasn't the good son because I didn't get an 'attaboy.' They agreed I was not wrong, but knowing that they knew *everything* made me absolutely sick. How did they know? Who told them? When would I have my own life? Would I ever have my own life? Would they always know everything? What else did they know that they weren't telling me? I wanted to know all they knew because we could have settled a lot of things that day. Right then. Right there. But parents never tell you all they know. It was all so innocent, and their reaction wasn't that bad, but it really affected me.

That was then, this is now. The second beer was as good as the first and inhaling cigarette smoke settled me as I sat on the front porch. I hadn't made eye contact with Miz Leola, but that didn't mean she wasn't watching from somewhere.

So this is it, my time on the cement sofa. Working out the reasons for my manufactured life thus far. Damaged goods. Who would want to buy them? Who would want me? Might as well be in the fifty-percent-off basket, hoping someone will find me among all of the other discounted stuff. What I need is a label listing all of the ingredients that I am made of. So the buyer knows exactly what's in the package. No surprises. A happy buyer is one who can make an informed decision. So, begin with the end in mind. The end is a happy buyer. The beginning is truth. Just like my father taught me. There should be no fancy packaging, no bright colors and no marketing ploys promising that life would be perfect if the buyer acquires this product. If the product is good, the buyer will buy.

This is going to be a good meeting with my *Self.*

I need an agenda. Why didn't I think of this before? But who uses an agenda in a counseling session? Am I having a business meeting with myself or a counseling session with myself? Both. If I'm successful at this, maybe I can start a new business. Coaching. Do I need initials behind my name to do that? I really don't want to go back to school. I don't do well in the classroom anymore.

Stop. Focus. You are here for a reason. Begin with the end in mind.

Okay, an agenda. We already know the purpose of this meeting. We already know the balance sheet shows no assets, many liabilities and the only equity is the breath in my body.

So what next?

Scratch the agenda, we'll make this a brainstorming session and stay here until we've made progress. Where should we start?

What brought you here?

The dream. The one. A woman. The buyer.

Go on.

I used to say all the right things. Well maybe not *all* the right things. But I used phrases like: "my job doesn't define me"; "how much money I make doesn't matter"; "I could be happy working at Burger King if that's what I wanted to do"; "I believe I can be anything I want to be"; and "I am a whole person without a woman constantly on my arm." Over time, I learned my communication skills were a great asset when it came to dating. I love to talk. And I don't mind listening. But more important than the ability to communicate was what I was marketing. A few things that sold well were my devotion to my parents; I'm from a large family that is more intact than most; I have a good relationship with all of my brothers and sisters; I spend quality time with most of my nieces and nephews; I love God and have always been active in church without being forced to do so; and I cook well, nothing fancy: just good down-home soul food and I love to do it.

There were two things I hardly ever discussed more than once or twice, but each time I talked about them with a woman, something happened between us. I learned these two things were the bait and the hook. I never knew exactly when these topics would come up, but if I wanted to continue the dating process and keep the buyer interested, these two things definitely needed to be put out there.

The bait is about the only sex education I received as a child. To this very day, the only thing my father has ever told me about sex is that it is natural from the gnat to the elephant. But it was my mother who made the lasting impression on me. She told me that I would never shack up with a girl, and that if I got a girl pregnant, I was going to marry her. That was it. Plain and simple. And to this day I have never lived with a woman and I don't have any children.

Now comes the hook. The hook was my dream. My wedding day. Women find a man who has a plan for his wedding day almost irresistible. Not that I had worked out all of the details, but the fact that I was actually looking for a wife and wouldn't have to be dragged down the aisle, balls in a noose and a double-barrel shotgun to my head, sold very well.

One of my sisters once told me I must be part Italian because I talk with my hands. When making my pitch to a potential buyer, I always got excited and passionate about it. I used my hands to make strong, masculine, and maybe even presidential gestures, and I may have even glowed a little too. All to sell the idea. I would begin by explaining my belief that a wedding is not just a ceremony where you get married, but a celebration of your marriage. I would explain to her that it was my responsibility to take whatever precautions necessary to prevent pregnancy so that I/we could have the day that I dreamed of. She could do whatever she thought she needed to do about birth control, but I always took my own precautions and she should not question me about it.

Next, I would explain that for me to even have a wedding day meant that I had found my best friend in the world. And divorce was not an option. I would explain how I had set up a general budget for the wedding on a spreadsheet with a five-percent increase per annum for each year I didn't get married. The budget was set up in 1989, with a very modest base of $20,000 that included $5,000 for her wedding ring. The budget was set up when I was twenty-six, after which I had at a minimum four years to save the money. I didn't want to get married before I turned thirty. I would explain that, in my opinion, the bride's parents should pay for the wedding if you marry in your twenties, but after thirty, the couple getting married should foot the bill. Actually, I felt that it was my responsibility to pay for it. I never revealed exactly where I was on the savings plan. I would explain that the budget wasn't a lot of money but that I thought I could pull it off.

Then I would explain the few details I wanted for the day and the rest either she could decide or we could decide together. I didn't want to have a church wedding. From the Bible research I had done, the wedding ceremony we use today isn't what they did back then. We've made it up by piecing things together. As far as I could tell from the Bible, a man and a woman are considered married in God's eyes when they have sex: "*Therefore a man shall leave his father and his mother, and shall cleave unto his wife: and they shall be one flesh.*" This part of the explanation was a test to see if she could follow me. Thought-provoking conversation is important to me.

I would take a brief tangent from my discussion on the wedding day to do a little theological exploration. I would ask, "What does one flesh mean?" Often, I didn't I get an answer. Actually I never got an answer. So I would simply explain that man and woman are made physically to "fit together" and that sex was designed for one thing but reserved for another. Designed for procreation first and pleasure second. You have to like it to want to do it. If you want to do it, then you'll do it more and increase the chances of having babies, which populate the world. But, it was reserved for married people. And marriage is a commitment, not a ceremony. Just like love is not an emotion, it is a commitment that lasts after the intensity of the emotions subside. At this point I would open the floor for discussion or debate by admitting I really didn't know if God recognized the commitment first, but I was definitely sure He considers you married when you have sex. Then would come the question for her: "So, how many people have you been married to?"

I'm not the sharpest knife in the drawer, but it really surprises me that some people don't think about these things. Rarely did I find a woman who just jumped right in for a discussion, debate, or to tell me that my understanding was bad. Mostly I got looks of bewilderment. Sometimes I wanted to fall out laughing, but I had a fish on the line and had to reel it in.

I'd continue to explain that months, maybe even a year before the actual wedding day, I wanted to get married by a Justice of the Peace. I figure, once you're engaged you might as well go ahead and make it official by the state. Besides, you're probably already having sex, so God thinks you're married anyway. So why not? But should we live together before the actual wedding since we were already married? Living together would be more real and save money, but living apart would be more intriguing and make the process seem more like a transition and I like that. I have often joked with friends that I wanted to make enough money so that my wife and I could live next door to each other and visit each other every day and most nights. But when I wanted my peace and quiet, I could go to my own home. Anyway, living apart for the time before the wedding would give the two of us time to know if we're still happy being married. They say things change after you say "I do." And if things did change I wouldn't get a divorce, I just wouldn't have to spend money on a big "celebration."

I have bought too many wedding gifts and attended too many "celebrations of love" only to see the couple split up shortly after. It has frustrated me to the point of wanting to ask for my gifts back. I have sat in the audience wondering, 'what are they doing?' then lo and behold, they wound up divorced. And I believe that at least one of them knew it was a mistake while I was at the store buying their gift. If it's not going to last, just leave me out of it. Don't send me an invitation to the engagement party, the co-ed shower, the bachelor party or the wedding. Just send me an email with your wonderful announcement and I'll bounce a congratulations back at you. Then twenty-five years later, when time has tested you, invite me to a party and I'll buy you a gift. So I think getting married before the wedding celebration is a good idea. Maybe I don't want to wait twenty-five years before I have the party, but it's an effort to address the issue.

I would go on to explain that even though I wanted to be married before the celebration, I would like to keep it a secret from everybody. I know for a woman that would be impossible and would add a level of frustration to my life that I just didn't need. So, even though I wanted secrecy, I would concede. A couple of days before the wedding I wanted to have time with as many of my male friends as possible. Maybe those from out of town could come in on Wednesday night and those in town would take off of work Thursday and Friday. Thursday, we would just have fun. Not a bachelor party with naked women and all; I've done enough of that. But instead, just hang out and be crazy for a while. Maybe go bowling. Friday we would catch the stragglers coming to town and just chill. Many of my guy friends don't know each other and I would like for them to get a chance to meet before the big day.

Then . . .

What's the matter? Why are you stopping?

This is . . . so . . . weak.

What do you mean?

I mean, I can't believe I said this stuff.

Is it the truth?

It's the truth, but I don't think she'll understand that . . .

Just tell the truth.

Well, finally, she would get to hear my plan for the wedding celebration itself. It included a huge facility where all of the events would take place in the same room: a live jazz group, the best singers in town, a babysitting service, an open bar with beer and wine, and good old-fashioned finger-food. You know, like chicken salad sandwiches with the crust still on the bread, spicy meatballs and fried chicken wings, and gut-fillin' side dishes. I want the guests to get *full*. I also want a movie director, to produce a film-quality movie, not just a video; a choreographer and whoever else my wife thought we needed. I really want those things.

The facility needs to be elegant, so the money would go into the rental, not in decorations. What decorations we end up with could be her choice, as long as it was simple. The movie director can set the mood with lighting. The room should be rectangular and large enough to accommodate the plan. The main entryway would be in the center of one side of one of the longer walls. As you enter the main doors, directly ahead is the main aisle down which the woman of the day will walk and it leads to a three-tier circular stage. Surrounding the center stage are round tables, which seat eight guests each. Tables of this size are more conducive to guests talking to one another during the reception. There are two other aisles running at an angle from each corner of the room to the left and right of the main entrance. The attendants will enter down those angled aisles in a theatrical, choreographed processional. As you can see, I've put a lot of thought into this. It's a celebration, but it's also a show. I insist on high production value. By this time, her eyes are glazed with incredulity.

Standing in the main entryway, this is what I see as I look into the room. On the opposite side of the stage is a jazz band. To the right of the main entry, along the short wall at the end of the rectangular room, is the bride's table with an ice sculpture, cake, punch and food. Opposite her table and at the other end of the room to the left, is my table with the same. There are four other food tables in the room, one to the right and one to the left of the main entryway, with an identical setup on the opposite side of the room. Outside of the main entry in the foyer are two bars with three attendants each, a registration table and a large gift table. Also, somewhere in this facility is the babysitting area where guests can leave their small children for games, movies and even bedtime if their parents wanted to stay that long. And they will want to. Since the final video of the wedding will be of cinema quality, I don't want to hear any crying children on it. The invitations will specifically say that no children under the age of eight will be allowed in the main area during the wedding. Once the party starts, fine. But not before. And anyone who doesn't like it can stay at home. The director will be given the authority to yell "Cut!" if a baby is heard crying. I'm serious.

As I wind up my lengthy description of my vision of the celebration, I soften. My gestures become less grandiose. The look in my eyes becomes more intent. I describe the center stage. It is round like a wedding cake and has three tiers. The top is just wide enough for the two of us, and God's representative. It is elevated just enough so our guests can see us. The attendants are on a lower level and the stage rotates ever so smoothly and slowly around and around while we exchange the vows that we each wrote for the other. And every guest in the room will see my wife's beautiful face and my tears of happiness as we affirm our love for each other.

It sold like hotcakes. Over time I practiced and refined the presentation and updated the budgeted amount. Even with all of the holes in my dream, in my plan, no one ever called me on them. No one ever pointed out the inconsistencies. What I found was that the woman I was talking to saw a man, and heard two things: "ring" and "wedding." Nothing else I said mattered. Blah, blah, blah. She would be stuck back at ring and wedding. In the beginning, I really believed in what I was selling. As a matter of fact, I wasn't even selling it back then. I was just talking. Don't ask me where I got the vision from; it's been stuck in my head just as I described it for a long time. I've seen it clearly for years. Even though the who and the when and the where and the colors and all the other details aren't there, I sold exactly what I saw. Did I find it strange that a man had such vivid images of his wedding? Yeah, but that's par for the course for me. This idea was in my head, so I had to use it to some benefit. Then, it lost its value.

Now, sitting here sipping on this Corona, thinking back, I remember: the time I first shared my dream with a woman, I really did believe in it. When I told her, I was looking for that person in my life whom I could tell anything to. A person I could dream with. I was young. I hadn't yet learned that what you say isn't necessarily what the other person hears. And if you talk a lot, like me, then there's more room for one-sided confusion leading to mass hysteria. But what happened to me changed me from that point on. It changed my approach to dating. It didn't change what I said, no, that sold too well; it changed how and why I said it.

So now, sitting here, I realize that the vision might not be a vision after all, but a dream. And maybe a dream is just that; only a dream. Something you awaken from.

Getting Down
Isn't as Easy as Getting Up

Chapter Five

I'm proud of myself. I haven't even finished my second beer yet and I've had a realization. Any other time, I would have downed a third by now and maybe not even come up with a summary or a conclusion. And what's up with the sun? It is still falling into the evening. Has it even moved? That means I still have time before night comes. This meeting with my *Self* is going very well. Just let my brain go wherever it needs to, to find some peace about my current situation. It's all so clear to me. I'm tired of being alone. But the approach I have taken so far hasn't been a very good one. In fact, even when I was dating someone, I still felt alone. If a woman found my sales pitch appealing and moved a little closer to me, I could look into her eyes and see that she was looking straight through me. To this day, I can go to some restaurants in Austin and remember which woman I was there with as she sat across the table looking through me. And without her noticing, I would study the look in her eyes to try and figure out why she was looking at me that way. Of course, the best way to find the answer to any question is to ask it. But who would ever admit they were looking through me and into their own future? Who would admit that they were trying to see if I could provide what they were looking for? So many times I just wanted to yell out "Stop! Stay here for a moment! Here! Right here! In this moment! Don't go anywhere else! Just stay right here!" But they might have focused and seen the real me. Did I want that?

Okay, wait.

What?

I have to back up and tell the truth.

About what?

There was one woman I dated who didn't look through me. This woman agreed to take what I considered to be the perfect approach to dating. Maybe she saw me for me instead of buying what I was trying to sell.

Really? What was her name?

Her name was Kathy. She had the prettiest bright smile; dimples; down-pillow-soft skin, and shoulder-length, coal-black hair. She and I had been acquaintances for a while before we started dating. We started hanging out more and more, and one sunny, Sunday afternoon, while having lunch at a small restaurant in Austin's Hyde Park, conversation gravitated to dating. We talked about all of the frustrations. Then out of nowhere, we simply agreed we should date each other. It was more like a business meeting and we were about to enter the phase where we negotiated the contract. But it was she who presented the terms and conditions, not me. Kathy suggested we proceed only on the basis that we were looking at each other as potential mates. I was so amazed at her candidness. I chimed in about how that made perfect sense. We were thinking about it, so why not just put it on the table? And that's how it began.

Kathy was in graduate school working on her master's degree. She had recently been on one of the local television newscasts discussing a program she had created that matched senior citizens with children in daycare. The program was a success and I was proud of her accomplishment. As usual, I was busy working long hours, pretending my career didn't define me. I cooked for her and she for me. I love it when a woman asks me what I want her to cook for me. There are so many microwave queens in the world, I find it refreshing when a woman is not intimidated by my own culinary skills and has some of her own.

Being with Kathy was becoming very comfortable. The sense of peace I got from knowing that we were inspecting each other made me feel good. But when the holidays approached I started to get nervous because I never know what to buy for a woman. My favorite person to buy Christmas gifts for is my brother Darrell. He and I exchange wish lists each year; we can buy as many items from the list as our budgets allow. It makes life so much easier. But with a woman, I get anxious as soon as I see the first commercial on television, which in my opinion should start no sooner than the first day of November. In fact, I want a law passed so that stores can't advertise Christmas anywhere, in any shape, form or fashion, until the first day of November.

My disdain for the holidays increased during the time Kathy and I dated. I was managing a law firm and was responsible for decorating the office, selecting and ordering Christmas cards, updating the addresses in the client database, determining who the top clients were, planning the firm's Christmas party, and, on top of all that, I felt responsible for making sure everyone in the firm had a good time at the party. It always seemed at least one of the law partners would throw a wrench in my life every year just to make me miserable. And to top it all off, December was the end of the fiscal year and I was responsible for organizing the firm's finances. I came to hate all of it. I found it hard to have a personal life around the holidays. So my big event was my annual New Year's Day dinner. I would coordinate with several friends to help prepare the meal and would invite as many as thirty people to my small, two-bedroom apartment to eat, drink, sleep and watch football all day. So although I'd like to think that what happened with Kathy was inevitable, I know I could have done better.

Things at the office were going badly over the holidays, as usual, but I did manage to get people lined up to help with my New Year's Day dinner. I wanted to be sure I had a good holiday after the frenzy. Lee and Cherry, a married couple and my very good friends, agreed to cook whatever I needed. Another friend, Glenn, would take a key to my apartment so that he could go over each day on his lunch break and clean chitlins (more formally known as chitterlings). Chitlins are the one thing I had to have at my dinner. While I don't mind the smell when I'm cooking them, I hate cleaning them. On the other hand, Glenn loved to eat them and had no problem with the cleaning. So when it came to chitlins, Glenn and I were a match. Glenn was an investment broker and fellow member of the finance committee we both served on in a non-profit group, Texas Organized Professionals (TOPs). He was also a fellow musician and while I thought I was better than he was, he simply had more courage than I did. He was tall with freckles, a red face and sandy-red hair. He was divorced with a child somewhere else. He had married again and that marriage was shaky too. He was a good guy to be around and I trusted him with the key to my apartment. But more, I appreciated him for taking on the awful task of cleaning my chitlins.

Meanwhile, Kathy finished up finals and made plans to leave town for Christmas. I was busy at work so I didn't mind her being gone. But what was I going to buy her? Before Christmas I decided to invite her out to dinner to go ahead and just ask her what she wanted. Before going to dinner I reminded myself that this was the woman who had negotiated the terms of our relationship. I was nervous for no reason. I would ask and Kathy would tell me exactly what she wanted. I'd go out and buy it and move on to the next crisis at work. That thought process gave me much comfort. I remember the conversation we had over dinner. It was pleasant. She was cute as ever. I asked her what she wanted for Christmas and without hesitation, she poised herself to give me the answer. My excitement must have shone in my eyes. But the answer was "world peace." I sat there for a brief moment before I broke into laughter. Not at her answer, but at myself for thinking this was going to be easy. I told her I couldn't buy her world peace so she should be serious and tell me what she wanted. Then she calmly said, "Nothing. I really don't want anything for Christmas." I don't remember much after that, but I do know that I left dinner comfortable that I didn't have to buy her anything for Christmas. I was more taken with her than ever that night.

The day came for Kathy to leave town and I would not see her again until my New Year's Day dinner party. She called and said that she wanted to have lunch so I left the office madness and met her at Luby's. When I arrived, I was glad to see her until I noticed a big box wrapped in deep blue paper with a silver bow on it. My heart quickened as my steps slowed. I looked down at my empty hands. Too late, there was nothing I could do about it now. But she was pleasant. We went through the line getting our food as she juggled the box, which I hoped wasn't for me. When we sat down, she presented me with the gift and told me not to open it until Christmas Day. The conversation after that is a blur. I didn't want to be there. I didn't want to deal with her disappointment. She was *definitely* disappointed I didn't get her a present. I got heartburn trying to eat fast so I could get out of there and back to problems I could handle. She told me she couldn't believe I didn't get her anything. No matter what she had told me, I should have gotten her something. I felt so stupid. How could I have believed her? And if she hadn't told the truth about that, were the negotiated rules for our relationship a lie as well? I had to get out of there! We shared a cold embrace before she left for Christmas.

New Year's Day. I had been brutally scolded by my female friends over what happened with Kathy. My male friends said I did the right thing, so I conveniently bought into what the men said and pushed the female perspective out of my mind. I don't remember whether I went out and bought something for Kathy or not. I just know that I poured myself into work and my party. I had been up most of the night cooking and getting the apartment ready for my guests. I usually took down the bed in my bedroom and shoved it into the walk-in closet to make room for fold-out tables and chairs. The second bedroom was my home office and there was more space for people to sit in there. Each room had a television with cable so people could go from room to room to watch different football games. People started to arrive about ten o'clock in the morning. When Kathy came, she had on her cute pink Alpha Kappa Alpha warm-up outfit with a cake in tow. She came right in and started helping me host the party. She was so nice. So I relaxed and thought we were past that little bump in the road. More people showed up than I had expected. My friend Wilbert even brought four other people with him from San Antonio. There was plenty of food for everyone. I always had enough and encouraged people to take food home with them. It was a good day. Almost twelve hours after the party started, the last person left. Kathy stayed to help me clean up. When we were done, we lay on the floor talking and dozed off for a minute before she decided to go home. I walked her down the three flights of stairs and we kissed and embraced warmly. We said the usual, "see you later," and she drove away. That was the last time I ever saw Kathy. And that was over six years ago. I kept up with her through friends. She graduated with her master's degree and married Glenn after he divorced his second wife.

So maybe Kathy saw the truth and found it wasn't worth buying?

I don't know. I just know she left.

CHAPTER SIX

A brief summary of what we know so far: you built a life, real or fake, to impress women; you're tired of being alone; you feel like you're on a pedestal and can't get down; and you're forced to deal with it here and now.

It just hit me.

What just hit you?

I know how I got up on this pedestal!

How?

No one put me on this pedestal! I put myself on it! Wow! I . . . put myself . . . on this freakin' pedestal!

Really?

Yeah!!!

And . . .

No one can put you on a pedestal; you have to buy into the idea of being on a pedestal. No one ever told me what they expected of me; I always expected the best of myself. Why in the world is that so clear *now*? It makes perfect sense. I . . . did it . . . to myself. But why in the hell would I do that to myself? Why have I made life so hard for myself? Arrrrrrrggggggghhhhh! I really frustrate myself sometimes. If I put myself up here, then I can just get down. It should be that easy. I can get down, and start learning about life down there with other people. And this will all be over.

The sound of the empty bottle hitting the cement made me notice how quickly I'd finished my third beer. How many cigarettes? Four already. I should slow down. Starting to tingle a little bit. But I don't want to interrupt the flow. I want to keep up the energy of this session.

Hmmmmm. . . . I did it to myself. The answer is so simple. Just undo it. Maybe that's enough for now. Maybe I can stop, write down what I've learned, meditate on it every day and watch the change happen. No! No! No! That's another thing about me I need to be honest about right now.

And what is that?

The fact that I'll start something, set a goal, move quickly toward that goal, get close to it, figure I've done enough and stop short. I really noticed that with the last workout program I started. The idea was to run 1.3 miles from the corner of Abilene Trail and Escarpment up to the silver traffic box at the corner of William Cannon and Escarpment, touch the box then jog back as far as I could before walking the rest of the way. I had planned to run every day and increase the distance as I increased my endurance, as long as I did the minimum 1.3 miles. I planned to eventually lose the weight I had gained since I turned thirty and summon the body of my mid-twenties to come forth. Granted, the body of my mid-twenties wasn't that great, but was at least better than the body of my thirties. After college I used to jog five miles a day, three days a week. I like jogging and it's something I could do alone. No teammates to depend on or to depend on me. Just me. Alone. Against myself.

The first day I started to run to the silver box, I was so proud that I still had a little bit of running ability after not having jogged in years. I got within one block of the box and just quit. As I walked toward the silver box, breathing hard but smiling, my brows started to furrow as I saw it getting closer and closer. I attempted to control my breathing. Then I stopped smiling and got mad at myself for not pushing harder to reach the goal. I remember standing at the silver box looking at it and wondering what passersby were thinking about this man standing and staring at a traffic box. I had walked up to it, not run. I didn't want to touch it, and I didn't. I just turned around and walked home. Mad at myself. I quit jogging.

So now, I'll finish this. I will. I will not stop. If I have to drink twelve beers and smoke three packs of cigarettes, I will do this!

Good. I'm ready when you are.

As I sit here reaching beneath the cold ice for another beer, I look down at the ground and wonder how to get down. My feet seem to dangle in the wind, high above the sandy brown dirt and pebbles. It would hurt if I jumped off. Has Nike created a shoe that would absorb the shock? I should be able to do this. But I can't. It should be easy; just go down the same way I came up. But it's a *long* way down.

CHAPTER SEVEN

I'*m waiting. Do you know where you want to start?*

Relationships.

Okay.

Whether with family, friends or with women I've dated, I have always felt distant, isolated, alone. I never felt that anyone ever really knew me. Because I was busy trying to be someone else.

Why?

Because . . . that's what I expected of myself. That's what I wanted for myself.

Why?

I have to figure out that part.

Well, who are you?

Right now? I don't know. I know who I was trying to be . . . but now I don't have the things that I thought made me me.

Then . . . , who do you want to be?

I want to be me.

Okay . . . . Let's try this angle. What do you want your family, friends and/or women you date to know about you that will close the gap in your relationships?

The truth.

The truth about what?

My life, my thoughts, my being.

Why?

Because . . . if a person knows you completely and stays with you, then you can be close.

47

Can you explain what you mean by that and to which person, family, friend or woman that applies?

Hmmm . . . let me see. A woman can become your wife, which is family. If she becomes your wife, then she should already be your friend. And in either case she's still a woman. So if I explain my thoughts about a relationship with a woman, then in some way, I will cover all three. Not that you have sex with your family members and maybe with only a few of your friends, but it's the concept of unconditional love that should exist among all three that I'm looking for.

Hmmm . . . Go on.

How many times have I heard a woman say, "If had known that about him, I wouldn't have married him." Entirely too many times! Every time I hear those words, it scares me. I hate divorce. And because it's so common these days, I wanted to do everything I could to prevent it before I got there. I thought that my approach was logical, but now I don't know anymore. When I hear a woman say something like, "I didn't know he smoked before I married him," I wonder how could you date a man for two, three or even four years, kiss him on a regular basis and not know he smoked? Or she says, "I didn't know he drank so much before I married him." Again, I wonder to myself, "While you dated him, he probably drank just as much as he does now and you liked him then." Or she'll say, "I didn't know he liked to flirt or cheat so much." I say to myself, "Isn't that the same man who was married when you met him? Didn't he flirt with you and flash his wedding band in your mesmerized eyes? And you still wanted him? Help me! I don't understand!"

I have seen too many divorces. I have seen too many people coexisting in misery. I have seen too many couples living separate lives and staying together for the kids. And I just didn't want that for myself. Yes, I got way off track. I have always wanted the woman I married to know everything about me before we got married. But the process of dating is not conducive to that level of relating. Taking the time to get to know each other, to learn to communicate and understand exactly what the other person is saying, is not something we humans do very well. Allowing the other person the opportunity to express themselves and to make mistakes and recover from them is something else we're not good at. I started out wanting things to be open and honest, but I fell face first into a process that took control of me instead of me taking control of it. It changed my approach and left me empty.

But how does divorce equate to family and friends?

Look, don't over analyze this yet, just let me get it all out. Have you ever heard a parent say that if they knew their child was going to be . . . let's say . . . an ax murderer, they wouldn't have had him? So in a family, divorce is like an abortion of the child when the child is outside the womb.

Oh . . . ooookay . . .

As I was saying, I found out it takes a long time to share your deepest thoughts and fears. I'm not one to just jump right in and start saying things like "I wonder what it would be like to have sex with sheep?" Not that I really wonder about that, it's just as an example. I also discovered that in typical dating situations, we don't wait before we have sex. First, second, but definitely by the third date, if a man hasn't approached the woman for sex, even if it's just for her to have the opportunity to say no, she starts to question his manhood. At least that's been *my* experience. It is so strange to me how women shape the way we are, and then blame us for being that way.

When I was pretending that my job didn't define me, my friends asked me how I could put up with certain things in the professional world. I'd tell them, "When you play football, you have to play by the rules of football. When you play baseball, the rules of baseball apply. You can't play football and use baseball rules," meaning that you didn't have to agree with the rules of the professional world, you just had to play by them if you were going to be in the game. In the dating world, after years of seeing how sex changed the dynamics of the male/female relationship, I tried to back off from going for it so early in the relationship. I came to believe that in addition to making the pitch to sell the product, the dating rules included keeping your thoughts about sex with sheep hidden and not going for sex early in the game. I thought my strategy would help ground me in this pretentious process and allow me to get to know women better. But resisting sex became a strategy that guaranteed that I would get it. And that eventually backfired on me too.

There were at least two women who became physically violent with me for saying no to their sexual advances. One stood toe-to-toe with me in her apartment, hitting me on my chest and telling me I needed to wear the pants instead of her. I remember rumbling inside of myself that night. I had to get away from her or I was going to do something I would definitely regret. I still can't believe what happened with the second woman. She and I had just started dating. She was divorced with two daughters, eight and twelve years old. I had a hard and fast rule: I wouldn't meet a woman's children until I knew that I wanted to be around long-term. One weeknight she asked me to cook dinner for her. I reluctantly agreed, but wondered what her daughters would be doing on a school night while their mother was out on a date. Didn't they have homework? Didn't they need to be fed? Didn't she need to bathe them and get them to bed? But I got past all of that and let her use her own judgment. Besides, I was nobody's parent. I didn't have a master's degree like she did, and I was not on the executive track at Motorola. Who was I to try and tell her how to raise her kids?

I prepared a tasty pasta dish with shrimp and chicken and a salad. But I was delayed getting into the shower when my ex-roommate's girlfriend came over to pick up some of his stuff. I had put him out after he almost burned down my apartment trying to make french fries, got third degree burns on his hands and legs, had no insurance and expected me to pick up the medical bills when he couldn't work or pay rent. But he could have sex with his girlfriend and other women, one of whom was married and got pregnant by him. Drama. I strongly encouraged him to go back to Philadelphia and live with his momma. That was over five years ago and he is *still* there.

Anyway, my date and my ex-roommate's girlfriend must have passed each other on the stairway to my apartment. I understood how it must have looked to her. She sees a woman leaving my apartment and I need to take a shower before I serve her dinner. But what happened still doesn't make sense. She knocked on the door. I answered, rushed and flustered because I was trying to get into the shower. I opened the door and she stood back, waiting to be invited in. I gathered my breath and told her to come in and relax while I jumped into the shower. She said no, that she would leave and come back when I was ready. I argued, but she insisted. So she left. But I took note of what she was wearing. She was clearly overdressed for an evening at home—black sleeveless dress, black shoes, pearl necklace and bracelet, and a big black bag. The black bag caught my attention. It was too large.

I showered, then poured two glasses of white wine. All in five minutes. I stood outside my apartment waiting for her. Forty-five minutes passed before she returned. I ran down the three flights of stairs with both glasses of wine in my hands to try and make up for not being ready. She took her glass and walked past me up the stairs. She was not happy.

I watched her angry hips switching from side to side. I followed her into the apartment, closed the door behind me, then followed her to my sofa. I sat next to her on the sofa and tried to start the evening with compliments and small talk but she was not having it. She leaned forward, put her glass of wine on the coffee table, threw her arms around me and started kissing me. She was strong. She kicked off her shoes, lifted her black dress, spread her legs and straddled me. She told me I was going to have sex with her. I wanted to eat dinner.

I tried to remove her arms from around me and slow things down, but she was determined. Then she started saying, "Love me! Love me! Love me!" Something was wrong. I forced my way from underneath her and went into my kitchen. I could see her from where I stood but she didn't look at me. She sat on the sofa, heaving from the struggle. It was as if she really couldn't breathe. I stood looking at her. I just wanted some space between us, and some emotional closeness before we made love. Then she took a breath and held it. She fixed her eyes on me, lowered her chin, keeping her eyes on me. Evil. She became so enraged that she charged me like a Dallas Cowboy defensive lineman. I didn't even know I had the ball. When our bodies collided, my head struck the cabinet door behind me, rattling the dishes. I almost passed out. She pounded me in my chest. I felt the anger rumbling inside. I was scared for me and for her. Then she collapsed in my arms and started to cry. I tried to console her but she was out of control. I helped her back to the sofa and then . . . she passed out . . . cold.

Luckily I had the number to the neighbors' house where her kids were spending the evening. They were a married couple I had met a time or two. I just needed to call somebody and see if something else had happened that I wasn't aware of. I called and her neighbor gave me the impression that she didn't expect my date to come home that night. That really pissed me off. Especially since it was a school night. I hung up and checked to the see if she was awake yet and she wasn't. What happened? Why did she pass out? She didn't smell of alcohol. I just knew I wanted her out of my apartment before one of us hurt the other. I tried to wake her but she was out of it. I put her shoes on her and got her purse. I put her arm around my neck and held it tightly at the wrist. I stood her up and steadied her with my other arm around her waist. I struggled to get her down the stairs, wishing those angry hips would switch away under their own steam. But the reality was our trip down the stairs was much different than our trip up. I put her in my car. I was going to take her home.

On the way to her house she started to come to. She noticed that she was in my car and asked where we were going. I told her just for a ride. She bought it until she saw her exit. She exploded. She said she didn't want to go home. I told her we would work it all out the next day. I'd get her car back to her and it would all be okay. She fought me in the car but gave up quicker than I expected. Once we were at her house, she asked me to come in and talk for a minute. She was visibly upset and there were people out on the street in her neighborhood. She said she didn't want to air her business in front of her neighbors. So I went inside. She locked the door and set the alarm and told me that I couldn't leave. My brain went into distress. I couldn't believe this woman was holding me hostage! I struggled to move my body from where I stood over the short distance to the stair leading to the second floor. I flopped down on the stairs, put my head in my hands and tried to figure out what was going on and how I was going to get out of it. She kicked off her shoes, lifted her black dress, spread her legs and tried to straddle me. AGAIN! That's when it came out. I knew I had it in me. I delivered an Academy Award-winning performance complete with tears, heaving chest and a lengthy monologue about how all I want to do is please a woman and I keep ending up being a victim. She tried to dry my tears but they kept coming. She asked me how she could make it better. I told her to open the door so I could go home. She did. I left. But I didn't go home. I was afraid she'd find a way to get back to my place. I went to a friend's house and stayed the night.

All of this really happened?

Yeah. You know it did.

Well, if I didn't know, I do now. What else do you want to tell me?

Here is something else: I rarely took a woman that I was dating to church with me. With the exception of a year or so out of my life, I have been to church most every Sunday. But I could never bear the guilt of having the woman I was having sex with, or that I intended to have sex with before I was married, sitting next to me in church. Go figure. It wasn't logical. It's just the way it was. I also wouldn't date self-professed atheists or agnostics. A woman who had a belief in God but was not a Christian wasn't acceptable either. Women always knew where I stood when it came to religion. I was, and still am, a Christian. On the few occasions I took a woman to church with me, I couldn't stand it. My time of worshipping God and hearing the Word was marred by her presence. So I stopped taking them. I tried finding a woman in the church to date but found the level of drama way too intense. Typically, I met women from my church in outside-of-church in social settings. But I quickly found out that I didn't have enough status in the church to be desirable to them.

Here's another strategy, albeit a weak one, from my personal playbook. When I thought enough time had passed in the dating process, and I felt it was time to test the unconditional love factor to see if we could progress further, here's what I would do: I would wait for the next argument. No relationship is without them. There was always something I did or didn't do, or could have done, or should have done, or would have done, if she just would have given me enough time to do it on my own instead of wanting it when she wanted it, which was not in my own time frame. Oh . . . sorry . . . I digress. The point is, the argument would eventually take place when she would say, "Why do you treat me like this?" To that I would calmly respond, "What do you mean why do I treat you like this? It's just the way I am. I make mistakes. I'm not perfect. As a measure of what you can expect from me, here is the one thing you need to look at. I am a Christian. I believe that God is my Creator, my Father. Just look at how I treat Him and know that you can't expect any better from me."

This brainstorming process is getting a little deep. Some of the things I'm remembering are surprising even me. I can't believe I ever thought and did them. But it *is* true that alcohol brings out what is already inside of you.

Try and stay focused on the topic at hand. Please.

Oh yeah. . . . Like I was saying, that was my strategy and those are the conditions under which I would use it.

And was the result unconditional love?

No. The sad truth is that not one woman ever heard me when I said it. Not one woman ever discussed it with me. Maybe it's because I'm just a man, but to me, the ultimate exposure was to share with a woman my inconsistent behavior with my Supreme Being. I was trying to have a conversation that would set the tone for our life together. How can a person stand before God and make a commitment to another human being that he had not even been able to achieve with the Creator Himself? I longed to have that conversation with a woman, but it never happened. Maybe the timing was all wrong when I used that strategy. Maybe it should have been under different circumstances. I don't know. The games are over. Hindsight is twenty-twenty. No Monday morning quarterbacking.

So what do you want now?

I want to put everything on the table up front. Whether it is sex with sheep or the need to know that someone will walk with me through whatever life brings, I want someone to know that I understand I am a culmination of all that I have experienced in my entire life. I am who and what I am because of what I have experienced and done. Nothing is constant but change. And people change constantly. We change based on the way we are wired early in life.

Years ago, one of my sisters did a demonstration for me. She told me to fold my arms. I'm a little slow, so she had to help me with the demonstration. She said, "You know, like if you're waiting in line or if you're mad at somebody." She took my arms and crossed them. I finally understood what she was telling me to do. Then she told me to look at my arms and describe how they were folded and how it felt. Instinctively, my left fist was underneath my right elbow with my thumb pressed against my rib cage. My right hand rested in the crook of my left elbow with my thumb near my triceps and my open palm and four fingers rested atop my biceps. Then she told me to switch positions. I did, and immediately it felt uncomfortable. She could see the uneasiness on my face. She said, "See!" I asked her what the point was. She said that by the time a child is eight years old, he has already learned which way is comfortable for him. She said that children learn many things around that age and they are basically wired for who they are going to be. My sister had no idea how much her little demonstration absolutely floored me. I tried to become comfortable folding my arms in the opposite direction, but it just never felt right.

I want my family, friends, and the woman who will become my friend and my family, to know the *me* that is me. I want to tell her my experience. I want her to find out what my family and friends think about me. I want her to know what they have seen in me over the years. I want them to tell her what they have experienced with me. And hopefully, *I* will come to a new understanding of me. That's it. I will come to know and will share with others, the me who has to stand naked in the world without possessions. No-frills packaging. That will be my new existence. I will lay out the plan now, sitting here at 521 Harter Street where it all began, drinking and smoking on the front porch of the place that I call home. That will be my path, my ladder down from atop the pedestal I climbed up.

Hey Darryll, would you? Tell her how you know me?

My friend and brother Winston is as different and unique as his name. Just think, how many people do you know named Winston? He wears his uniqueness proudly and it is sometimes mistaken for arrogance. I would like to explain this uniqueness, using his name:

W – Like the wind, he is refreshing but cannot be possessed or controlled.

I – Intelligent in things most people take for granted. For instance, he knows when it is time to take care of himself so that he can be at the top of his game for those he cares about.

N – Noble in his beliefs and convictions.

S – Spiritual in a way most people cannot understand. His spirituality comes from within. He must first feel what God wants of him before he can commit to anything that you or I want from him.

T – Tenacious. He will stick to his guns until you can prove to him that there is a better way. However, it sure must truly be a better way. He will not be deceived!

O – Obligatory. Obligated to what he feels is the Truth. Don't expect him to lie to you just so he does not hurt your feelings. Because he cares, he will always be truthful with you. By the same token, don't lie to him; he can handle the truth!

N – Non-conformist. He does not conform for conformity's sake. He has his own mind and he uses it! Don't try to browbeat him into submission, it will not work!

One last suggestion in dealing with my friend Winston: be kind, gentle, honest and, most of all, patient and you can expect a long and productive relationship with him.

That's my story and I'm sticking to it.

Darryll Stewart
Austin, Texas

Left-right, Left-right
Getting in Step with the Others

CHAPTER EIGHT

I actually have a memory of the day I was born. It only gets a little fuzzy when I try to think of whether I actually remember that day or whether I've created images in my mind based on what I've been told. It was a sunny day. April 1, 1963. I floated down from the sky going around in spiral circles, passing though thin light clouds against a clear blue sky. I remember seeing the tops of the buildings in Marlin, but for some reason, I particularly remember seeing the icehouse close to downtown next to the railroad tracks. I remember seeing my father parked on the eastbound side of Live Oak Street at the Commerce Street intersection, near Pilot's Supply Store, just a block from the railroad tracks. His car was pointed in the direction of the hospital that was just on the other side of the tracks.

My father had just left his job at Houston's Restaurant to make it to the hospital when the policeman stopped him and told him he needed to change the plates on his car. It didn't matter that my father had a child on the way; the plates needed to be changed. My father already had the plates but hadn't had a chance to put them on, so with his ingenuity, he wired the new plates on top of the old ones and was allowed to proceed to my arrival.

I waited awhile before taking possession of my body. I hovered in the room just long enough to see my mother's silhouette resting in the hospital bed. But I wasn't in her arms. Someone else had me. My mother and I both listened to the nurses talk about how dark I was. Before I could say anything in my defense, my mother made it known she was not asleep and that she could hear what they were saying. She asked them to hand me to her and it was at that time I entered my body and held my head up with pride for the nurses to see before I rested in the arms of my mother.

My next memory isn't until I was little more than a year old. It was the morning my crib-days ended. The day that I met Harrell and Darrell. It seems like it was autumn or early winter. There was a fresh, crisp coolness in the house that morning. My father had already gone to work. I was standing in my crib, which was in my parents' room. I stood there peering through and over the bars of my crib. I looked at my mother and tried to remain quiet while she had a few final minutes of rest before the sun completely flooded the room. I remember the bedroom door burst open and these two *things* burst in, terrorizing the peaceful morning my mother and I were enjoying. They woke her up. Their movement was darting and constant and loud. I tried to make my eyes follow them around the room but I couldn't keep up. Their hands, faces and feet were on my crib, in my crib, off my crib. I remember thinking, "Why won't they be still?" The noise they made got louder. I wondered, "Why won't they be quiet?" My mother rolled over, wiped her eyes and touched her head. She looked at me looking at her and asked the two things to hand me to her. The bigger one grabbed me under each armpit and handed me to my mother. As she sat up in bed, my mother turned me around and placed me in her lap facing the crib. Before I could enjoy the comfort, I saw those two things climb into my crib. They jumped hard and the crib crumbled. The two things slid down the mattress as it fell to the floor. I gasped, my mother gasped, their eyes grew big, but at least they got quiet. Only the backside of my crib leaning against the wall remained standing.

They stood side by side, one looking behind him at the broken crib and the other looking at my mother and me. Their faces and movements were frozen, as though they were waiting for something else to happen. What they waited for, I don't know. What more could happen? My crib was gone. That's all that mattered. Could it be fixed? I knew from looking at it that I wasn't the first to have used it, but did anyone need it after me? What else had these two things broken? My mother put me on the floor beside her.

I remember pulling myself up by the bedspread that drooped near the floor and standing on my wobbly legs. My mother went to do something about the crib. It didn't matter. Something told me that it wasn't going to be fixed.

I later learned that the two things were my brothers, Harrell and Darrell. They were not twins. Darrell, whose real name is Aubrey, was actually a little more than a year older than Harrell, but Harrell's name always came before his. Harrell was a little less than two years older than me. I was the third of the trio. Harrell, Darrell and Winston. Most times you heard all three names together because, like them, I became a terror. More out of the need to survive and through guilt by association, but a terror just the same. Winston Gordon Williams was my full name. It would take me over thirty years to know how to spell my middle name correctly: 'don' and not 'den.' Like I always said, I'm a little slow.

One day, I became aware of all of the people who lived in our house. Besides my mother and father, all of the rest of them were my brothers and sisters. I was around three years old. It was another sunny and crisp fall day. There must be something about fall and my memories. But I remember these two tall guys came to the house and everybody was glad to see them. They arrived in a shiny blue car with blinds in the back window. They were both as tall as trees with almost bald heads and they both wore jackets with footballs on the front and patches on the sleeves. I vaguely remembered that these two guys had lived with us but for some reason they had left. There was John. He was the oldest and was named after my father, but my father's friends called my father J.C., and this guy's friends called him Johnny C. The other one was Randy, but his real name was Elliott. Then besides me, Harrell and Darrell, there were three girls who were all older than me, Harrell and Darrell, but younger than John and Randy. There was Linda, then Vern, whose real name was Viola after my mother's sister, then Stine, whose real name was Esstine. I learned that when I wasn't with my mother, Stine was the one responsible for what happened to me. She was only eight years older than me, but she was very responsible.

On that fall day, everyone was laughing, talking and playing with each other. My mother was preparing food and my father was doing something. I was happy to be around all of these people. My older brothers amazed me. They were so tall and I could hardly bend my head back far enough to see their faces without falling backwards. I knew I liked them. And I wanted to be wherever they were.

I remember going into the backyard where they were and feeling like I was one of them. The older one, John, picked me up and looked me right in the face and I wanted to hug his neck like I did my father. He looked at me, then turned me around so that I could see the other one, Randy. Then he tossed me to over to Randy. John laughed, Randy laughed, so I laughed too. Randy tossed me back to John and I laughed even harder. I couldn't believe that we were having fun with each other. I really liked these guys. Then John tossed me back to Randy. The time I spent in the air seemed a little longer than the first time, but it was still fun. Randy tossed me back to John. When John turned me around so that I could see Randy, I noticed that Randy seemed to be a long, long ways away. I remember wondering if the fun had ended. Was the game over?

Then I found myself flying through the air and the feeling was not joy anymore but something else. Randy caught me and quickly turned me around to face John on the other side of the backyard. Again, I found myself flying through the air and at the same time letting out a yell. John caught me and I could feel my face was wet. My eyes were letting out water, my heart was pounding really fast and the sound coming out of my mouth was very loud. John turned me around to face Randy yet again and I looked down at the ground to see the green grass and I wondered if it was as soft as it was green. My arms and legs began to flail wildly and I wanted to wipe the water from my face but even more I wanted to get away from these two guys, so I continued to swing my arms and legs to try and get free. I could hear John and Randy laughing louder. Then John put me down. I don't know where I went or what happened next, but it was over. I knew then that I needed to keep my distance from those two guys.

Their visit came to an end and they were preparing to leave our house. Good! That's when I noticed it. The entire family was walking out the front door. That day, my father led the way, followed by my mother, followed by John, then Randy, then Linda, then Vern, then Stine, then Darrell, then Harrell. They were all walking one behind the other, in step with each other. That was the day that I joined in the line. Right behind Harrell. The family had been marching in step, left-right, left-right, long before my arrival, and that day I joined in right behind everybody and felt that this was my place. No one was behind me and even though the pace of those in front of me was a bit fast, I did my best to keep up. I was at the end of the line, far enough away from those two guys who had caused my eyes to water but close enough to peek around and see them from my rear position. Close enough to see Stine and feel safe because she was only a few people ahead of me.

We filed out into the front yard, spread out across the sidewalk, gathered around the two guys that were leaving and shared warm embraces with them before they drove the shiny blue car with blinds in the back window off down the dirt road. There would be many visits like that. And each visit left an indescribable range of emotions.

Hey Linda, would you? Tell her how you know me?

Keep in mind that I am president of the WGW fan club!

I would share with your woman about your integrity. The fact that you believe in "doing the right thing" even when no one else is looking. You have a high sense of right and wrong but also understand that in life, there are gray areas and your compassion allows you to look at the gray and still maintain your integrity.

I would share about your compassion for all God's creations and that you would never intentionally hurt another person, even if you had experienced hurt. That you take the Golden Rule seriously and actively practice it.

I would share about your deep love, devotion and respect for your parents. That you are supportive, committed and just in love with your Momma and Daddy. A man that treats his momma the way you do will really honor the woman he spends his life with.

I would share what a profound family man you are. That you hold "blood" in high esteem and that you love your family, even the unlikable ones!

I would share about your generosity. That you have a giving, sharing spirit and will make sacrifices, when the spirit says so, for the welfare of another.

I would share about your being an honorable man. One who has high self-esteem, self-respect and self-worth. One who, when experiencing a "valley" episode, will still carry himself in a manner that earns the respect and adoration of others.

I would share about your ingenuity! God has blessed you with an entrepreneurial spirit and you are always aggressively seeking ways to develop a project, improve it, train others, make the income and share the knowledge.

I would tell her about your passion for "toys," cars, gadgets, technology, adventures, travel and new experiences.

I would even tell her about your sexual appetite. You LIKE it! At least, that's what I've heard.

Also, I would share about your tendency toward perfectionism. You have certain standards that exceed those of most people, and in many ways, you do not bend beneath those standards.

I would explain that you and I are related by blood but connected through a deep friendship and that I met you when you were about fourteen and have learned to love and respect you as a close confidant and personal friend.

I would tell her that you are still evolving into what God wants you to be and that you have a few dark secrets that she may never know or understand. You may never tell her all about yourself but would let her know that you can be loved for the pieces she is allowed to have.

Linda Williams Porter
Los Angeles, California

I Saw and Knew
What Grown Folks Didn't Think
I Saw and Knew

CHAPTER NINE

I can't figure out why the sun hasn't moved. Is this the day that time stood still? Just for me? Am I that special? Never mind the sun. I know for sure that's one thing I can't control: the rising or the setting of the sun. Thank goodness I don't have to deal with that today. When did I build up such a tolerance for beer? There goes my fifth one and I know I am going to want . . . no . . . *need* more.

I return the same way I came the first time but now with, hopefully, enough beer to take me to the end of this brainstorming session. Like a superstitious athlete, I want to do things exactly the same way so I can have the same outcome as I've had so far. But I don't. Instead of parking in my father's spot, I think I'll pull into the driveway now, my mother's parking spot. Like the street and like my father's parking spot, it is also made of dirt. As I open the door of my car, it brushes against the hedges, just like my mother's car door used to. My car is so much smaller than the big four-door cars my mother had over the years. But she had a lot of kids to haul around. She always had a four-door sedan and my father always had a station wagon. I don't remember all ten of us ever taking a trip together. The two older guys were already gone by the time we took the first trip that I remember. My father's station wagon had the third and fourth seats in the very back that folded up so the people sitting in them could face each other. That's where me, Harrell and Darrell would sit and terrorize each other.

Looking back, it's inconceivable to me how my father did it. When he was just about the age that I am now, he had a wife, eight children, a house, two cars, a full-time job, and a restaurant of his own. That doesn't include all the part-time jobs and two or three thriving gardens. He did it all with no more than a tenth-grade education and with only twenty-four hours in a day. My mother was amazing too. I tell people when it came to certain things, the lines that divided the roles in our house were often blurred. My mother could swing a hammer just as well as my father. My father could cook just as well as my mother. And here I am by myself, barely making it. I can't hold a relationship together long enough to even call it a relationship. Where did I go wrong?

Remember . . . that's what we're trying to get to.

I remember . . .

Then . . . continue . . .

I love my father and my mother. They are amazing people, but right now, in order to repackage myself, I am going to have to look at some things from the knee-high view of a child.

It's okay. Just do it. Tell the truth.

After I learned how to march in line and stay in step with the leader, life pretty much rolled along for me for a few years. There were enough people ahead of me to keep my parents busy and their attention off of me. I hadn't graduated to a full-fledged terror yet. So, fortunately, I saw what happens when you step out of line. And being born a logical and rational child, it made perfect sense to me to watch and learn so I wouldn't make the same mistakes. I decided to watch everybody, listen to everything, and try to put the pieces together and learn. Once Harrell started to go to school, there were a couple of years when it was just my mother and me during the day. She was a busy woman. We went a lot of places and did a lot of things. Only now do I know she was taking care of business. Me? I was just having fun being with her.

By the time I was born, my mother had stopped working as a domestic. She was busy coordinating the household, all the kids' schedules, working the noontime lunch rush at our restaurant, Williams' Snack Center, selling Stanley Products, caring for her mother who was in a nursing home in Waco, and renting out two of her mother's houses, one of which is behind our house. When it was gardening season, my father would organize the entire family effort to get each garden plowed and the seeds planted.

Once that was done, my mother would make the rounds to check on them during the week and take time to pick vegetables for dinner. As soon as I was able, my hands were busy helping out or getting in the way. In my house, you couldn't have two working hands and expect not to put them to use doing what needed to be done to keep the family going. There were six of us still at home and even though things were running fairly smoothly for that many people being in the same house, it could get pretty hectic. My parents were very active people and they still are. I have no idea where they get the energy. Even today, I tell them the only reason they still keep busy is so that rigor mortis won't catch up with them.

Later in life I learned that the two guys who left shortly after I arrived at the house had both been quite active in high school. They had both played football for the Booker T. Washington Wildcats and played instruments in the band in the off season. My parents were boosters and did a lot for the team and the band. To hear the stories about those days, the Wildcats were a tough team. They took long road trips, shared cold winter nights in the bleachers, had big homecoming parades and hard-fought championship games. The classmates became friends for life. They both got scholarships to college. One in football and music, the other just in football. And both my parents were right there with them the whole way.

Even as a young child, I knew the time I had alone with my mother was precious. I enjoyed experiencing each day with her: seeing each of the others off to school, watching the chaos on days when somebody made everybody late, riding in the car with her to Waco to see her mother, Big Momma Taylor, in the nursing home. Then back on the road to Marlin, listening to my mother sing as she drove fast to make it back to open the restaurant in time for the high school students and factory workers who came to eat lunch. My older sisters came to the restaurant on their lunch breaks and worked while they grabbed something to eat. Being in the midst of all those tall people made me want to grow up real fast and join in with them. They were all so full of excitement. But I had to wait. So while I waited, I watched and tried to learn. When the lunch hour ended, sometimes my father's father, Granddaddy, would come up to the restaurant. He and Big Momma Williams lived just a few houses up the street from the Snack Center. Granddaddy was tall and slender with a thin face. Most of the time he wore a fedora tilted to one side. His name was Sam.

The story passed down to me was that his father, whose name was also Sam, married a woman and they named their first son Sam. Then she fell off of a wagon and died. So he married another woman and she too had a son she wanted to name Sam. By the end of the story, there were five children named Sam: Christmas Sam, Easter Sam, Baby Sam, and two other Sams whose distinctions I can't remember.

I don't know which Sam my grandfather was, just that we had fun together. He had a piece of land across the railroad tracks behind the Snack Center. Momma would give Granddaddy and me the scraps from the lunch hour and he and I would go across the tracks holding hands and laughing, about what I don't remember. Granddaddy always laughed with me. Even when he put me across his knee and took the black leather strap he kept hanging on his front porch for bad little boys and pretended to give me a whipping, we laughed. Once we were safely across the railroad tracks, he would let go of my hand and let me climb on the rickety wooden fence made of old, gray planks, while he meticulously undid the intricate locking system of old clothes hangers and fence wire. He would swing the gate open with me going along for the ride until the bottom of the fence scraped the ground underneath. Then he'd give me the leftover lunch and send me along the trail that led to where he kept his dog Blackie tied up with a rusty chain that must have weighed more than she did. I'd feed Blackie and wonder why she was always so frail and why her ribs always stuck out through her shiny black coat.

I don't know how old Blackie was when I first met her, but I spent many hours with her and she was my friend for years. She lived in a run-down tin-roof house befitting her station in life. Blackie's house was just inside the fence and only a few feet away from the railroad tracks where the train screamed past many times a day. It seemed to me Blackie birthed a new set of pups several times a year. Once I thought I counted nineteen puppies at one time. But that may have been because I couldn't actually count yet. I always felt sorry for Blackie, and hoped the time I spent with her made her happy. I didn't know exactly how she came to have the pups, but I was sure it had something to do with the tracks and the chain around her neck. Her milk bags were always full and swinging. As soon as she had a litter, her babies disappeared, one by one, and there was nothing she nor I could do about it.

When I finished feeding Blackie, I would join Granddaddy while he fed and watered his horse. I don't know much about Granddaddy's life and what brought him to have that piece of land and that one horse, but he tended to them both everyday. There was a pile of rubble that rose out of the middle of Granddaddy's piece of land like a mountain. It was made of tin, old tires, iron tractor pieces, lumber and God knows what else. On the backside of the pile, there was an old barn that leaned to one side. It was a wonderful place to explore, full of bales of hay and crokersacks that were either full of horse feed or empty and primed for the next crokersack races at the festival down in the south part of Marlin. The barn had gallon-sized tin cans, bridles, saddles and just stuff. I loved it. It was always cool, too. No matter how hot it was outside, the darkness of the barn and the smell of the hay and the feed took the edge off. Granddaddy would yell to the horse, "Ya, ya!!" and we would laugh while the horse pranced around the pasture remembering its glory years.

The horse had a much better life than Blackie. It was a boy. I remember the first time I saw it. You know . . . its thing. I didn't know what it was and my mind didn't know how to process it. I didn't have anyone to ask, since everybody else was so busy marching ahead of me and they hardly ever turned around to talk to me. I had to wait for information to be passed back. Not much came in words. Mostly it was action. So I filed the image of the horse's thing away and hoped for the day when someone would tell me what it was so I could understand and make sense of it. It was huge.

Sometimes my mother would drop me off at my grandparents' house before heading up the street for the noontime rush. I loved visiting Big Momma and Granddaddy. Their house was so comfortable. It was old, but well kept, painted white with white around the window frames. The porch stretched from one end of the house to the other with chairs on either side and a small wooden bench for me. I would sit with Big Momma and Granddaddy and watch the world go by. The house faced Commerce Street and the love they surrounded me with seemed to flow out into the street. Big Momma was much shorter than Granddaddy and her body was full and round. She had a smile I will never forget. Her gray hair was streaked with black, and she kept it bound in two plaits that rested at the nape of her neck. She wore cat-eye glasses and dipped snuff. Her spit can was always near and, oddly enough, had an aroma I grew to love.

Grandma Easter lived with Big Momma and Granddaddy. She was Big Momma's mother. She was almost full-blooded Indian with distinct Indian features, reddish golden skin and long, flowing, gray hair. She also had the gift.

One day Harrell and I were playing in the ditch on the north side of the Snack Center. We were barefoot and Harrell stepped on a piece of glass that put a gash in his foot from just under his toes to just past his arch. There was blood everywhere! Grandma Easter just happened to come along in the midst of the panic. I don't remember another adult being around. All I knew was that my brother was hurt and I didn't know what to do. Somehow, Harrell made it to the front steps of the Snack Center. Grandma Easter took Harrell's bleeding foot in her hands, squeezed it tight and started to hum. I remember her humming. I remember how it made the air whisking around my head change color and texture. Why do I remember that? Within minutes, Harrell's foot was healed. There was no more blood. No scar. No evidence of what had just happened. Grandma Easter was calm, like it was no big deal. I stood with my eyes wide and my mouth gaping in shock. My mind didn't know what to do with what I had just witnessed, so I filed it away and waited. Sometimes when Harrell and I reminisce about that day, the only conclusion we can come to is that a miracle happened to him right in front of me.

Grandma Easter slept in a little room just behind Big Momma's room. Big Momma's room had two beds in it. But Granddaddy didn't sleep in either one of them. He slept in a room in the middle of the house in between the front room with the television and the kitchen. As much love as I felt from and for my grandparents, I always had an uneasy feeling about their sleeping arrangements. Maybe Granddaddy didn't sleep in the same room with Big Momma because she sold Lucky Heart Products and had boxes of stuff scattered all around the room. In any case, at the age of four or five years old, I knew that mommas and daddies were supposed to sleep in the same bed.

I also knew that in the middle of the night something happened. Sometimes at night, when I got scared, I used to find the courage to make my way to my parents' room and climb into bed with them. Like clockwork, my sleep and the security of my haven would be interrupted because I couldn't breath. I would wake up in my parents' bed gasping for breath because these two large bodies had rolled toward each other. This happened time after time until I decided to confront the things in the darkness rather than risk being suffocated. I was away at college before I realized I had probably prevented one or two people marching in line behind me!

So my grandparents' sleeping arrangements just didn't make sense. Something was wrong and my own confusion only got worse. In our family, at our house, we all ate together at the table with plates, knives, forks, glasses and serving bowls. I knew all six of Big Momma and Granddaddy's children were grown and gone away from home so they didn't need to have the same rituals for meals as we did. I saw Big Momma cook for Granddaddy many times. But when it came time to eat, she would set his place at the table, place his plate of food on it, call him into the kitchen to eat, then make her plate and take it to her room. He would eat in the kitchen at the table and she would eat in her room. Both of them eating at the same time, but eating alone. Just like the way they slept.

It just didn't add up. If my father was their son, then where did he learn to have the family eat together and to sleep with his wife? It didn't make sense to me and there was no one to ask. Years later, some of us kids gossiped about the separate bedrooms. But the tales didn't matter. My eyes experienced the truth I knew. I saw a truth and I knew I didn't want that to happen to me.

Regardless of the way my grandparents chose to sleep and eat, their love for me was beautiful. It must have been great for my mother to have them so near to watch after me whenever she needed. When my mother picked me up from my grandparents', she and I would be off on another adventure. We would go to the freight station and I would pick up boxes of Stanley Products. We'd take the products to our house, where I helped her separate them into groups. Pretty bottles went with pretty bottles, gold liquid with gold liquid, and blue liquid with blue liquid. Then she'd read her orders and give me a bag big enough to hold the items. She handed the different products to me and I put them into the bag. We spent what seemed like hours doing this, but actually it only took a little time. Our work would be interrupted by us having to go and pick up someone from school or make sure someone else got to piano lessons or to choir practice.

In the meantime, Daddy would come home from his job at the restaurant and settle in for his afternoon nap before he had to either go out to collect insurance money or go to the restaurant and open for the night business or maybe head to a lodge meeting. Based on the stories I had heard about my oldest brothers, I figured out that after I arrived and they left, Daddy cut way back on things like the booster club and following the football team. He participated in school activities through my mother because he had too many things to do for the family, and I understood. I also understood that Daddy's afternoon naps were very important. He would be gone in the morning before anyone else woke up and wouldn't get home from the restaurant until we had gone to bed. Even with his schedule we still saw him a lot.

Sometimes I would snuggle up next to him on the sofa in the den. I remember how hard it was to balance myself on the small space between him and the edge. I always moved the black ashtray stand away from the edge of the couch because it was full of his cigarette butts and the smell stung my nose. I would still be getting situated and Daddy would already be in a deep sleep. Sometimes I would fall asleep and sometimes I would just lie with him and listen to him snore. The noise that came from inside of him amazed me. His stomach moved in and out, and I wondered if I would make that noise when I grew up.

I learned a very important lesson being at my father's side there on the sofa. When I grew up enough to walk home by myself from school, I had to use the back door to come into the house. The two front entrances had fancy screen doors that creaked really loudly. But the back entrance had a screen door that didn't creak. And no matter which entrance you used, you needed to walk very softly and be very quiet, put your books down and go back outside until Daddy's nap was over. It didn't take much for me to learn that lesson. The first time Daddy and I heard the front screen door creak and noisy children coming into the house as if no one was trying to take a nap, Daddy's stomach popped out and pushed me to the floor. He barked at the noise and demanded the presence of the persons making it. I learned that I never wanted to have an audience with Daddy after having disturbed his sleep.

CHAPTER TEN

Sometimes in the evening after dinner, my mother would take me, and sometimes Harrell and Darrell, to church with her for mission or choir rehearsal. Most of the time she would be late and I would brace myself for the ride. Upper Zion Missionary Baptist Church was outside of the city limits and the dirt roads were not kept as well as the ones inside the city limits. There were bumps and chuckholes in the road and I would bounce along inside the car making noise just to hear my voice shake with the bumps. We would arrive and hurry inside. Upper Zion is one of the biggest churches in Marlin. It can seat hundreds of people and has a U-shaped balcony that wraps around it above the pews facing the pulpit. When I was a child, the choir stand was so steep it scared me to be up there. I had nightmares about that choir stand.

Like so many families of that time, we were in church all day on Sunday, including Sunday School and six o'clock evening worship. We were there again on Monday night for choir rehearsal and again on Wednesday night for mission or midweek service. But why were we hearing the same thing over and over? At choir rehearsal they rehearsed the same songs they had just sung on Sunday or the Sunday before that. At mission they repeated the same reports from the week before, said the same words to God that they had just said on Sunday. I knew they were getting something out of being there that I didn't understand and they really enjoyed it or else they wouldn't be there so much. So I set out to find out what that was.

On mission nights, my mother would give me something to do, usually something to write with and a few cards from the children's Sunday

School class. The cards were always so colorful and peaceful looking, with a message about doing good and loving everybody. I loved to stare at those cards and think about what they were trying to tell me. The colors alone kept my attention. If Harrell and Darrell were with me, they would usually get us into some kind of trouble that would make Momma separate us into different parts of the sanctuary. Then I could be alone to ponder the cards and maybe try to draw peaceful pictures myself.

Sometimes things at church got interesting. Especially when the people in the meeting were not behaving like my little cards said they should. I would hear and bear witness to things I knew definitely didn't belong inside the church or in people's lives, period. In one mission meeting, some women got into an argument over who was going to bring the bread for the dinner after Sunday afternoon service. Or was it potato salad? I can't remember. But I remember I sat there and wondered, were these the same people who shouted and testified on Sundays?

Sometimes I overheard stories about which woman was dating which married man, or who was drunk on Saturday night, or which woman was marrying men then killing them for the insurance money, or which man was a swindler, or which women practiced voodoo. I would think to myself, didn't they just get finished with a lesson about loving one another like Jesus did?

My mother was never involved in any of the ruckus at church. She participated in the lessons, responded occasionally to the pastor as he delivered his message and on rare occasion, cried aloud. She prepared and delivered her dishes. She appeared on the program when asked, taught the children and led her favorite song in the choir. She greeted everyone with a genuine smile, gathered her children and took us home to feed and care for us. On very rare occasions, when some woman would stretch my mother's patience to the limit, she would wait until she was off church grounds before she let the word "heifer" slip from her lips. I knew my mother's patience had truly been tested when that happened! She had taught me it was a bad word and that people shouldn't use such language, but I understood when she just couldn't help herself. Besides, she had such a dignified way of saying it. "Heffa."

I determined that the people who raised fusses at church were the ones who were too busy yelling back at the pastor when he was yelling at them during his message. So I decided to be a little like my mother; I would sit and listen to the pastor or teacher to understand what they were saying, and maybe I wouldn't behave like those other people.

Some evenings, Momma would have demonstrations for Stanley Products or Tupperware. She would have a woman host a party, invite friends over and my mother would show them the product the company offered and take orders. There would be food, fun and money for my mother. I loved to help my mother in business. By the time I was in the second or third grade, I had a lot of practice helping her with product demonstrations. Her business had expanded to other small towns around Marlin. Around that same time, my father bought another car. He replaced her old green batmobile with a white 1969 Chevrolet Impala with a black top. I loved to wash that car. Getting it from dirty to white was so rewarding to me.

I thought everything was fine with my mother's business. I could see money changing hands and she paid me for helping. But one particular evening when my mother was getting ready to go to a demonstration at her cousin's house in Calvert, Daddy was upset about something. I saw him get dressed to go to the restaurant and thought that he had already left. But instead something else happened. I heard rumblings from their bedroom. By then, I was familiar with that rumbling. Daddy's temper usually exploded when he was under pressure at the restaurant or when he was fed up with us. Whenever I heard that sound it would make me feel like there was a change in the very air and there would be a small rumbling that echoed inside of me.

My mother came out of their bedroom and my father followed her, still rumbling. I stood still and kept quiet to hear what was going on. My father was telling my mother that he didn't want her putting a lot miles on the new car and that he didn't want her going all the way to Calvert for her demonstration party. I peeked around the corner and saw my mother in the bathroom putting on her makeup. She didn't say much but my father continued rumbling. I listened.

When my mother finally spoke, she told him that she helped contribute to the family. She told him that the kids needed shoes and clothes and the money she made helped buy those things. I thought what she said made perfect sense and what he was saying didn't. Not that I wanted to side with my mother, it just made sense. Daddy continued rumbling and Momma continued putting on her makeup and calmly told him that she was going to go. I wondered why he kept going on and on; he had made his point and she had told him what she was going to do and that should be the end of it. When it was all over, Daddy went to work and Momma went to her party. She continued to go to Calvert after that. I never understood what the big deal was. But I knew at that point that the small rumbling inside of me was a part of my father and I never wanted it to explode. I decided that I didn't want that part of my father coming out, and I would do whatever it took to keep my rumblings buried deep inside of me.

One morning after Momma and I had seen everybody off to school, there was a knock at the door. My mother answered and I heard a woman talking to her. She and my mother chatted while I lay across my bed waiting to go somewhere. Momma was in the mirror in the bathroom putting on her makeup and I peeked around the corner to see who the woman was. I recognized her as a relative, but I didn't know how we were related. She stood near the bathroom door talking to my mother. I drifted in and out of their conversation until it got interesting. The woman was telling my mother about her husband having had an affair that produced a child. I found it strange that my mother didn't stop and give this her full attention. But the woman kept talking. From what I could understand and put together, I knew the other woman and had actually seen the child. This relative was obviously upset, but the way my mother kept preparing to go to work seemed to mean something. Next thing, the woman left our house and my mother and I went to the restaurant. The next time we visited the woman and her family at their house, I wondered if she and her husband slept in separate bedrooms. It would be years before I heard another conversation about the other woman or the child. But she and her husband are still together to this day.

One evening when I was about six years old, we kids were eating dinner and Daddy came into the kitchen and said something that made Stine act funny. I was enjoying my mother's delicious casserole of rice, wieners, chili, beans and corn chips topped with a lot of cheese when I saw water coming from my sister's eyes. I stopped in mid-crunch and looked at her. Is that how I looked when water came from my eyes? She looked funny so I started to laugh. I looked at Darrell and water was coming from his eyes, too. I didn't understand why something that Daddy said to Stine would make water come from Darrell's eyes. Harrell seemed unconcerned. Stine wiped her eyes and saw me laughing at her. Then she yelled at me, saying Grandma Easter just died. I didn't know what it meant, but my sister who took care of me had water coming from her eyes so maybe water should be coming from my eyes too. I bowed my head and pretended to have water coming from my eyes just like them. After a minute or two, I wanted to get back to my meal so I did. Stine hadn't touched her food so I asked her if I could have it. She said yes and left the table.

Several days later, I had to put on my Sunday suit, even though it wasn't Sunday, and go to the building that my father's cousin owned just up the street from my grandparents' house. I missed school that day. My mother took me by the hand and led me down a short hall to a small room with five or six rows of chairs. We sat down. I looked around to try and figure out what was going on. Then I saw Grandma Easter lying in a bed at the front of the room. Nobody ever explained to me exactly what was going on, but I knew. I knew that Grandma Easter's healing days were over. I bowed my head and real water came from my eyes.

Even though no one explained things to me, I wondered if the grown folks knew I had questions in my head. I wondered if they knew that I saw, and wanted to know more.

Hey Niece, would you? Tell her how you know me?

I have several uncles and aunts, but Uncle Winston always stood out in my mind. He was young, cool, and close to our age. I always felt more comfortable around him than the others because he was easier to approach and talk to about personal issues. I liked how he always took the time to talk to me and see what was really going on in my life. He showed genuine love and compassion toward me, even though I am his niece through marriage. That was important to me because I sometimes felt different because I was a part of the family only through marriage.

One recent incident that stands out really opened up my mind and heart even more to Uncle Winston (that's what I'll always call him no matter how old I get, or how young he gets.) One of my closest cousins and I were not getting along and without even knowing or being told, Uncle Winston could sense that something was wrong. I didn't think he or anyone else would pay that much attention during the time that this was going on because my cousin was getting married. However, as always, Uncle Winston could tell that something was not right in his family. He waited until I was alone so as not to make me feel uncomfortable, and he discreetly asked me what was going on. I initially had no intention of talking to anyone about it because I felt it was something between me and my cousin. But because he showed genuine concern and care for me, I decided to open up. I think, to do what he did, you have to really be in touch with your family, not by phone or mail, but spiritually and emotionally.

I really look at him as a great role model and teacher. Growing up was hard, and at times we did not attend church as a family. But one day Uncle Winston took the time and initiative to teach and explain to me the ABCs of going to heaven. I thought that was important because even as a young adult, I did not know some of the things he taught me. I really appreciated that, because I always wanted to know, but never asked. Now knowing these things, I try to consistently practice the ABCs. Since then, I have come to know and love Uncle Winston even more for opening me up to the Lord. I want to learn and know more from him, so I need to stay in touch more (smile).

One more testimony and I'm through. I have had to overcome many obstacles to achieve things. I learned some positive characteristics from my uncle. Recently, I told him that I wanted to work for the federal government. Now that dream is finally going to come true, thanks to him and God! I told him my interests, but he knew already from past conversations that I've had this goal since I started college to earn my BS in Criminal Justice. Uncle Winston knew people and had connections. He was always the one to call if you wanted to know about something or somebody important. So I did and of course he came up with positive results. Soon after we talked, he e-mailed the contact information to me. I was really happy and excited that he took the time to do that. I quickly called the contact, had a great interview and was hired! Thank you Uncle Winston. I will never forget what you have done for me.

Kiata Carlette Gude
Houston, Texas

Terror Begins
Learn to Terrorize or Die

CHAPTER ELEVEN

The sun has finally fallen to the top of the horizon. Standing on the porch, I have a better view of the sun's rays between the trees and the beginning of evening's dusk. The mild wind is humming in my ear. The coming darkness seems to be reaching for me. I wonder if it wants to heal me. Maybe. But right now the only thing on my mind is relieving myself. That sixth beer was it; I have to go.

The west side of the house was not meant for passage, at least not for people the size I have grown to be. It is very narrow with a rusty, chicken wire fence and shrubs separating our property from the neighbors', but I manage to navigate it. I begin to relieve myself outside of the bathroom window like we all had done many times before. Living in a house with one bathroom and as many as ten people required alternative locations for relieving oneself. When I was small, we kept a "pee pot" outside the bathroom door. It was plastic, shallow and dingy yellow from years of use. In my early years, it was easy to use the pee pot when the bathroom was occupied. I could either kneel down or hold the pot in one hand close to me. Either way, I could turn my back to the passing public and face the corner of the closed bathroom door and the dirty-clothes closet for privacy without having to go outside. Over time, I began to notice that I was the only one using the pee pot.

The message was passed back to me through the line that it was time for me to go to the spot outside the bathroom window. This was the place those in front of me had used and now it was my turn. I never understood why we all had to use the same place and why that place had to be just outside of the place that was already occupied. Why couldn't we relieve ourselves outside the kitchen window or on the side of the storage house? Was there some kind of underground drainage system that made all of the stuff flow to the same place? Years later, when I thought I had learned about fertilizer and what it was made of, the scientist in me became curious. So I planted a garden on that side of the house. Corn, green beans and some flowers. At first when it all sprouted, I was excited and couldn't wait to report my findings to somebody, anybody. Then the corn grew taller than me and the green beans and flowers grew as well. But the vegetables that grew on the stalks and vines were withered and never matured and the flowers were dingy and scrawny. I thought it had something to do with us and our pee.

I wonder who will be the first woman to hear all of these memories. I wonder if what I want to communicate to her will make sense or if I'm just wasting my time. I could be subconsciously setting up the rules for a new game that might backfire on me too. She might take my life, my thoughts and my heart and twist them around to hurt me. Maybe this isn't the right thing to do. Maybe I should stop. My seventh beer would taste so much better if I only had a lime, but I decide against returning to the store because the shadows are still reaching for me. I'll take the beer as it is and deal with the need to pee. This meeting with my *Self* will continue so that I can get all of the product information documented in my head and ready for packaging. Tonight I will go all the way and touch the silver box. There is no turning back.

CHAPTER TWELVE

Are you ready to continue?

Yes.

Then go on.

My time alone with my mother came to an end when I started kindergarten. We waited for the bus while I ate the breakfast she had prepared especially for me. We sat there in the two metal chairs my father had painted blue, and I remember her looking at me. Just looking. The bus came and I gave her a hug then walked to the bus, not even wanting to look back. And I didn't. But I knew our daily adventures were over, or would be very different, for both of us.

We were all busy. For my brothers and sisters still at home, it was school activities, church activities, social activities and of course friends. But for all of us, there was work. By the time I was five, I had already received my first pay for working. I became pretty good at cleaning the tables during the lunch hour rush. My kindergarten classes would be over by the time the big kids let out for lunch. Our school, Booker T. Washington, was just down the street from the Snack Center, so I could walk to the restaurant by myself. Cleaning the tables gave me a chance to hang out with the big kids and learn how to be like them one day. They would laugh and pat me on the head to acknowledge my presence. Cleaning the tables also made me feel very useful. I couldn't stand just sitting in the chair in front of the television while my mother and sisters were running around trying to keep up with all of the orders. When I helped, I felt like I was contributing to the family. I could barely see the tops of the tables I cleaned, so I would climb into the booths or on the stools at the counter and take as many plates or glasses as I could and get more on the next trip. The plastic container that held the dirty dishes was underneath the counter and was easy for me to get to. Then one day my mother handed me five one-dollar bills. I held them in amazement. I just stared at them. That day, I felt myself grow into a tall man inside. I came to learn that none of the children ever received an allowance and neither would I. My parents would provide the basic necessities, but we worked for the rest.

While I didn't have that much time with Momma anymore, I still got to see Granddaddy and Big Momma Williams. Either I went up to their house or one of them came to the Snack Center to visit. If Granddaddy came to the Snack Center and didn't take me to feed the horse, he and I would sit in the booths and pretend to play checkers with soda bottle tops. We would set up on the black table where lovers and thugs had carved their messages over the years. There would be hundreds of bottle tops and Granddaddy would tell me to crown him, then let out his infectious laugh. Even though I had started school and didn't have the mornings with my mother any more, I thought that if life was like this—go to school, go to work, get paid and then play with my grandfather—I was going to enjoy it a lot.

CHAPTER THIRTEEN

Harrell, Darrell, and Winston. We were bad children. No, I was a good child until I joined them. I officially joined them when I entered first grade. Our school days ended about the same time. We did household chores together. Life just put us together sort of naturally. So my name was added to the end of theirs, but I hated being at the end. By this time there were only five of us left at home. The others had followed what I would come to know as the unspoken rule. High school graduation meant you had to leave the house. It didn't matter where you went, but you had to leave. So they went to college. Daddy gave all of us the opportunity to go to college and we all did, whether we graduated or not.

Once I left the comfort of my mother's attention and was placed under the watchful eye of my sister Stine, Harrell and Darrell pledged me into their fraternity. Right under everybody's noses, my reign of terror began. They were learning the ins and outs of marching in line. I don't know if they were as attentive as I was and I definitely know they didn't have the same objective as me; to march, left-right, left-right, stay in line, and out of trouble. Harrell and Darrell found trouble and dragged me right along with them. There was a hard and fast rule in our house that had developed by the time Harrell and Darrell and I started our reign. Boys didn't fight with girls. I think it had something to do with one of the older guys breaking Vern's arm. Some say she fell out of the tree, others say she was pushed. I don't know, but for whatever reason, it was a rule.

Vern and I only had one scuffle before she had to leave the house, and instead of handling it herself, she had Harrell do her dirty work, which just added to my brotherhood pledge program. She told Harrell to lock me outside because she and I had gotten into it. I don't know where my mother or Stine were, but there was no one there to protect me. Harrell struggled to get me out the back door and lock it behind me as he had been instructed to do. I fought back hard. I was determined not to have a girl make my own brother put me out of the house. Harrell was older and bigger than me and he finally won. The upper half of the pink wooden back door had blue textured glass in it. When Harrell pushed me out the door, my body burst through the screen door and I fell onto the red brick walkway. I was more mad than bruised. I jumped to my feet and was glad to see the screen door was still intact. Seems like my mother had to replace that screen every other week because we were so hard on it. I ran to try and force my way back into the house before Harrell could close the door. Right when I was about to press against the door, Harrell slammed it shut. I couldn't believe he didn't have the sense to put his hands on the wooden part of the door instead of the glass. Blue glass flew at me before I could put my hands up to protect my face. The glass cut me. Only a little blood came from my forehead, but I still have the scar to this day. That day I learned what I needed to survive.

It was early in the pledge program, but I had seen enough from Harrell and Darrell to know I needed some leverage. I had no personal experience with the old cliché that says the youngest is always spoiled. My life was nothing like that. All I knew was that everybody was bigger than me. They were okay with being in trouble, and I needed to find a way to survive. So even though I wasn't badly hurt, I pushed water from my eyes, made my chest swell up real big, then let all the air out of my lungs like I was going to pass out. For good measure, I made my entire body shake. And it worked. They panicked! Of course they tried to convince me not to tell. But I knew I wouldn't have to. The evidence was already there. The broken window, the cut and the blood. Perfect! I didn't care if they got a beating or not. I couldn't give up the act. I played it so well that Big Momma Williams requested my presence at her house so she could see my scar. My goal was to get Harrell and Darrell to leave me alone. But do you think they learned? No. They just became more cunning. I tried to spend more time with Stine, but there was no escaping Harrell and Darrell.

Every day, at least one of us cried and at least one got a beating. Years later, I told my mother I figured out why her arms never got flabby; she had a good workout every day by swinging a belt at us. My father must have had great confidence in my mother's disciplinary abilities. Not once did my mother ever tell us to "wait until your father gets home." She handled everything in real time. And she was good at it. Like the time when I was in the ninth grade, and Darrell and I were getting into it over something in front of my mother. He was a senior and you'd think he'd know better by then. I was the closest to my mother and her gold "I Dream of Jeannie" pixie shoe was the closest thing to her hand and that was it. That was the last lick I got from my mother. I remember going to school with the welt from a pixie shoe on my leg. Yes, I deserved it.

CHAPTER FOURTEEN

Stine was my friend. When she watched over me, I always behaved and tried not to get in the way. Even when she had to run the Snack Center on Saturdays, I wanted to be there with her. Her friends would come by and I would just hang around and be a good little brother. Stine was growing into a very popular and beautiful girl. Daddy dealt with so much grief from all of his kids, he didn't need me telling him anything else. So when I saw Stine kissing her boyfriend, Carl, in the Snack Center's big dining room where we had special events, I kept my mouth shut. Besides, I liked Carl. He eventually became my brother-in-law and is like my brother to this day.

Stine was about the only one who would talk to me and give me advice. Me, Harrell and Darrell were chunky little boys. Each year before school started, we dreaded having to go to the Sears mail order store to get our husky jeans. It was Stine who told me to watch out because no woman wanted a fat man lying on top of her. I was still quite young when she told me that and I didn't know what to do with the information, so I filed it away for later and started eating salads with my fried chicken.

Not only was Stine my friend and caregiver, she was my protector. Somewhere along the way, Halloween in Marlin took a wrong turn. I enjoyed several years of homemade costumes, plastic masks and goo-gobs of candy, but then it started to change. Down the street from the Snack Center, just across the railroad tracks, was a neighborhood grocery store. An Italian family owned it and one of their sons was in the same grade as me. Somebody started a tradition of breaking out the grocery store's big glass window every year. Even worse, all over town people climbed into trees and threw rocks at trick-or-treaters. Cars got egged. Rotten tomatoes were thrown on houses. Turf wars raged between people from different sides of the tracks or different ends of town.

This particular Halloween, Stine and me, Harrell and Darrell wanted to go out, get candy and then just walk around. We thought as long as we stayed together and on our side of the tracks we would be fine. It was at the beginning of the Halloween problems, so we were still quite green about what was actually going on in our small town. Looking back, I realize I was too small to be out there at that time of night, but there I was. When the sun finally went down, the darkness took on a different look than any other night of the year. The thrill of danger crackled in the air. We came across some folks we knew. Stopped to chat. Then continued to walk. I saw people perched in trees and they let us pass because they knew us. Stine kept my hand tightly in hers. For some reason, we decided that the Snack Center was neutral territory even though it was on the other side of the tracks. So we decided to walk over there and stroll down toward the south end of Marlin to our cousins' house across the street from the old Booker T. Washington school campus.

I remember how dark the night was and how my heart pounded with each step. I wanted to go home. But I was a typical little kid, not wanting to be called a chicken. I gripped Stine's hand. Darrell and Harrell walked on the other side of me. Maybe to protect me. Maybe not. We made it to our cousins' house but again, for some strange reason, decided to press our luck and walk a little farther. The south end of Booker T. Washington's campus was another dividing line in Marlin. The people down there were said to be rougher. It was a place where you didn't want to be caught on a night like this. But we were foolish. We kept walking. There were other people out as well and it seemed like we were all just trying to find fear. We found it in the guise of a boy named Male Cow Evans.

I think his real name was Malachi, but everybody called him Male Cow. People said that he did things to cows. I had filed that information way back in my brain along with the image of Granddaddy's horse. By day, Male Cow was frightening for me to look at and I would have rather died than find out what he turned into at night, especially on Halloween.

Male Cow was lurking in the shadows that night. He was a long distance away, but I knew it was him and he must have known it was me because it sounded like he called me by name. I think I heard him growling, but I know for sure he started to chase us. Stine had one hand, Darrell grabbed my other and they started running and screaming. I didn't know where Harrell was and I didn't care. My feet left the ground and I was airborne, flapping in the wind like Superman's cape. I opened my mouth to scream but couldn't. Nothing would come out. They ran and ran and ran. I thought I heard Male Cow getting closer. I could almost feel his rough hands against my legs, his nasty breath on my neck. I closed my eyes and prepared to die. When I opened them, we were at the grocery store standing underneath a streetlight. The big glass window hadn't been broken yet.

My feet were back on the ground and the water started to well up in my eyes. I felt like if I opened my mouth a sound would come out but it would be a sound that went with the water. I thought everybody was as scared as I was so letting the water fall and letting the sound out would be okay. Then, I couldn't believe my ears. Those crazy brothers of mine were laughing. They were bending over, hands on knees, out of breath and wasting what little air they could suck in . . . laughing. What was so funny? I didn't get it. Then Stine got caught up in their madness and started to laugh too. I was so confused. Grandma Easter dies . . . I laugh . . . they get upset with me. Now my life was about to end and they found it funny. Who was I going to turn to, to help the world make sense?

How could I tell my mother to take me back? How could I explain to her that I didn't like being with Harrell and Darrell? How could I make my parents understand I didn't like being in line behind them? They weren't teaching me anything worthwhile. How could I make my parents understand I wanted to stand by myself and get private lessons on how to march? Didn't my parents see the hell Harrell and Darrell were putting me through? Did they even care? So it continued. I had nightmares about Male Cow for years. And I do mean years.

CHAPTER FIFTEEN

Not only was Stine beautiful, she was talented. She was in the band at school, played piano for a church or two, sang in the choir at our church and performed with the Hampton Specials, a gospel group. On top of all that, she was a cheerleader. So when it came time for me to transition into spending even more to time with Harrell and Darrell instead of with her, I understood. She was busy living her life. I had to go and fight for mine.

Momma's confidence grew in Darrell's ability to be in charge when the three of us were left alone. But I wanted to tell her so bad that he was evil. Not like Satan, but mad scientist evil. And Harrell was no better. Being younger and not as sharp as them, sometimes I needed their skills to fight back. This was a little tricky because for a while it was always the two of them against me. When they found out I hated small, dark places, they locked me up in a closet or rolled me up in quilts so I couldn't see or move. Once they even rolled me up then locked me in the closet. When I entered my bed-wetting years, they poured water on me at night to make me think I had wet the bed. When I had to share a bed with Harrell, he supposedly marked the headboard dividing the bed down the middle, so I would have my side and he would have his. Then after being kicked and punched silly night after night because I couldn't stay on my side of the bed, I found out he had taken a lot more than just half for his share and given me a sliver of the mattress to sleep on. They were in together on my pledge program and I had to find a way to drive a wedge between them to get one of them to side with me against the other. I don't know how I did it, but I did.

Part of the pledge program included being given a nickname. Even though they were bound and determined to drag me into their brotherhood, I was not going easily. So when I was given a nickname, I made sure they each had nicknames too. Each one of us wound up with three names each. Names that, if uttered, could easily cause a fight. The intensity of the fight depended on the name used. I endured such relentless teasing, or meddling as we called it, that it causes me anxiety to this day.

As a child, I felt my lips covered my face. I never told anyone about it, but my brothers had a sixth sense about such things and used it to torture me. They nicknamed me Lippo-bippo-jet. They said I looked like some creature on *Star Trek* and I got fighting mad each time they said it. Eventually, they shortened it to Lipojet. Darrell's first nickname came from *Star Trek* as well and was also based on a physical feature I found to be quite amusing, and I still have some scars to prove it. I found it strange that my mother couldn't see the evil scientist in Darrell—all she had to do was look at the way his eyebrows were shaped. They each started in the middle, rose to a sharp point, then went back down, sort of like Mr. Spock's eyebrows. Hence Darrell's first nickname: Mr. Spock. Darrell could hit real hard and I took my share of punches for calling him that. Harrell's first nickname was based on a physical attribute too. Harrell had bright red, puffy gums, so I called him Bubble Gums. The second set of nicknames we gave each were reserved for times for when we wanted to be *really* nasty. Which for them, the evil ones, was everyday. Darrell's second name was JB for Juicy Booty. Like I said, we were all very chunky as children, but he carried his weight in his behind. Harrell's second name (and he'll kill me for telling this) was JT for Juicy Titty because he carried his weight in his chest. My second name was Mooooo because of my intense fear of Male Cow Evans. Not a single day went by without them saying "Mooooo" to me. And if they didn't say it, I thought I heard it. I refuse to explain the third set of nicknames. My third name was Qwack-qwack-qwaoo, Darrell's was Hammerhead and Harrell's was Boomerang. And that's all I'll say about that.

CHAPTER SIXTEEN

So many things happened when we were left alone. Over time, I learned to go deeper and deeper into a trance to numb myself so I could just to make it through another day. One day, the three of us were at home alone. I was in the den watching television, minding my own business, hoping, just hoping, my brothers would leave me in peace. Harrell came into the den with a look of horror on his face. He told me to hurry up and come to Darrell's room, because something was wrong with him. He ran out of the room and I followed. Darrell's bedroom was a small room in the back of the house just off the kitchen. It was a creepy little room because it was so small and I hated small spaces. But he wanted his own space. When my older brothers lived at home, the room was theirs. When they left, my mother made it into her sewing room. Before Darrell moved into the room, I had only been in it a few times. There was an old manual Singer sewing machine with the wide pedal that had to be see-sawed back and forth to move the needle. I used to sit on the pedal and hold the round wheel and pretend I was driving. But I only did that when my mother was in the kitchen. If she left the kitchen I left that room.

I arrived at Darrell's little room and found Harrell standing in the narrow doorway with his back to me, peering inside. I stood behind him hoping he would handle whatever was wrong. He moved to the side and told me Darrell had fallen on a knife by accident. I peeked around Harrell, only to see Darrell lying across his bed with my mother's favorite long, black-handle knife sticking out of his stomach. He was bleeding badly. There was blood all over him! I screamed in horror and grabbed Harrell and told him to do something. Harrell just stood there, unconcerned. Doing nothing. I ran to Darrell even though I didn't know what to do. Salty water started coming from my eyes. I knew then that while I hated the way he treated me, I didn't hate him. Not enough to just stand by and watch him bleed like that. I yelled for Harrell to call somebody, get somebody, do something! He just stood there. I didn't know whether to pull it out or what. Darrell was moaning from the pain. I thought if I pulled the knife out, his guts would come out too. I felt so useless. My vision was blurred by the water in my eyes. I hung my head and lay my hands on Darrell's stomach, hoping I had a little of Grandma Easter in me. I noticed Darrell's stomach felt very soft and it started to shake. I didn't know what was happening. Was it working? I squinted to see what was happening. I wanted to wipe my eyes, but I didn't dare move hands; they might be healing him. I stared at the knife. It was shaking real hard. I looked at Darrell's face and he was laughing. The water continued to fall from my eyes to my cheeks as Darrell sat up in his bed and pulled the knife out of the pillow he had stuffed under his shirt. The "blood" was catsup. The days that followed were a delight to Harrell and Darrell. With each rising sun, they opened a new box of torment for me.

Like I said before, in our house, every day somebody had to cry and somebody had to get a beating. That was just the way the days went.

"Moooo!"

I hated when they called me that. If I could only disappear then they couldn't see me and I would be left alone.

"Spock!"

"Moooo!"

I can't just let him do this to me. I have to fight back. But I'm so tired of fighting. I'm so tired.

"Spock!"

"Moooo!"

That's it. "J.B.!"

Then the chase began.

There were limits as to how far from the house we could go when we were left alone. If it was at night, we couldn't leave the house at all. Daddy had already taught me one lesson about disobedience and I wouldn't have even gotten that lesson if I hadn't felt pressured by my brothers to prove myself. I was in the midst of their pledge program and even though they didn't tell me to, I felt like I needed to give them a report of something I had done and gotten away with. For my birthday, I got a new bike, having outgrown the one with training wheels. I wanted to go over to the new projects to ride on the paved sidewalks and the huge cement square in the middle of the complex. All of the apartments were built on one large block and the four streets around them were all dirt. However, the sidewalks were paved and I could go real fast on my new bike. I don't think there were any other sidewalks on our entire side of town. Our cousin Etta Mae and her two girls, Jackie and Shae Shae, lived in one of the apartments. It was early evening and Momma was in the kitchen cooking dinner and Daddy was about to lie down for a nap. It must have been a Monday because Daddy was off on Mondays so the Snack Center was closed too. Momma cooked big meals on Mondays, kind of like Sunday dinner. We hated washing dishes on Sundays and Mondays.

Anyway, I asked Momma if I could go to the projects to ride my bike. She told me dinner would be done soon and I should ride around outside our house. But I explained I wanted to ride on the sidewalks because we didn't have paved sidewalks at our house. She told me that we did, in fact, have paved sidewalks, right in front of the house and to just go right on out there and ride all I wanted to. Our sidewalk wasn't good enough for riding a bike. It was good for getting wet in the summertime and putting soap on it to skate and slide back and forth, but not for riding fast like at the projects.

I walked through the house and saw Daddy on the sofa. I stood in front of him and struck my innocent "Shawty" pose; that's what he called me, "Shorty," but when he said it, it came out "Shawty." I caught him just in time, before the first snore. I asked him if I could I go to the projects to ride my bike. He never even opened his eyes when he gave me the go-ahead. I left before he could ask any questions. Went out the back door, got my bike, and took the back route to the projects so my mother couldn't look out the kitchen windows and see me. When I arrived at the projects, I let the wind beat against my face as I rode real fast on the paved sidewalks. I was sensible enough not to stay gone too long and to get back home before the sun went down and before dinner was ready. So I did.

I parked my bike in the backyard and re-entered the house through the back door because Daddy was asleep. I thought that I had pulled off the perfect caper. Was I the Penguin or the Riddler? The back door led to the bedroom Harrell and I shared. To the left was the kitchen where my mother was still cooking dinner and to the right was the bathroom. I needed to go pee so I tiptoed through the doorway of our bedroom. I stopped and stood still, facing the blue door. I kept my arms stiff and breath shallow. I didn't want to disturb the air Daddy would be sucking in if he was asleep. He typically slept with his head on the sofa away from the doorway to our bedroom. He had one hand behind his head and the other lay across his stomach. His eyes were closed but he wasn't snoring. What I saw in his hand stopped my heart. The room rotated around me until I was facing him. I started to back into the bathroom. I shut the bathroom door and stood against it. Why did Daddy have his belt in his hand? It couldn't be for me. My little caper was perfect. Flawless. Simple. Easy. I concluded that the belt must be for one of my siblings. Didn't matter which one, there were enough for him to choose who he wanted. As long as it wasn't me.

Daddy called out for me to hurry up and come out of the bathroom. I flushed the toilet though I had not used it and ran the water in the sink trying to figure out what I was going to say or do. I had stalled long enough. I didn't want to make Daddy tell me to hurry up twice. I opened the door and dragged myself to his feet. He was in the same position but this time his eyes were open and he patted the belt gently on his stomach. His eyes looked at me, not with anger or malice, but with justice. I braced myself for what I knew I deserved and went somewhere else in my mind, as I had learned to do. He talked to me, asked me questions. I must have answered because usually he didn't stop talking until everything was said by both parties. Then he beat me like I deserved.

"Moooo!"

"Spock!"

"Mooo!"

"Spock!"

"JB!"

When Darrell started chasing me around the house it was at night, so running out the front door was not an option. I knew better than to break the rules. We learned how to move fast over and around the furniture in our house. We could make a circle through the house by going clockwise from the bedroom Harrell and I shared, to the kitchen, to the dining room, to the living room, through the den and back to our bedroom. Our bedroom, the living room and the bedroom behind me now, all had exits to the outdoors. But like I said, that was only an option at certain times of the day. Our second round through the house made a lot of noise. The floors shook as we tromped from room to room. The floor in the dining room seemed especially vulnerable to our chunkiness because the china cabinet and the matching buffet trembled and I could hear my mother's precious holiday china clinking together. I finally stopped in our bedroom. I made sure the bed was in between us. I was breathing hard but proud I had made him mad enough to start the chase instead of just hanging my head and holding back the water in my eyes. He made several lunges at me but each time he knew it would give me a chance to head for the kitchen door and start the circular chase all over again. I knew he was about to go to another level when I saw his eyebrows rise. He looked down and grabbed the covers on the bed in both of his fists and pulled everything off of the bed. The bedspread, the blanket, the sheets and the pillows. He threw them all on the floor, walked to the den, sat down and started watching television. Like it was all over and he had won.

At first, I thought it wasn't a problem. It was actually good he pulled the covers off of the bed. It was Harrell's bed too. Darrell would have to deal with me *and* Harrell. But then I came to my senses. If Momma came home and our bed wasn't made up, Harrell would get in trouble and beat me too. I looked up to the sky and asked God, "How long?" But I didn't have time for God to answer; I had to survive in that house and if Darrell wanted to take it to a new level, then I was going right along with him. I turned and walked through the kitchen to Darrell's room, grabbed a handful of covers in both fists, lifted, and threw them all on the floor. Then I walked into the den, sat down next to him and started watching television too. It took him a few minutes but he finally figured out I had given up too easily. He needed to figure out what the deal was. He asked if I had made our bed. I calmly said no but that he should go and check his. He jumped up from the sofa and shook the house as he stomped to his room.

I just sat and watched television. Harrell was getting interested by now but didn't get involved. For once he remained a spectator. Then we both heard a loud thump. It sounded like Darrell had fallen in our room and hit the floor real hard. Harrell and I ran to see what had happened. I couldn't believe what he had done. Darrell had taken both the mattress and the springs and dumped them on either side of the bed. Only the headboard with the frame and the slats were left standing. You could see all of the dust and stuff under the bed. Had he lost his mind? Then he took his chunky butt back to the den, sat down and resumed watching television. I didn't hesitate. I didn't think twice. I just reacted. I would be dat-gummed if I let him get away with that. I went straight to his room and did the same thing to his twin bed. Just left the headboard with the frame and the slats standing. Then, I let him know.

Typical, typical, typical, what happened next. We could see the head-lights of Momma's car pulling into the driveway. She was home. Her house looked like a . . . like a . . . I don't know what it looked like. I just knew she was going to beat us senseless. And judging from what we had done, we weren't too far off from being senseless. We sent Harrell out as a decoy and hustled to put everything back in place. We did it! We pulled it off, together. My mother never knew a thing.

It was that day I realized that even though I had to live with those two brothers, maybe I couldn't survive without them. Because even though they would get me into trouble, they could also get me out. I was still in my formative years and trying to figure out the world around me, trying to make sense of everything. This new realization was a strange and complex comprehension, but it was all I had. I either had to suffer in silence and learn to terrorize, or be framed by my brothers and be beaten to death at the hands of my own parents. The choice was clear. I joined my brothers. I learned to terrorize.

There were several instances when Harrell almost killed me. One day he and I were meddling each other and I started getting the best of him and made him really mad. I had already learned that no matter how many things they said to hurt my feelings, I should never, ever, let them know how much they hurt me. I had also learned to laugh real hard at the things I teased them about, no matter how weak my bantering was. If I didn't think what I said was funny I would look like a fool. I learned it so well that on this day I made water come from Harrell's eyes. His mouth twisted and I could tell he wanted to grab me, strangle me and rip my heart out. Earlier that day he had found a stick to play with. It was the cross-piece that connected two legs of an old wooden chair. What had been a toy became a weapon. He grabbed the stick and came at me. Even Darrell saw we were going to a dangerous level. I guess he knew there was no going back if we went there. Harrell really could have killed me that day. Darrell tackled Harrell and they landed on the sofa in the den. I stood near the doorway to our bedroom still laughing at what I had brought out in him. The student getting the best of the teacher. Harrell tried to throw the stick at me but Darrell held down his arms. And I kept coming closer and closer to the edge of the sofa trying to get as much out of this day as I could. I never will forget Harrell's eyes; they hated me, they wanted me dead. He freed his hand and flung the stick at me. Luckily I saw it coming and moved just in time. The piece of wood went deep into the sheetrock wall right where my head was. I was frozen. What if I hadn't moved? How many times would I escape death in this house before it caught up with me? We hung a picture over the hole in the wall and told our mother that we just thought the picture looked better there.

Once Harrell pulled his .22 rifle on me. Another time he pulled a knife on me. We got into a fight outside the Snack Center near the rail-road track, and he hit me in the face and tore up the entire inside of my jaw. The list goes on and on. Harrell was good at what he did.

CHAPTER SEVENTEEN

Stine graduated from high school when I was in the fourth grade, leaving me to fend for myself with my brothers. The three of us continued to follow the path ahead and were assigned age-appropriate responsibilities and rewards. We had our parents fooled, but only because we were in it together. One year, all three of us got BB guns for Christmas. Harrell and Darrell were older, so they got guns with a pumping action. They wanted pellet guns but Daddy knew they were not ready for those. I got a gun that to me resembled the Rifleman's gun except it didn't have the large round cocking mechanism. Mine had a regular cock. I loved that gun. We all loved our guns.

One day we decided to be big-time game hunters. Marlin had lots of wooded areas within the city limits. We struck out hours before we had to be back at the Snack Center. Our big hunt started with us going to the store to buy lots of BBs. We also bought cigarette lighters to start the fire that would cook what we killed. Then we were off. We didn't have to go far from home to find a good wooded area with lots of things to shoot at. It was right at the west end of our street. We entered the forest and began to step slowly, carefully and quietly. We crouched down and peered through the site with our weapons. We pointed toward the game to determine who had the best shot, and signaled silence. That day, we killed two or three sparrows. We called them chee-chee birds. We were big-time hunters. We knelt down in the forest to pluck our kill and prepare them for eating. It was almost time for us to go home and get ready for the Saturday night shift at the Snack Center. Sometimes, if Daddy's nerves could stand it, all three of us would work together. We had to hurry to finish our adventure. We plucked the small birds, but we didn't gut them. We skipped a real fire and decided to cook the birds with the cigarette lighters. Then we stood there in the forest, huddled together and ate half-charred chee-chee birds with guts and feathers; they tasted like lighter fluid. We thought it was a fine meal.

Looking back, I knew Harrell and Darrell had me in their grips and that I was a full member of the brotherhood by the summer after my sixth-grade year. Our worlds seem to separate that year. It was Darrell's first year in high school. Harrell was doing the sports thing and that kept him busy. I was dealing with my own world. We still had our time at home together, and it was still challenging, but just having Darrell on another campus during the day and taking a different route home after school gave me a little peace. Harrell was quiet and shy when he was at school, so he didn't bother me there. But when the school year ended, I noticed I had changed and probably would not become the nice young man I had started out to be a long time ago.

In Darrell's first year in high school, he took FFA—Future Farmers of America. In the second quarter, FFA assigned him to raise an animal. He chose to raise a rabbit. He bought the rabbit and a cage and hung the cage on the side of the storage house in our backyard. He made sure the cage was high enough off of the ground so that no animals could get to the rabbit. He took care of the rabbit, but I could tell by the look in his eyes that he didn't really care for it. I helped feed it because I liked it. But something happened that Darrell didn't plan for. The rabbit was a female and must have been carrying babies when he bought it. He didn't line the bottom of the cage, so when the babies came, they fell through the bottom of the cage onto the ground. I don't know if Darrell ever told his teacher, but I do know we took the babies and buried them in the backyard. We put them with the dogs that had died; rats that had been caught in the house; possums that had crowbars smashed against their necks, their tails lifted until their necks popped; and the four or five chickens Harrell had killed during the time he was trying to breed a prize-fighting chicken. He had fed those chickens everything from hot sauce to gunpowder trying to make them mean enough to fight other chickens. But all they ever did was die. Then he'd get another one.

So, the rabbit's babies went the same way as the other dead things in the backyard. When the school year ended, we were glad to be out of school and have the summer ahead of us. That excitement lasted the Friday night school let out. Then it was terror as usual. But this time I played a different role. On Saturday morning, out of simple curiosity, I asked Darrell what he was going to do with the rabbit. By that time he hated that rabbit. I don't remember what he said he planned to do with it but something in me connected with those evil scientist eyes. I had an idea. I gathered Harrell and Darrell around for a demonstration. In sixth-grade science we had studied flammable substances. I don't know what made me experiment on that poor rabbit. But I did. I took the cage off of the wall and placed it in the middle of the backyard. Then, I went into the house and brought out some alcohol, a can of hairspray and a lighter. Dear God. . . . I poured alcohol over the rabbit, lit the cigarette lighter and sprayed the hairspray near the flame. When the spray met the flame, it created a blowtorch. When the blowtorch met the alcohol on the rabbit, me, Harrell and Darrell had a real live show. The rabbit bucked inside of the cage like a wild bronco. The blaze was magnificent. The rabbit screamed and bucked and bucked and screamed. Then it lay still. A black charred mass lay in front of us and we were filled with exhilarating excitement. We laughed. Hard. It was demonic. We got a shovel, dug a hole and lay the rabbit to rest with its babies and the other dead things in the backyard. To this day I don't know what drove me to do that. But whatever it was, I have had to suppress urges like that, because they had become a part of me. Though I didn't burn any more rabbits, life would present some unusual situations and in return I would have strange thoughts and do some strange things. Back then, I learned to terrorize and I didn't die.

I want a woman to know this about me because the man who wants to give a woman all his love is the same man who burned that innocent rabbit. Some of the things inside of me scare even me. I've worked hard to suppress my rumbling, my temper and my evilness, but the mere fact that these things have to be suppressed . . .

Hey Robert, would you? Tell her how you know me?

You asked me to do this quite some time ago and I have been dragging my feet about it. For some reason it made me a bit uncomfortable. I don't know why, it just did. It was not until recently that I was able to do it.

Here is how I know him. . .

I know him as the friend to whom I owe a BIG FAT THANK YOU! I told him this story last week about how the pastor in his message said that we all have someone to thank for leading us to Christ. In my life, Winston is that person. Over the years, we have always shared stories of our religious experiences. As it turned out mine was just that, religious and not spiritual. I was going through ceremonies of tradition because of my rearing. His was real. He had an honest personal relationship with Christ and God.

I remember a piece of art that he had in his apartment in Austin. The painting was inspired by a dream that he had. He told me that, as he was painting, God was arranging the paint just as he had envisioned it in his dream. He went on to tell me that he was talking to God as he was painting. What has stuck in my mind over the years was the way he talked about the conversation he was were having with God. It was as if God was his close, if not best, friend. He even went on to say "Man, You are crazy," referring to God, for something that happened while he was painting. Now, a person does not get that comfortable with God unless He really knows you and more importantly, you really know Him.

I remember Winston telling me stories (they are personal so I will not go into details because I do not know what he has in mind for this commentary) of him arguing with God over him doing certain things in his life and God showing him visions of what was going to happen for his disobedience. All of the time I'm thinking to myself, this is God you are talking to, are you crazy?

As the saying goes, hindsight is 20/20. I understand now that all of this was a result of him having a relationship with Jesus Christ and God, and not a religion. He has taught and shown me the difference.

Here is what I want to say thank you for. In July of 1992, I was in a one-bedroom apartment in Arlington, Texas, with a couch that someone had thrown away, a computer and computer desk, a dining room table with no chairs, and a waterbed. Winston visited me in my palace and humbled himself as if it was just that, a palace. As we drank a few beers and discussed our affairs, our conversation, as it had so many times in the past, shifted to religion and Christianity. He made a profound statement that evening, whether he knew it or not. He said, "Salvation is simple." Of course, I asked him what he meant and he began to explain that the Bible says that "God so loved the world that He gave His only begotten Son so that whosoever believeth in Him shall not perish but have everlasting life." He said that it is our belief in Jesus Christ the Son of God that saves us, not our works. What really drove this home to me was his explanation of man having a physical and spiritual make-up. And just as our physical side has physical needs food, water, sleep etc, so did our spiritual side. These spiritual needs can only be met/satisfied by a relationship with Jesus Christ. He voiced his disdain for religious leaders and the church for making this point so convoluted that a lot of people, including myself at the time, were missing what Christianity was all about.

What I have to thank him for is, as a result of that conversation, I realized that I was not saved and that I needed Jesus Christ to come into my life and satisfy my spiritual need. A need that I was trying to satisfy with worldly pleasures. You see, that was the night of my salvation. Shortly after he left that night I asked God to forgive me of my sins and I asked Jesus to come into my life and make me whole.

So, how do I know him? I know him as a close friend who has a deep personal relationship with Jesus Christ and God Almighty. I know him as vessel, a mouthpiece that showed me the way to Christ and changed my destination for eternity. I know him as the one to whom I owe a "Thank You!"

Robert Moore
Arlington, Texas

The Gift
That I Never Wanted

CHAPTER EIGHTEEN

The sun has fallen from the sky. It is dark now. There is no moon in this night. No light in this darkness. But I won't let the darkness keep me from moving forward with this meeting. There is still work to be done, and I will do it before I leave the spot where I now sit. My body is tingling from the beer, I can feel it in my toes. It has made me content. I'm glad I'm a happy drunk. But I can't stand to look at the cigarette butts in the bottom of the empty bottles. I can't stand the smell, either. I'll put the empties back in the carrier so I can't see the butts. I can't believe how much I smoke when I drink. And to think I hate the smell of smoke on other people. People will smoke during the day, at work, at home, in the car, in the church parking lot. Everywhere! I don't do that. In fact, not many people even know that I smoke. I have kept that a nice little secret too. I only smoke in front of a select few.

Why?

Because I cared what people thought about me. From now on, I will smoke when I feel like it, and I don't care who knows.

How bold of you!

Thanks. I think so, too.

115

Chapter Nineteen

Why do people laugh when they find out I was born on April Fool's Day? And why do they look at me like they're thinking, "I *knew* something was wrong with you!" After I figured out I couldn't change my birth certificate, I made the best of being born on April Fool's Day. And after I figured out I couldn't depend on other people to make my day special for me, I decided to make it special for myself. It took me a few years to understand what April Fool's Day was all about, and to expect pranks around my birthday. Daddy always did a good job of making our birthdays special. He always baked our favorite cake. And even though Darrell's birthday is only a few days before mine, Daddy made us separate cakes until we got old enough not to care so much. Then we told him we would share a cake. One year, Big Momma Williams called me on my birthday and told me to come on over to her house and get my gift. Wow! A gift! I knew what Granddaddy was going to give me. He gave all the grandkids the same thing for Christmas and on birthdays. We laugh about it now, but thinking back and remembering how sincere he was about presenting the gift to us, it has become very special. Granddaddy would beckon each of us to stand right in front of him while he went in his pocket and pulled out his coin purse. He would twist and unsnap the top of the coin purse then pour out the contents into his palm. He used his aged index finger to move the coins around in the palm of his hand until he found what he was looking for. A shiny dime. He would take that shiny dime and place it in our hand. A dime. He would give us a dime. No matter if you were two or twenty, he gave you a dime for Christmas and a dime for your birthday. It was sweet. I loved Granddaddy.

So as I walked over to Big Momma and Granddaddy's house, I knew what I was getting from him, but had no idea what Big Momma had gotten me. I arrived at their house anxious to go inside, but Granddaddy met me at the door. He came outside laughing and sat in his chair on the porch. He put me across his knee and gave me a gentle birthday spanking, laughing the entire time and talking about it being my birthday. He did that to all of his grandkids. He hugged me and I felt the whiskers on his narrow face and inhaled the scent of his plaid flannel shirt. Granddaddy had a unique aroma. The warm scent of an old man. I laughed with him while wiggling away from his embrace so I could go inside and get my other gift. He held my arm and led me back to stand in front of him while he pulled out his coin purse, emptied it into the palm of his hand and placed a shiny dime in mine. I showed genuine excitement over his gift but ran quickly into the house to see Big Momma.

She sat in her room with a dip of snuff tucked in her lower lip, spit can at her feet. I gave her a big hug. Her perfume and snuff filled my nostrils, replacing Granddaddy's scent. She had a beautiful smell. She knew I was eyeing the room for my gift, but I didn't see it among the Lucky Heart products. She got up and went over to one of the beds and pulled out a beautiful box from under the bed. It was a large box. I couldn't figure out how it fit under the bed. I was really excited by then. She handed it to me and told me to open it. Like a champ, I tore into the paper. The box was good and heavy, and that meant it was expensive. I got through the paper and stood to place it on the bed. I took the top off and saw lots of paper covering the gift. My heart was racing so fast! I knew this was going to be good. I took both hands and scooped the paper out and over the top of the box onto the bed. And there it was. My gift. Rocks. Rocks? Rocks! My mind just shut down. To this day I don't remember what happened after that. I don't know if she gave me a card with money in it or what. God rest her soul, but that's what I remember Big Momma did that year for my birthday. So I decided right then and there that I was always going to be good to myself on my birthday. I expect nothing on my birthday from anyone. And if by chance I get something, that's icing on a cake that I baked for myself.

When I was twelve, something happened that I thought would change my life. By this time I had settled into our family church routine. Darrell was fifteen and had been moved into the role of Sunday school secretary. My sisters had also been the secretary, and I knew one day I would have the role. I had already memorized the script they read from the black book each week, and memorized the songs and who would receive the banners for attendance and most money raised, neither of which seemed to change from week to week. In Sunday school my brothers and I were set apart by age, which worked out well for my mother because she didn't have to coordinate that part of our church attendance. But when the eleven o'clock service started, she had to divide the sanctuary up and send each of us to our respective areas. We terrorized the church ladies and each other so bad that we had become known as the Three Desperados. Women would watch in fear to see if we were going to sit in their row. They were warned to watch their toes if one of those Williams boys was anywhere near. So Momma assigned us to empty parts of the church. We were not to try and sneak near each other, talk via code to each other, look at each other, or send notes to each other. Nothing. And if one of us passed the other one during the walk-around collection, we were to keep our hands to ourselves. If we were in the congregation, that meant Momma was in the choir and she had a perfect view of what we did. We could never tell when or if Daddy would be at church. He had to work on Sunday mornings and usually only went to evening service before going to the Snack Center to open on Sunday nights.

So during my separation from my brothers, I would prepare to go to sleep once all the physical activity of standing and singing and reciting was over and done with. I had already followed my brother and sisters before me and marched in line down the aisle to the front of the church to request to be baptized. I understood the pictures on the Sunday school cards and who God was, but I didn't really care for Him that much because I was suffering so much and He wasn't helping me at all. I knew that He had a Son named Jesus and that He was sent to earth to suffer on my behalf. But I couldn't understand why a father would do that to his own son. I had decided not to deal with God. I also knew Jesus was loving and kind and always pleasant, unlike some of the people who went to church, who were supposed to try to be like Him. I didn't feel like the preacher told me anything new when I went to church, so I usually went to sleep. But on that Sunday, I remember Reverend C. S. Sanders made it to the podium and opened his Bible. I was sitting in the pew next to the space heater. On that side of the church, the rows of pews stopped to make room for the space heater that was close to the wall under a faux stained-glass window. Then the rows of pews began again and continued to the front of the church. My left hand gripped the top of the pew to serve as a makeshift pillow for my head. My nap had to get under way before Reverend Sanders started shouting to the point where I couldn't sleep. I already had my eyes closed when he began. He announced he was going to talk about a man named Lazarus that Jesus had raised from the dead. What? Reverend Sanders had caught my attention with something truly magical. I didn't lift my head but I kept my eyes and ears open. What Reverend Sanders said intrigued my very soul. When the shouting part started, I was still pondering a dead man coming back to life. And who did it? The man named Jesus. My mind concluded that Jesus was the answer. He was the one who could do what even my parents couldn't do. He could give me life. He could make everything in my life better. He could make sense of everything. I also concluded that I didn't have to deal with God or my feelings toward Him. His Son would be my friend. After that, I never slept in church again. At least not on purpose.

I was a junior in high school when I discovered something about myself. I didn't notice it at first, but it became more and more evident. At the time I was the only child left at home. Harrell and Darrell both were in college. The three of us had only spent one year together in high school. I had survived by staying out of their way as much as possible at school, but by then we had become thick as thieves. We couldn't stand being separated, but we couldn't stand being together either. We had our own way of being good brothers to each other. So by the time Harrell left, I could finally present to the public the image I had been working on for years and no one would be at home to tear it down. I became president of my junior class. I was still first chair in the tuba section in band, and had been since my freshman year. I was nominated for president of the band but threatened to beat up anybody who voted for me. I was on the honor roll, and moved up in class ranking. I was setting up a good little finish to my high school years.

The one thing missing was a girlfriend. In my biology class I became close friends with a classmate I had known since middle school. Her name was Lowanda Massingile. Lowanda was slender and voluptuous. She had a sweet, soft voice that I really liked. Back in middle school there had been rumors about her dating a high school guy and going farther than a middle school girl should. I was very curious, but didn't dare ask her. That rumor made me a little apprehensive at first about even being friends with her because she was possibly quite far ahead of me in life. But we sat next to each other every day and she and I would cut up during class. She laughed at my stupid jokes. She would look at me with such interest. But Lowanda had a boyfriend. A senior. I think he was voted most handsome in his class one year. I couldn't compete. So I put Lowanda in the "friend and nothing more" category. I can be a real good friend and know which boundaries never to cross.

The time came for the annual trip to Six Flags Over Texas in Arlington. The Spanish Club went each year. Lowanda and I both had been members since our freshman year and I always looked forward to going on the trip. For some reason, Lowanda's boyfriend didn't go, so we sat together on the chartered bus. We laughed and talked as usual but something wasn't right. I felt something. Deep down, I knew what it was, but I had no idea where it was coming from. I didn't say anything and just went along with the day. We arrived at the park, received final instructions from the chaperones, and took off. We were young, energetic teenagers. We stood in a long line for one of the roller coasters. I love roller coasters. I hate the way they make me feel, but I love to hate that feeling. I remember when we reached the top, just before the first big drop, the feeling hit me again, but this time real strong and I looked at Lowanda and was afraid for her. It changed me for the rest of the day, but I tried hard not to show it. I got it again on the ride that sucks you against the wall when the floor drops out. Lowanda was stuck to the wall across from me, screaming. Again, I was afraid for her. I still didn't say anything, just continued running around all day until it was time to load the bus and return home.

I think it was the next week when someone told me Lowanda was really sick. Then she called me and told me she had been in the hospital. I asked why and she was very straightforward about it. She told me that she had had a miscarriage. My feeling was right! That is exactly what I thought when we were on the bus, on the roller coaster, and on the other ride. How did I know? Why did I know? I had never experienced that before in my life, but I knew she was pregnant and no one had told me. I just knew. And what's worse, I didn't say anything. I didn't try to steer her away from those rides. I don't even know if there were warning signs for pregnant women riding roller coasters back then. Anyway, we were only teenagers. We were tall enough to ride the rides and definitely not supposed to be pregnant. So if they did have a warning, it wasn't for us. But I knew and said nothing. Now a child was gone. I had too many other things in my life to deal with so I blocked it all out and tried not to think about. Lowanda and I remained friends. She and the guy had problems and broke up. She started dating another guy from another small town and I continued looking for someone for me.

CHAPTER TWENTY

Back when I was four years old, my mother dressed me in a dark green velvet jacket and pants and a bow tie. Then she handed me a small white pillow with two rings sewn onto it and made me walk down the aisle at our church to where my oldest brother was standing with some other guys that I didn't know. Later, I came to understand it was the day John was leading the way for the rest of us. He got married to a girl he had dated in high school. Her name was Sara Denman and I came to know and like her over the years they were together. She was tall and thin with long, straight black hair. She had dimples that framed her perfect white teeth. She looked like she should have been on television or in a magazine. They moved to Houston and had a child. They visited us on holidays and we visited them sometimes. Several years after they were married, on one of their visits to our house, me, Harrell and Darrell overheard John talking to our parents about us. He was asking if he could take the three of us back to Houston with him for a visit. We kept out of sight with our fingers crossed hoping that our parents would say yes so we could be off on another adventure. It happened. They took us to Houston with them. On our way to Houston, me, Harrell and Darrell sat in the back seat of the car. We were on our best behavior, acting like we actually got along well. I was having a real good time with my two brothers. We arrived at their apartment and settled in for fun. I don't remember what we did, it was just good getting along with Harrell and Darrell for a change.

But one morning, I heard rumbling. It came from the room where John and Sara slept. Harrell and Darrell heard it too. We listened. I tried to make out what the rumbling was about. Toothpaste? I thought I heard it right. Toothpaste. That wasn't interesting to me. I tuned them out but it continued, louder and louder. Their argument ended, along with our trip to Houston and their marriage. I don't know if one had anything to do with the other, but I couldn't understand why people had to rumble anyway. And why when they rumbled, it was about things that even I, as a kid, understood weren't important. I continued to hate rumbling. I hated when other people did it and I hated when I did it with my brothers. I decided that when it was my turn to stand at the front of the church, I was not going to rumble with the woman once we were at home.

After my brother's marriage to Sara ended, I found out that she had many sisters. None of them were as tall as she was, but they were all very beautiful. There was one in the same grade as Darrell and one in the same grade as me. Her name was Delila. Over the years, I came to know Delila. Besides being as beautiful as her sisters, she was smart, athletic and funny. As far as I could see, our two families got along despite whatever went on between my brother and her sister. I, like every other guy in my class, always thought about having Delila as a girlfriend, but her mother was really strict and very religious: a holy roller. Her family even went to church on Saturdays. So I waited in line, behind other guys, for the years to roll by before I could find out if Delila wanted me. She started to date when she was a sophomore, but I felt sorry for the guy because he had to go through Delila's mother. I waited until I was a senior before I started setting the stage to find out if she was interested in me. Periodically, I joked around with Delila and tried to figure out who she liked.

One day my mother and I were at the Snack Center, alone like old times. It was a Friday and school had let out early for an out-of-town basketball game. I was starving and had gone to the Snack Center for a cheeseburger. There were no customers, and my mother sat at the counter watching me move about as I explained where I had to be and by what time. Then she said the oddest thing to me. She said, "I hear you trying to 'cote' [court] one of them Denman girls." I said, "What?" Not to try and deny it, but in amazement that she knew it. Then she said another odd thing to me. She said, "I knew it! I knew when the time came for you to get serious about a girl it was either going to be a white girl, or a Denman."

I stood there behind the counter looking directly at my mother as her words floated above my head. I was silent. Stunned. I was rumbling inside. I figured out why my mother had given me the sex talk and why she did it when we were near the Denman's house. The rumbling welled up inside of me and I suddenly got scared of what I was about to do. Not necessarily because of what my mother said, though I didn't like it, but because I was dealing with the fact that she knew so much about what I did. The rumbling inside of me intensified because neither one of my parents had come to know me as a person. They had no idea what went on in my life, what I had been through. And if they could find out so much information about who I liked, then maybe they did in fact know what had happened to me and just chose not to deal with it. That made it worse. Much, much worse. That thought made me want to explode. How dare she jump right into the midst of my life and say something like that after leaving me alone to fend for myself and figure things out on my own! Maybe what I did next wasn't the right thing to do, but I did it. I leaned forward, put my elbows on the counter and moved my face close to hers. I pointed my index finger at my mother's face and explained to her that she had no say in who I chose to date, or 'cote' as she called it, and I would date a Denman or a white girl or whomever I felt like dating. She didn't hit me. She just explained how she felt. Delila's mother had played a big part in John's marriage to Sara and the subsequent breakup. She said my brother's interaction with Delila's mother had affected him deeply and she didn't want the same thing for me. I didn't hear those words until weeks after she said them. Right there, right then, I was trying to contain my anger and it took all I had to control it. Our conversation was a missed opportunity for us to have a real conversation about life. But I like to think that that particular interaction set a new tone for my relationship with my mother. And it was all because she didn't slap me when I got in her face.

CHAPTER TWENTY-ONE

I continued to joke and flirt around a little with Delila until I jokingly slipped the possibility of 'us' into a conversation. She laughed and said I had to know our mothers weren't going to let us get together. Maybe her mother had had a conversation with her. I dropped it and moved on. I still talked to Delila like I always did, as a friend. One day I got to school early. I was headed to my usual routine, but stopped to deal with a little drama brewing between my cousins, Jackie who was in the tenth grade, and her sister Shae Shae, who was in the ninth, about some guy. Afterwards, I went and stood with Delila and some other friends at the snack counter in the activity center outside the gymnasium. I put my books down and something hit me. I had felt that feeling before. No! Impossible! I looked at Delila. Life stood still. Not Delila! My eyes locked on Delila. She said she felt sick. A minute later she fell backwards to the floor like she was having a seizure. Then she threw up. Everyone panicked and hurried around her. I stood there in shock because I knew what it was. But how did I know? What was this I was dealing with? Sure enough, Delila was pregnant.

Lowanda was without a boyfriend long enough for us to get together. I would say she was my girlfriend, but just recently I found out she never really considered us boyfriend and girlfriend. After eighteen years, my high school sweetheart tells me she never thought of us that way! That's another issue. Regardless of what she thought we were, it doesn't change the time we spent together and how we spent it. Lowanda was a great person to be around and I loved her soft kisses, which matched her soft voice. We spent a lot of time together and we talked on the phone a lot.

125

We went to the prom together. It was a very romantic evening. I promised myself that I would not get Lowanda into trouble. Partly because of my mother's sex talk with me, but also because of what had happened to her. She didn't have to do that to be with me. Like I said, I thought we *were* boyfriend and girlfriend. I was naïve and stupid. That's probably why she was with me.

I remember one Saturday afternoon I was taking a nap in between shifts at the Snack Center. I had a dream. In the dream, I saw a classmate named Johnny Jones driving a car and a girl was in the passenger seat. There were two other people in the back seat of the car. One of them was Lowanda. The other person in the back seat was a guy. In the dream, I was behind them and I could see the shape of his head and the outline of his face when he turned to the side. The dream was very clear. The next time I saw her, I asked Lowanda how her weekend was. She said it was fine. I asked her what she did, but before I let her answer, I told her I knew where she was and who she was with. I was half joking because I didn't believe what I saw in the dream was real. She looked at me with a bit of surprise and said if I knew, then maybe I should tell her. I had nothing to lose. I explained I had a dream and what I saw in the dream. My stomach sank when she told me that I was right. I remember pretending to be very smug and saying something like she'd better be careful what she did, because I would know. But inside I was scared. I didn't tell anybody else about what I was experiencing. I just filed it away.

By the time this happened, I had developed a bad habit of storing things away in the back of my mind and not dealing with them. It was the only way I could cope some times. Lowanda and I continued going out until I left for college. We had a very emotional goodbye and she quickly married after I left, then divorced. We are still friends and both still single.

CHAPTER TWENTY-TWO

My cousin Jackie is the same age as I am, but during the course of our school years, she had to repeat two grades. People had their opinions about Jackie, but I think she just didn't like school very much. When she and Shae Shae discovered boys, all hell broke loose. My cousin Etta Mae, their mother, raised them by herself. Their father had left years ago. Etta Mae was a nurse and worked hard to keep her girls well dressed and in a nice home. Etta Mae was proud of the brick home she had built for the three of them and the fact that she was able to move her family out of the projects. While Etta Mae had her own share of man drama, Jackie's issues changed life for all of us.

Jackie came across Freddie Campbell and thought she had found something good. Why she thought that I will never know or understand. He was so far from what Etta Mae wanted for her daughter. Far from what I thought Jackie deserved. The two of them were like the drama you see in the movies. Only worse. I had nothing against Freddie, but then and now, I grapple with words to describe him without being harsh. Let me try. Freddie was . . . sub-human. Okay, I failed. It is harsh. But that's how he came across to me. The morning Delila passed out, I had just pulled Jackie aside and asked her what the hell was on her mind because I had heard she was seeing Freddie. But there was nothing I could do for either of them. Etta Mae punished Jackie. Made rules. Set limits. But nothing worked. Jackie was determined. I loved Jackie, Shae Shae and Etta Mae. And I didn't want anything to happen to any of them, but it did. Jackie got pregnant. She was smuggled to Houston for Stine to arrange an abortion.

I went to Houston to see how she was doing. It was over and she was recuperating. She returned to Marlin and picked up where she left off. Freddie was upset but no one knew how much. The world was going mad around me and I was going crazy right along with it.

It was a Sunday night. I went to sleep and dreamed that Freddie made his way into Etta Mae's house with a gun. There was a gunshot. Etta Mae was dead. I don't know how long the dream lasted, but late that night the phone rang. Something had happened at Etta Mae's house. My parents and I rushed over there, but it was too late. The last things I remember were the lights, the screams and the confirmation. Etta Mae was dead.

Days, maybe weeks afterwards, my mother sat me down and asked me a question. She said she found me in the street in front of Etta Mae's house holding my head and wandering around saying, "I don't want it! I don't want it!" She wanted to know what it was that I didn't want. I explained the dream. I told her I didn't want the gift.

Hey Ron, would you? Tell her how you know me?

OK, here goes:

I met Winston through my wife, Gwen. We weren't married when I first met him. He seemed like a really nice guy. The one thing that really caught my attention was the easy way he smiled. He acted like he didn't have a care in the world, you know the "happy to be nappy" kind of guy. What you have to understand is I was going through my own insecurities at the time. So many of my perceptions of 1992-1994 come from a skewed point of view. But Winston's personality was easygoing and he was nice to be around.

I really got to know him better when I moved to Austin in 1994. I initially stayed with my brother-in-law and his family, but after six months it was time to go. Gwen told me to call Winston and ask him to help me find a cheap apartment. We looked for a couple of weeks and I thought I found a place, but Winston said Gwen would not approve. So he invited me to stay with him. They say you don't really know a person until you've lived with them. That was definitely the case with Winston.

Luckily, our schedules kept us from bumping into each other during the week and I came back to Houston on weekends. But I found out a lot about Winston. He is one of the most driven people I've ever met. Here's what I mean by that: a person who thinks of what they would like to be, but doesn't know how to make it reality, is a dreamer. A person who thinks of what they want to be, or do, and sets out a plan to make it reality is a driven individual. Winston is driven. If there's something he wants to do, he'll sit down and make a plan to make it a reality. It may not be what other people think it should be, but it'll be what Winston wants it to be. There are very few people in the world like that. In this respect, he has encouraged me to be less of a dreamer, and become more driven.

In terms of Winston's social life, I don't have much to comment on. This is because we come from different backgrounds and have different life experiences. I don't envy many people. But in a lot of ways, I envy Winston. He traveled where he wanted. He bought the house he wanted. He decorated it the way he wanted to. He bought the car he wanted. He lived in the part of Austin he wanted. I've never had that experience and I think every man should before he gets married and has to deal with the wishes of the wife and kids. Then you don't do shit you want. Anyway, I digress.

What I don't understand about Winston is his view on relationships. He comes from a two-parent home, but he behaves as though his parents were divorced. I think there's something that has him gun-shy about marriage. But understand, I say this about marriage, not commitment. I think Winston is perfectly capable of maintaining a committed relationship, until it gets to the point of marriage. Then it seems to fall apart. But I stand on the outside looking in. The women I've known who Winston dated were mostly college-educated professional women. I've only met a few, so I can't comment on Winston's idea of the perfect woman. However, I think it has to be someone who will give him space to be Winston, and love him for who he is, and not what they think he should be.

Over the years I've known him, I must honestly say, if I were to get in a fight, I'd want Winston at my side. I trust him and I think he knows what he's doing, most of the time. He's not an easy person to understand, but how many men are? So, my only real advice would be to buckle up and get ready for the ride of your life. You'll have fun, and somewhere along the way I'm sure you're going to shed a few tears. But that's life, isn't it?

Ron Goodwin
Houston, Texas

I'm Waiting
For Someone to Talk to Me
To Tell Me What to Do
Where to Go and Who to Be

CHAPTER TWENTY-THREE

My father and I didn't have as much time alone together as my mother and I did. But I wanted us to. I thought I could begin to build the same type of relationship with him that I had with my mother. So I watched his patterns to figure out when would be a good time to jump into his life and become a more meaningful part of it. My father was so busy. Most of what he did was for us and very little was for himself. There were just too many people ahead of me requiring his attention, his support and his instruction. So I kept my place in line, marching behind the others, watching my father teach them how to stay in line. But I continued to watch for an opportunity to jump ahead and get his attention.

My father became a scoutmaster when my oldest brothers were young. When I came along, he continued for a while, long enough for me to experience the Boy Scouts. It was in his position as scoutmaster that I noticed he treated other boys the same as he treated us. He provided, instructed by example, corrected, then sent them on their way to do what he showed them. He taught us to swim, took us to the rodeo and fair, helped us prepare our exhibits and made arrangements for us to usher at the Baylor Bears football games in Waco. He did a lot. I enjoyed seeing my father interact with other boys. I enjoyed the way they looked up to him. But I also enjoyed the fear in their eyes when he rumbled. Over the years, my father would help raise several other boys from our community. They would become my brothers and call him Dad. I liked them all.

Before my father stopped being a scoutmaster, I had a chance to go on a cookout that he organized. I was so excited. We were going out into the woods and cook over an open fire! We were supposed to learn how to be prepared. Me, Harrell and Darrell bugged Daddy all day long about what we were going to cook. I don't think he told us because we were still excited when we headed to the woods. He put all three of us in his group for the cookout and allowed the other boys to bring whatever food they wanted to prepare. After helping us get our fire started, he went around to each group, helping them start their fires and inspecting their food. I remember hearing him laugh deep and hard out in the distant darkness. Some of the boys had made strange food choices that amused my father. We sat around rummaging the food he brought, trying to figure out what it was. Daddy returned and I remember how excited his face was when he laid out the menu. Daddy loved food and still does. He had brought meat and vegetables for the cookout. What? Meat and vegetables? He'd brought potatoes and vegetables wrapped in foil. And meat. Maybe it was beef but at that point I didn't care. Me, Harrell and Darrell looked at each other wondering the same thing. Had Daddy lost his mind? We were kids. We wanted hot dogs and hamburgers. For goodness sake, he owned a restaurant with plenty of hamburger meat and wieners in the refrigerator. And he had brought meat and vegetables? It was a somber meal for us and the other boys in our group. We didn't dare say too much about our opinion of Daddy's menu choices. We were in public and we knew our father.

Daddy was a well-known insurance man in our community. In those days, an insurance man went from door to door collecting the monthly premiums. Daddy always referred to his insurance route as his 'debit.' He collected from a lot of people. He even had to go to Waco to collect insurance money. Sometimes he would take the three of us with him. Once he announced we could go with him, Marlin or Waco, it didn't matter, the fighting started. The first fight was over who could sit in the front seat. Making sure we were out of Daddy's presence, we'd fight it out and then present ourselves as happy little boys when the time came to leave. Then the fighting would progress. When Daddy stopped at a house and went inside, we'd start calling each other names. As soon as Daddy came out of the house, we stopped. He'd walk to the next house and go inside, then we'd start again. He'd come back to the car, we'd be angels. This went on from stop to stop. We'd make faces at each other. Back seat to front seat.

Front seat to back seat. In the side rearview mirror. Punches would start flying. Then at the next stop, back seat to front seat, front seat to back seat. Daddy would come back to the car and we would be breathing hard. Daddy stopped at the next house and we'd start kicking each other. The person in the front seat would straddle it and kick somebody in the back seat, punching at the same time. Daddy would come back to the car and we'd stop. But the person behind the passenger seat might put his foot under the seat of the person in the front seat and move his foot up and down so that the person in the front could feel a poking in his butt. That would be it. The final straw. Somebody had to cry! Daddy would stop at the next house and when he returned to the car, somebody would be crying. He would ask what was wrong and of course, no one knew. We were bad kids. No, *they* were bad. They just dragged me along.

At that time, Daddy drove an old white station wagon with bad shocks. He had become a pack rat. I noticed that, as the number of children in the house went down, the amount of stuff in the back of his station wagon went up. He kept shovels, paint, wire, hedge clippers, paperwork, bottles, cans, pecans and God only knows what else back there. The front and back seats grew debris like neglected pasture after a rainy summer. It got to the point where he had to work to make room for the three of us to ride with him. And when we did ride with him, the car would bounce up and down, even on paved streets. To me, Harrell and Darrell the bouncing was fun. At first. One day, Momma and Daddy went somewhere in her car and left the three of us home alone. They never learned. It was still daylight, so we were allowed to go outside, but we couldn't leave the yard and we couldn't have any friends in the yard, either. Anybody who came by the house had to stand in the street to talk to us. That day, we had become weary of agitating each other, so Darrell decided to find something for us to get into. And there it was. The old white station wagon. Parked right there in front of the house. Darrell said we should try and see how far we could rock it. At first I didn't understand. I watched him climb onto the very top of the car where the luggage rack was. He stood up facing the front hood with his feet spread apart. His head brushed against the low branches of the Chinaberry tree. I was still confused but curious. He started to lean from one side, then to the other and the car moved a little with him. Harrell jumped onto the hood of the car, faced Darrell and moved in sync with him. Then I understood what they were trying to do. The car was really beginning to rock back and forth from left to right. I went to one side of the car to help. We were laughing hard and we knew, without saying a word, that we wanted to see if the tires would lift off of the ground. That station wagon was really rocking! Harrell and Darrell looked like professional surfers riding a big white wave. We ran out of breath before we made the tires lift off the ground but we thought it was so funny. We laughed for what seemed like hours. We didn't think about evidence, we didn't think about consequences. We didn't think about being seen. When Momma and Daddy came home, we were in the house watching television. Daddy came into the house and told us somebody had broken into his car. The three of us looked at each other in silence. Better to let him think that.

He drove that car until it fell apart. When we were in high school we dreaded cold days when Daddy would be the one who had to take us to school. The heater and air conditioner had died long ago and the floorboards were rotted out. It was like something out of the "Flintstones"— we could actually see the ground pass underneath our feet as we drove down the road. In the winter, Daddy covered the holes with plastic floor mats, then put candles in empty gallon-sized coffee cans and placed one on the driver side and one on the passenger side to keep the ice off of the windshield. The station wagon had developed a loud squeaking noise due to shockless bouncing. The three of us would be bundled up inside, miserable. I always wondered if maybe Daddy knew what we did that day and punished us by driving us to school.

Even though we terrorized that station wagon, I cherished it during its early years. When I was eight, I found a way to jump into my father's life to spend time alone with him while he was awake. I knew his schedule. I knew the days that he went on his debit. I knew the long debit days and the short debit days. I also knew Harrell and Darrell's low tolerance for the long debit days, especially when the weather was hot. So on those days, I would ask Daddy if I could go on his debit with him. I loved it when he said, "Sho Shawty!" We'd leave the house and I'd grab his hand or stand on his feet while he walked to the car, pretending to take big steps just like him. I would get into passenger side, lock the door and perch myself in the corner of the seat and the door almost facing him and wait. Daddy didn't know what I was seeking and I didn't tell him. I just expected it to happen. For him to talk to me about stuff. I knew I was young, but I thought he could see the curiosity, eagerness and neediness in my eyes. I wanted and needed to talk to him, even at that young age. But Daddy commanded silence and seemed to bask in the sunlight of his life, of his accomplishments, of his responsibilities. He loved to hum. He would sing the words to a church song, and maybe even "Happy Birthday." But other than that, I never heard my father sing the words to a song by himself. He'd hum. We drove along from house to house. He gave me the option of going inside with him or not. Sometimes I did, sometimes I didn't. I waited, but what I needed and wanted didn't happen. I tried something else. I noticed my father didn't sit around with other men, talking and doing nothing. Everything my father did was centered around being productive. He taught by demonstrating. He came into contact with a lot of people every day. Maybe he had friends he talked to every day, but if he did talk to them, he was selling them either a hamburger or burial insurance. I noticed my father had to have a purpose to talk to you. So I found a purpose. After several evenings of riding in silence with him on his debit, I asked him if I could learn how to drive. I had heard he had taught my older brothers. Momma taught all of my sisters because they felt like Daddy rumbled too much and that made them nervous. Harrell and Darrell were still too young to make the decision of who would teach them. But I asked him. And he said, "Sho!"

We practiced on an old country dirt road where several of my father's insurance customers lived. Either side of the road had shallow ditches filled with plush, high, green weeds. He sat in the driver's seat and put me in his lap. At eight years old, I could still stand up and not touch the roof of the car. He maneuvered around me, steering the wheel, changing gears and pushing the pedals until the car was in the middle of the road. Not many cars traveled that road and I saw gravel and potholes ahead. The station wagon was a manual shift. Daddy told me not to worry about the gearshift on the steering wheel or any of the pedals, he would take care of that. We sat still while I gripped the steering wheel and got a feel for it.

Immediately, I started moving the steering wheel right to left and back again like Batman did on television and like I had practiced on the sewing machine. But Daddy told me that I didn't have to do that. He said to just hold the wheel steady and the car would go straight. He said whichever way I moved the steering wheel, the car would go in that direction. The car moved forward just slightly and my heart vibrated. Here was my time with my father. He was instructing me. We were close and he was awake, not sleeping on the sofa. But I thought that he would be worried because my heart made my body shake. I was scared he would stop instructing me because I couldn't take it. But he continued. He moved the pedals and the car moved very slowly. I gripped the steering wheel real tight and concentrated hard to keep it in the center of the road. And I did it! We didn't go very far. We just went from one house to the next. And I did it with my father's instruction. I knew we could do it. Together. I started to hate the times that Harrell and Darrell wanted to come along with me and Daddy. But Daddy and I got many chances to practice. I think he looked forward to those times as much as I did. Before long, I was sitting in my father's lap while he pushed the pedals and I held the steering wheel and shifted gears all by myself going as fast as seventy miles an hour down the highway.

My great accomplishment, finding something my father and I could do together, didn't produce the type of communication and instruction I was hoping for. It became clear to me that my place was in line, watching and learning from those in front of me. So I went back to the end of the marching line. Left-right, left-right. Watching the others and watching my father too. It was easy to see the things that made my father and mother happy and those that did not. So to the best of my ability, I tried to do what made them happy. But daily, I got caught up in some kind of trouble with Harrell and Darrell. The others in front of me had so many accomplishments that I couldn't always achieve more than they did. But I decided to strive to be the best at whatever I did and hoped that I could make a name for myself and receive my own recognition. It seemed like my parents saw that desire in me and let me do whatever I wanted to. They never pushed me to do anything. I was the eager initiator. Oh, wait. There was one thing my mother pushed me into doing that I really didn't want to do.

And what was that?

All of us were musically inclined. But Harrell and Darrell got to skip piano lessons. Harrell got to skip band too but I think that's because he was lazy and Momma was just too tired. When I was six years old, my mother put me in piano lessons. And after a few years I grew to hate them. Miz Ethyl Smith was my teacher. She was really good and very thorough at what she did. The others before me had been to her. I didn't dislike the lessons because Miz Smith cracked my knuckles with a ruler. I disliked them because of what I overheard the second oldest guy tell my mother. He must not have known I was in line watching and listening to him for direction or that what he said and sent down the line to me was important. I watched him leave the house, go to college and get married. But he didn't stand at the front of a church, he stood in a house. Anyway, he and his wife came home for a visit. It was a strange visit because they sat in the living room on the gold sofa and visited with my mother like they were special. I was in the den on the other side of the wall when I heard my name in their conversation. I listened. I heard Randy tell my mother that I was a sissy because I played the piano. What? I had heard the word sissy used to refer to other people. I sort of knew what it meant, but wasn't real sure. But I was sure that it wasn't nice. There was a mirror hanging on the wall in the living room just inside the doorway that connected it to the den. It was to the right of the gold sofa and there was a gold chair under the mirror. I stood in the den looking at my brother's reflection in the mirror as he continued talking about me to his wife and my mother. I didn't hear the rest of his words. My mind shut down. But I saw his teeth. And I saw the way his mouth shaped around his teeth. And I knew that he wasn't saying good things about me.

What had I ever done to him? I didn't even know him. And he didn't know me. I never even told anybody about the time he threw me across the backyard. I didn't tell anybody, not even Harrell and Darrell, that I saw him pulling on his thing in the bathtub. They could have used that information to make water come from his eyes. It hurt that he would say mean things about me. I tried to quit piano several times but my mother wouldn't let me because I was actually pretty good for our small town. What Randy said haunted me and made me not want to be any better at it, but I wound up being the best in the family.

I stayed in line and I kept watching. I watched my sister Linda leave the house, go to college and get married to the guy who drove my father's car when he wasn't supposed to. I later learned that she was pregnant and that's why they got married. I watched my sister Vern leave the house but Daddy drove her all the way to Missouri to go to college. She finished in a short amount of time and returned home. But it wasn't pleasant. One night she didn't come home. Daddy rumbled about that. I listened. She came home the next day, which I thought was fine. When she walked into the house, Daddy asked her where she had been. She just walked past him and went to her old room and closed the door. I guess that was the wrong thing to do because Daddy rumbled real loud and kicked in the door. Me, Harrell and Darrell stood in the distance as Daddy went on and on about how no daughter of his was going to act like a common street woman and then come to his house and expect to live there. I thought Vern was going to have to be sent to Austin with the other crazy people. She was huddled on the side of her bed with her back to Daddy. Her hands were trembling about her face like she was trying to find it. Her entire body shook uncontrollably. The next day her bags were packed. Daddy took her to the bus station and sent her to Houston. She got married soon after that. Then she got divorced.

Then it was Stine's turn. I had noticed the pattern of Daddy's joy and pain. Stine was as smart as she was beautiful. Since she was the youngest of the girls, I thought she was more like me and knew the routine—stay out of trouble! But then came miniskirts and boys. One drew the other. Sometimes I couldn't believe what my sister wore to school. I knew it was the fashion, but even from my point of view something that short couldn't keep anyone covered up. But she wore them. My cousins and sisters used to take material, measure out what they thought was enough, fold the material in two, lay it on the bed, then one would lie down on top of the material while another would cut around her. Then they would sew the two sides, hem it and presto, a miniskirt. That must have been the way Stine got her clothes, because I could never imagine my mother buying her something like that. But then again, she didn't sneak around to wear what she wore. She walked right out the front door wearing it. So maybe my mother approved, I don't know. But her looks combined with her clothes made Daddy rumble.

One Saturday evening, Daddy and I waited at the Snack Center for Stine to come and work the evening shift. She arrived on the back of a horse with a guy that I didn't particularly care for because he wasn't nice to me. Daddy started to rumble again. I think things would have been okay if she hadn't responded the way she did. Instead of just listening and pretending to absorb every word with fear and trembling, she turned her back, waved her hand and said, "Aw man. . . ." Daddy went on and on about how she needed to watch the way she talked to him and how she needed to watch who she hung around with. I tried to leave, but had nowhere to go. His voice rang to every corner of the building. He finally finished and each one of us did our work.

But Stine made Daddy proud too. He beamed with pride when he showed the old black-and-white films of the Booker T. Washington days. Parades, football games, dances, banquets, proms. Daddy would laugh and narrate and he could tell each person's entire family history. Being an insurance man gave Daddy inside information on a lot of peoples' lives, especially when a person died and the wife thought she was the beneficiary on the insurance policy but Daddy knew different. Or when men took out insurance policies on children who didn't live in the same house with him and his wife. Oh, where was I? Oh, yeah. When Stine was a senior in high school, she entered a Miss Teenage Texas Pageant. She also planned to marry this rich guy who drove a convertible and bought me real nice presents when it wasn't even my birthday. But he disappeared and I don't know what happened to him. Samuel Black. Later, somebody sent us a photo of him in a society magazine.

CHAPTER TWENTY-FOUR

How many beers have I had?

Eight.

I need to go around the corner of the house again.

It's dark.

I need to hold it together long enough to finish what I started. What was it that I started? I can smell my own breath.

Cigarettes and beer. Who would want to kiss a mouth like that?

Having somebody to kiss right now sure wouldn't be a bad idea.

Forget kissing. Concentrate.

Concentrate.

I know it's getting late and you may be getting tired but you have to focus. You're doing some great work and we don't want to lose the momentum. Drink another beer, it'll help you focus, relax and keep the flow going. Okay?

Where was I? Oh, yeah . . . Stine. . . . She worked hard to prepare for the pageant. My mother was right there with her and Daddy stood in the distance smiling. I watched them all. She made her own clothes for the pageant, including her evening gown. It materialized from five-and-dime fabric into something stunning. I knew my sister was beautiful but I didn't know she could look like that. She did her own hair, something that required foil and a brown paper grocery bag. I was even more proud of her than before. I sat and listened to her practice for the talent portion of the pageant. I would chuckle to myself when she hit the high notes. She would tilt her head back and to one side, close her eyes and her eyelids would flutter. But her voice was clear and pure. I remember where I was sitting

142

when the curtain went up at the pageant. There were all these girls, and there was my sister. I took my eyes off of her long enough to look down the row at Daddy. He was beaming, so proud. My sister was outshining every girl on stage. I couldn't take my eyes off her. She sang the song and her eyelids fluttered:

I believe for every drop of rain that falls
A flower grows . . .

Then she came onto the stage in her evening gown. It was a floor-length, deep aqua blue dress that gathered around her neck but left her back, shoulders and arms bare. Her hair was perfect. She had on long white gloves that made her hands appear to be so delicate it seemed she had to move them very slowly at her sides or else she would hurt them. She was perfect. I didn't have to look at Daddy when they announced the winner. I was a part of him; I knew what he felt. They placed the crown on Stine's head, put a black cape with a high Victorian collar around her shoulders, gave her a scepter, a trophy and flowers. Water came from her eyes. Water was coming from my eyes too so I knew it was coming from Daddy's as well. A few months later Momma took Stine to another pageant in Alabama. We couldn't go. After the pageant, Momma called home to report that Stine had placed ninth in the nation but only because another girl needed to really improve on her stage presence so Stine helped her. That girl ended up placing sixth. But that's the kind of person Stine was.

Stine left home and went to college at the University of Texas at Austin. I worked hard to make money to send to her. I guess I would have worked hard whether I sent her money or not because that was the house rule. Everybody worked hard. I worked at the Snack Center. I mowed lawns. I picked up pecans and sold them. I picked up glass bottles and sold them. I picked up aluminum cans and sold them. I even had a little racket going at school. I was allowed to go off-campus while some of the other kids in my class weren't. So I would stop at the U-Tote-Em and buy bubble gum for a penny and take them back to school and sell them for a nickel each. I made so much money. And I was only in the fifth grade. But I had learned from watching the others ahead of me. They never had enough money while they were in college. I didn't know why, but I figured that it would be the same for Stine, so I would just send her money every now and then.

Stine had been in college a few years when she came home with news. She was pregnant. When she came home, her stomach was already beginning to stick out a little. She and I sat in the booth at the Snack Center and talked briefly before she was to have an audience with my father. I don't even remember hearing what she said. My mind had shut down. Here was something else Daddy was going to have to deal with. I don't know what was said between Stine and Daddy, but the conversation continued in the presence of me, Harrell and Darrell that Sunday at home in the special dining room at dinner. Somebody said the word abortion and Daddy said he didn't believe in abortions and that's why he had the three of us.

What? What did I hear him say? He confirmed what I thought I heard. Me, Harrell and Darrell were accidents. My mind wouldn't shut down even though it wanted to. This wasn't the way things were supposed to be. This wasn't even about me. I hadn't done anything. This was about Stine. But I heard the words and they hurt me. Stine moved to California with Linda and the guy who drove Daddy's car when he wasn't supposed to. She had the baby. A few years later she came back to Texas and got married to Carl.

Chapter Twenty-five

After Stine left for college, just me, Harrell and Darrell were left at home. Life continued to make less and less sense to me. Though we had many, many good times, the bad times seemed to outweigh them. I tried to hold onto my mind but I felt it slipping away. One day I brought home my school pictures. I was so proud that I had managed to make the camera capture the happy little kid that was buried inside of me. I showed Daddy the proofs and asked if he would buy them for me. He said he wasn't going to buy those ugly pictures. I could see his teeth when he said it and the way his mouth shaped around his teeth. I didn't like the way it made me feel. My mother paid for my pictures. After that incident I tried to run away from home. I wrapped some clothes up in one of my t-shirts and left the house. Miz Minnie, a neighbor, saw me and asked me where I was going. I stupidly told her the truth. She sent me back home.

Somewhere along my path I became preoccupied with death. I felt like I wouldn't live to see my eighteenth birthday. I didn't know if I would die at the hands of Harrell or Darrell or by some terrible disease. Harrell and Darrell seemed to be accident-prone. Harrell fell out in the backyard one day while we were playing with a bunch of other kids. He lay on the ground, shaking out of control. Randy was at home from college that day and put his fingers in Harrell's mouth. He said Harrell was trying to swallow his own tongue. My mother rushed them both to the hospital with Randy's fingers still in Harrell's mouth. Harrell was having an epileptic seizure. Every other month it seemed like Darrell would get himself into a situation where one of his fingernails would be pulled completely off.

Watching them made me think that my time was coming but mine would be worse. Fatal.

Finally, my day did come. We were having bike races in the back alley. Harrell was going to race me. All the kids were using the same two bikes and Harrell got to the good bike first. I was mad but took the worse bike and went to the starting line. Harrell beat me by a lot. I was mad and wasn't looking both ways crossing the finish line, which was at the end of the alley at an intersection. I rode out into the street right in front of a car. I pushed back on the pedal to make the bike stop. The back wheel of the bike grabbed for the ground but the rocks made the bike spin. The car started to spin too. The back of the car hit me and the bike. I landed on the top of the trunk and ended up underneath the car in between the two back tires. When I came to, I was looking up at the gas tank under the car. Someone was pulling me by the feet out from underneath the car. They stood me up and asked if I was okay. I looked down and all I saw were my socks. Both my shoes were gone. A kid ran almost a block away to get one of my shoes. There was a cloud of dust rising from our front yard; my father was coming to rush me to the hospital. They found my other shoe a block in the opposite direction from the first one. Daddy took me to the hospital. I was fine except for a few bruises and the bump on my head that is still there today. Harrell and Darrell laughed about it afterwards. There was no choice but to laugh with them. But it would have been kind of nice to go and see my friend Jesus.

As he got older, Darrell pulled on his thing more and more. Finally, he learned how to make his thing bubble. Once he had mastered this technique, he showed me and Harrell. We tried to make ours bubble too. Harrell could, but I couldn't, no matter how hard I tried. I thought something was wrong with me, or maybe I wasn't trying hard enough. So I kept trying. It was hard finding time alone to work on it. The three of us had to bathe before going to bed, so that wasn't enough time. Daddy had to have his long smoke in the bathroom after work and before his nap. Harrell and Darrell tried to avoid the bathroom after Daddy, so I thought that would be a good time and place to practice. But someone would miss me and come looking. That didn't give me enough time either. I was determined to figure out why I couldn't make my thing bubble like Harrell and Darrell. But I had no one to ask, and no one to tell me why. I thought about spending time alone on the side of the house where we went when the bathroom was occupied, but I couldn't find peace there. We had nailed a bicycle rim to a square piece of plywood and nailed the plywood in a tree to make our own basketball goal. I was small and not very good at basketball, so I thought having our own makeshift goal would give me a chance to practice by myself. But other kids would come into our backyard and play even when Harrell and Darrell weren't there. I couldn't understand why, especially when there was a bigger and better goal in the back alley. But when they came, I forgot about wanting time on the side of the house and practicing by myself. I just tried to fit in.

A few of the kids were even older than Harrell and Darrell. They would talk about girls. I listened and tried to learn. I learned to laugh when they laughed but I never said anything. One day one of the bigger kids asked me what I was laughing at. I didn't answer. He said that he bet that I didn't even know how to get a girl. Get a girl? What was he talking about? I still didn't answer. He stopped shooting the basketball, held it in his hand and walked up to me. All the kids started gathering around me and looking at me. I backed up against the side of the pink house with blue trim around the windows. I looked for Harrell and Darrell to rescue me. They never rescued me when I really needed them to. The guy gave me a little shove on the shoulder and said he bet I didn't even know. I said I did know. He said, "Then where do you get a girl?" Where? Where? Not how, but where. My mind was struggling to add up everything that I had been storing away. I really didn't understand the question, but I knew he wasn't asking me where to "find" a girl. He wasn't asking me where you take a girl to do things you weren't supposed to do. Then I had it. I remembered the two dogs that Tanzes had separated. It must have been a boy dog and a girl dog. So the boy dog must have been "getting" the girl dog. I stood up from the wall straight and tall and announced my answer. In the booty. I started laughing because I thought I had said the right thing and they laughed when they talked about girls. They started laughing too, but harder than I had seen them laugh before. We were probably not laughing at the same thing. What did I say wrong? Wasn't I right? I kept hearing them repeat, in the booty, in the booty. Then one of them said that something must be wrong with me. I couldn't disappear. There was nowhere to go. I believed them. Something was wrong with me.

CHAPTER TWENTY-SIX

As I grew older, I felt more and more fragmented. With so many people around me, it seemed like I should have had all the resources in the world to get the information I needed to keep me together. But it just wasn't there. I kept struggling to find a place for the leftover pieces of me. Teacher after teacher called me by the name of one of the older kids in my family. I know it sounds really trivial and that other guys on the market have had the same problem, but this is what happened to me and it is a part of my packaging, so it's important to know.

That's okay. Remember, this is YOUR story.

When I was in the seventh grade, I didn't try out for football. I wasn't very good at sports, nothing like my older brothers. Harrell and I had played summer baseball for the Bankers. I was just average. Still, I had a good time wearing the uniform, belonging to a team, being without Darrell, and riding my bike to practice and to the games. Since I was not a naturally good athlete, I decided to be an academic and try and get scholarships for college. One of the coaches was my science teacher and kept telling me he could use me on his team. The seventh graders didn't play other schools. There were four teams and they played each other. He talked and talked until he convinced me that maybe I could be good at football. So I went out for the team. Here was a place where I could let my insides rumble and it was okay. Here was a place where people instructed you and if you did what they said, you were almost guaranteed to be good. I followed instructions very well. The pads felt good, the helmet felt good, the cleats felt good, the workouts felt good. Plus, the coach seemed to be happy with me. I played offensive and defensive tackle.

One day we were in practice. I was on defense and Big Luke Majors was opposite on offense. Coach had taught me how to handle Big Luke and it worked. Stay low so he couldn't move me away from the ball, then go for the man with the ball. Just that simple. And that's what I did when the quarterback handed the ball to Manny Mendoza. I made the tackle with little or no yards gained. I jumped up to go to the huddle when I noticed Coach Green and Coach Gooden watching me. I looked over at them hoping for praise, but that's not what they gave me. I heard one of them tell the other that I was good, but I would never be as good as my older brothers. I quit football that afternoon and never went back.

Earlier that same year, I had started to play one song each Sunday on the organ at church. My newest teacher, Miz Jesse Mae Lowe, had a full-size organ in her house. After my piano lessons, she would go in her back room and lie in bed while I played the organ. She would sing along in her beautiful operatic voice. The organist position at our church had been vacant for a few years. Vern had played the organ and Stine played it a little, though she mostly played the piano. Then another guy came but he didn't stay very long. So I knew what they were up to when my mother talked to the pastor and the pianists and volunteered me to play the song before the morning message. I didn't fight it. It was my turn to go. In the beginning, I was pretty mechanical. I played the song, whatever the song, note for note, got up and went to my seat. One day my mother told me she wanted me to play "Amazing Grace" and I said no, I wouldn't do it. I had seen the other musicians play that song and make people jump up yelling and screaming. I didn't understand that. But after playing the same song Sunday after Sunday, even I got a little bored with my playing. I decided to at least slow down the tempo so that I would only have to play it through once or twice instead of three times. Something happened to people when I slowed down the tempo. They didn't jump up, they didn't yell and scream. But some of them had water coming from their eyes. Church was the very last place on earth I wanted to pretend to be somebody I wasn't. But that's what happened. I learned how to make water come from the people's eyes.

One night, that same year, Darrell was taking a bath when he called out for help because he couldn't get out of the tub. It wasn't my birthday, but that didn't mean he wasn't up to something. I opened the door expecting some prank, but his face told me that it was for real. He couldn't act that well. He lay in the water, looking distressed. He couldn't move the left side of his body. Momma and Harrell helped him out of the tub and put his pajamas on him. She took him to the hospital. It was serious. He had to be transferred to Scott & White, a bigger hospital in Temple. It was a while before Harrell and I knew what was going on. Fear welled up inside of me so much that I couldn't breathe. No matter what they had done to me, I loved my brothers. I hated a lot of things they had done to me. And, as a result, I hated my own life. But in a weird way, I loved them more than I loved myself.

The doctors told my parents that Darrell had a brain tumor and that he would have to be transferred to yet another hospital in Waco for surgery. On his brain? How could he survive that? My brother was going to die. I wondered how Daddy was going to pay for what Darrell needed. It sounded so expensive. I didn't make any promises to God or ask Him for anything. I just prepared myself to be whatever the family needed me to be to help us get through it. I would be useful and not a burden. I watched my parents work as a team. They coordinated our lives so that me and Harrell would continue with our daily activities and they called in the troops for support and prayer. The day of the surgery, we made a big circle in the living room. I can't remember who all was there, but I remember my parents standing hand-in-hand as the preacher prayed for God's blessing on Darrell, strength for my parents and faith for us all. I heard my parents breathe deeply and sigh as they prepared for whatever was to come. When the preacher finished, there was water in everyone's eyes.

Darrell didn't die. He made it through the surgery and back home. He had a big question mark on the side of his head where the doctors had removed the tumor. His head was swollen and he couldn't talk or walk. But over time, he regained both of those abilities.

While Darrell was at home recovering, I went to middle school and Harrell went to high school as usual. I had made up in my mind to go straight home everyday after school and ask for more to do around the house and at the Snack Center. One day, the coaches of our P.E. class lined all the boys up in front of the basketball goal and told us to do lay-ups. I stood in line and noticed they were dividing the boys up on either side of the gym. The boys who made the lay-up were on one side and the boys who didn't were on the other. My turn came and I missed. I didn't really care. The coaches announced it was basketball season and there were going to be two teams. An A team and a B team. I was on the B team. But I didn't want to play basketball on a team. I had to be around in the evenings to help my family. That afternoon, when I got home, before I could ask for more to do around the house, my mother told me that Miz Betsy Craney, the pianist for the senior choir at church, had passed away. I was going to miss the Banana Bites and Chick-O Sticks she sold out of her black case after church. Then my mother told me they wanted me to take her place. The first thing I thought about was money. I would get paid. I could add that money to what I was making at the Snack Center, help out with the bills and be even more useful. It surprised my mother when I agreed so fast.

Darrell recovered fully and returned to his evil self. Daddy never asked for any money and I really didn't know how to offer, but I was definitely more financially self-sufficient. I became quite useful at church. I was only in the seventh grade and I was instructing people who were in their fifties and older. Teaching and leading them came so naturally to me. But most of all they respected and wanted me and I found a place to be useful.

The line in front of me was getting shorter, but I had lost hope of communicating with my father. Me, Harrell and Darrell worked hard at the Snack Center, the rent houses and in the gardens in addition to all of the activities we were involved in at school and in the community. Our lives were going along the same path as my other siblings. That was scary. By the time I was a freshman in high school, all of my siblings who had already graduated from high school had been married and there were already four divorces.

My freshman year in the high school band our football team made the playoffs. We traveled to Cleburne near Dallas. Randy and his wife lived in Dallas, but I didn't expect to see them at the football game. After our halftime show, I saw him waving at me from the stands. I was really surprised. I couldn't help but feel a little bit special in front of my friends because my brother had come to see me. I had a big smile on my face as I jogged up the bleachers to speak with him. I stood there just below where they were sitting, looking directly up at him as we talked. I noticed something strange. His wife hadn't spoken to me. So I turned to her. It wasn't his wife. His voice trailed off toward the night sky as I stared at her and tried to figure out what was going on. She smiled at me but I couldn't smile back. I don't even know if he introduced us. My mind shut down. I wasn't even going to try and figure this one out. I quickly bid my good-byes and went back to my own life, which I was having a hard enough time understanding without more family drama. Sure enough, he got divorced and announced he was going to marry this other woman. I immediately wondered if my father was going to cater that wedding too. My father had dutifully catered every one of their weddings with three-tier bridal cakes, chocolate groom's cakes, crystal glasses, glass plates, fine silverware, candelabras, champagne, color-coordinated punch, finger food, flower arrangements from his garden and bows that he made himself; the works. And he did it happily. And they kept doing stuff like this. I didn't want that for my life.

But I was already in line, marching along. I had seen it happen with the others and naively thought I could be better than them. I could be a good son who was eager and willing to learn and do what was right. But the big blowup between father and son was inevitable. It seemed like a strange test he had developed to see if you were ready for the outside world. "Grasshopper, when you can remain standing after a rumbling with me . . ." I don't know. Daddy's temper was like a volcano. His worst times were at the Snack Center. He would go way beyond rumbling and explode. If a customer lied and said they ordered mayonnaise instead of mustard, it was our fault. If Daddy misunderstood what we wrote down, it was our fault. If he rang the bell when an order was ready, he wanted it out of his way right then. Didn't matter how many customers you had. He rang the bell and you got the order. If the customer complained loud enough that Daddy could hear them, that was our fault too. He'd put one hand on his hip and swell up, his eyes turned a hellish red, he'd cock his head to one side and roar. He didn't care who heard him. My father didn't swear much. On his worst day, he'd say "shit." But he would call us names. We were called "gump" a long time before Forrest came along. We didn't even know what a gump was, but when Daddy said it, we knew what it meant. Then, when he'd had as much as he could stand, he would send one of us home. His favorite line was "Get on 'cross that track!" And we knew what that meant. To go home so Momma could humiliate us even further and send us right back to him. Then it would start all over again. The customers would come in and we would get real busy, he'd explode, and five minutes later, he would be humming a tune while we were still hurting. I grew so weary of that routine. I didn't understand it, but I knew I was also capable of the same mighty anger and I swore that not to be like that.

I tried real hard. To this day I am the best cook in the family. At least *I* think so. I became very useful for Daddy's catering jobs. I could make the potato salad just the way he wanted it. I could make the chicken salad just the way he wanted it. I could decorate trays just the way he wanted them. I could make a great-tasting punch of any color. I could make the barbecue sauce. I knew how to put the cloths and skirts on the tables. I knew how to trim the candles to make them all the same height. I could do all of that stuff by the age of fourteen. But it didn't matter. He still had to explode. I understood Stine's response to him the day she showed up on the back of a horse. She was just tired.

One night, just the two of us were working at the Snack Center and I made the mistake of thinking that things were going pretty well. It started over a chili-dog. He didn't fix it because he said I didn't tell him. It was all my fault. I didn't tell him all he had to do was use the system that he had set up (which I was following exactly like he showed me) and see that I had written the chili-dog down on the order ticket and hung it right in front of his face where all the other orders were. I didn't say any of that. He said he was too busy to fix it and that I needed to fix it myself. I said "fine." He rumbled back that I shouldn't start talking smart to him. I have to admit I had an attitude, but he was setting me up. Daddy never liked anyone in his kitchen with him.

There was room enough for three people in the grill area and Daddy acted like he needed all of it, all of the time. Wherever the other person was, that's where he needed to be. He would bump you and shove you and rumble because you were in his way. So I couldn't believe he had just told me to come into his kitchen and cook a chili-dog when he had all those other orders and I had customers up front. Why would he do that to me? I braced myself for battle. I moved around him timidly, trying to anticipate when he was coming to my spot so I could move before he got there. But he wouldn't let it go. Daddy had taught me how to make a chili-dog and wrap it to go. But that was a lot of activity for me to manage with hot chili and a hot man who wouldn't give me any room to move. I was bound to fail. He bumped me several times, but I was hurrying just trying to get to the end and doing a bad job of fixing the customer's food. I was finishing the final roll when he bumped me on my left side and rumbled for me to hurry up and get out of his way. I couldn't help it. My head snapped in his direction and I gave him a go-to-hell look and he . . . heard . . . every . . . word my eyes said. I was brave enough to hold my position, but only for a second. Then I almost ran out of the kitchen grabbing a brown to-go sack for the chili-dog on the way. But it wasn't over. He wouldn't let it be over.

Daddy liked to eat ice cream after we closed up. Sometimes he would scoop some into a Styrofoam cup and take it home or sometimes he'd scoop it into a bowl and eat it in his office at the Snack Center. After the chili-dog incident, we spent the remainder of that evening working together but not speaking. When the customers were gone, I sat at the counter and watched television while he sat in his office. We were alone and he didn't talk to me. When it was time to close, we did so in silence. I knew what to do and he didn't have to tell me. Then he told me to hand him the ice cream. I opened the freezer, reached in and pulled out a frozen square block in a blue cardboard container and placed it on the counter near him without any eye contact. When he finally noticed what I had given him, he started. He rumbled. He told me that I was ignorant. Just ignorant! Any fool ought to know the difference between ice milk and ice cream. What? What in the hell was he talking about? Ice milk? Ice cream? No, if there was a difference, I had never heard of it. I wanted to tell him that maybe if he told me, then I would know. Just maybe, if he talked to me I would know. But I didn't. I just returned to the kitchen to prevent an even larger explosion. But he met me at the freezer, still rumbling. And that was it. I was tired. I was not going to take it anymore. He was going to have to hear what was on my mind.

I stood squarely in front of him and looked up at him. I told him that yes, I may be ignorant of the fact that there is a difference between ice milk and ice cream but I was not ignorant in general. When I finished, I stood there, raised my eyebrows and blinked my eyes just to let him know it was his turn. And I was ready for whatever he decided to do. Both of his hands hit my chest, grabbed my shirt and lifted me to my toes. He didn't speak. It was my turn. I balled up my fists, brought them up through his arms and broke his grip with my forearms. Then I squared off with him and took my left index finger and put it in his face. When I spoke it was stern and very serious. I told him that he was not going to hit me, ever again. I told him I was a man and I could understand every word that came out of his mouth. And from then on, he was going to have to talk to me like a man.

He didn't hit me. I backed away slowly still facing him. He might have attacked me from behind once he realized what had just happened. I went to the front counter to sit down so my knees would stop trembling and my heart could stop pounding.

He busied himself in the kitchen for a long time, just humming. How in the hell could he hum after what just happened? Finally, he said we should go home. On the way home, I sat in the passenger seat of his junky station wagon with my back turned to him and my face pressed close to the window. I didn't want to be near him. I was hurt. What did I do to make him treat me like this? I didn't care if I was an accident; I existed. Why can't he see me for me? I am not one of his other children! My name is Winston! My name is not John, it is not Randy, it is not Linda, it is not Vern, it is not Stine, it is not Darrell and it is not Harrell! My name is Winston! All I wanted him to do was to talk to me. To tell me what I needed to know about life before I had to leave home. What had I done? If he didn't want me then why did he have me? If he could hear my thoughts, would he care? My name is Winston!

Are you okay?

No. I sit here in the grips of the darkness and today is the first time I've cried about that day. Right now, I'm not a happy drunk.

Can you go on?

I have no choice but to go on.

I see you are upset, take a moment if you need to. I'm ready when you are.

Darrell graduated from high school and left home to go to Texas Southern University in Houston. Harrell graduated and went to Blinn Junior College in Brenham, Texas. Then came my turn. Everybody except Vern came home for my high school graduation. It was an excellent day. My family cheered the loudest, louder that any of my other classmates'. When they had me stand up and announced my scholarships, more cheering. I had a music scholarship from my high school and an academic scholarship from the University of Texas at Austin. When the ceremony was over, we all gathered at the house. They had so many gifts for me. A huge trunk filled with things for college. But the most special thing they presented me with was a plaque. On it was a poem written by the second oldest guy. It read:

> *We are proud of you little brother*
> *Youngest child of our Dad and Mother*
> *We expect you to go further*
> *And achieve much more than us seven other*
> *So run on, climb high*
> *The world is yours to discover*
> *From the heart of each sister*
> *And the soul of each brother*
>
> * * *
>
> *John Columbus*
> *Elliott Randolph*
> *Linda Faye*
> *Viola LaVerne*
> *Esstine Denise*
> *Aubrey Darrell*
> *Harrell Dean*

Finally, here were my instructions! I had waited all my life for someone to tell me what to do, where to go and who to be. I would try to live up to their expectations.

Hey little cousin Nicole, I know you're only thirteen, but would you? Tell her how you know me?

I know him from my mother. He is a part of our family. He is very nice, he has a loud laugh (very loud), he speaks with kindness, truth, respect for people and he treats his family nice. He cares about his family, friends and God. I don't know what else to say. Oh, and sometimes, personally, I think he needs help.

Nicole Hill
Houston, Texas

Train Up a Child
In the Way . . .

Chapter Twenty-seven

I'm a mess. And I don't have anything to clean up with.

Are you alright now?

Yeah, I thought the cry I had about my father was bad, but when I remembered the poem from my brothers and sisters, the floodgates opened. I can't believe how many tears came from my eyes. Now I have to blow my nose.

Use your shirttail.

Gross. That's just plain old nasty. My shirttail is soaked. Beer and cigarette stench, snot all over me, now all I have to do is pee on myself and I'll finally look like the mess that I really am. Try to package *that* and sell it.

But it is all coming together now.

Yeah, it is. I feel like I let my family down, like I lost myself on graduation day. That day, I learned they expected me to go further and achieve much more than they had. I knew in my heart I would fail. But I lifted my head, put my shoulders back and buried myself. I know now that the packaging I created didn't start with women, it started with my family. What I sold to women was only a by-product.

The Winston that had it all together?

Yeah, the "everything is great" Winston.

Hmmmm . . .

Beer brings on certain urges. . . Those urges are calling me . . . But . . . I know there is nobody in this town who I want to satisfy them. My trips to the side of the house are kind of frequent now and no doubt will continue because there is still beer left. But another purpose may be added to those trips. For me, in times like these, usually, when I sow the seed of those kinds of thoughts, it leads to reaping the fruit thereof.

What do you mean by that?

I don't want to go there. Literally. At least not right now.

So, go on.

My parents drove me to Austin and dropped me off at my dorm room at UT. That's it. I wish I could say more about it but I can't. Not that they were being cold or insensitive; I just don't remember much about the preparation to go, the drive to Austin or the "farewell son, it's a new beginning for you" speech. We moved my stuff into my dorm room, they left and I had two hours to get to tryouts for the University of Texas Longhorn Band, The Show Band of the Southwest. I left the dorm in plenty of time, but what should have been a five-to-ten-minute walk took me two hours. I got lost and I didn't, wouldn't, ask for directions. I just *had* to figure it out for myself. The only way I found the band hall was to follow some students who looked as though they were going there. I followed them, trailing behind, up some wide and high concrete stairs, through some trees, past some buildings and then I heard the drums. I checked in just in the nick of time.

The band hall was full of hundreds of students wanting to be a part of this great tradition that I knew little about. They were full of spirit, jumping up and down, clapping and yelling. They were doing something with their hands that obviously meant something. I learned later that it was the famous 'hook-em horns' sign; forefinger and pinkie up, thumb folded across middle and ring finger. I began to imitate them. Anybody looking at me would think I really knew what was going on, but I didn't. That's how my college career began. That is how the other me began: faking it 'til I could figure out how to make it.

After a week of grueling practices in one hundred plus degrees, courtesy of the August sun, on Astroturf that burned a hole through my brand new Kaeppas, after carrying a heavy brass tuba (we used fiberglass in high school) that left a huge bruise on my shoulder, I made it. I made it through Hell Week and into the band. I called home with the good news and received the first post-living-at-home words of approval from my parents. My mother: "I'm so proud of you son," and my father chuckling, "That's good! That's real good!" They beamed through the phone. I could feel it. Was this the me they wanted? I liked it. Hmmmm . . . .

My college experiences, especially in the Longhorn Band, were the beginning of many life lessons. I was no different than any other student entering college. Nothing made me unique except my social security number. The band usually hosted a big party after the names of new and returning members were posted. It was held at an Austin landmark that I came to know pretty well, Scholz Beer Garten. It was already dark by the time I made it to the party.

I got a late start on the party scene; my parents kept us working too much. But thanks to Laura and Tracey, I caught up. Tracey was a rather large girl with long, thick hair. She was one of the smartest people in our high school graduating class. We nicknamed her "bedroom eyes." Laura was my best buddy and our families were friends. Laura was one of the tallest people in our class, so sometimes she slumped her shoulders, trying to be shorter. She also had long, thick hair and a personality that people either loved or hated. I loved it. She could make me laugh, any time of the day. Laura, Tracey and I were going to Austin for college. Tracey was going to UT on the same scholarship as I was and Laura was going to Austin Community College. We went out for dinner in Waco the summer before college started and that's when Tracey showed me how to guzzle beer. Back then, beer and alcoholic drinks were cheap, and poor students who drank loved happy hour. I guess they still do.

Tracey ordered a pitcher of beer like it was something she did all the time. I sat quietly and watched. I still wasn't used to the fact that I could drink legally. Then she showed us her big gulp technique. I wondered why anyone needed to know such a technique, and then I tried it. That's who I was, a follower. And following Tracey, I learned to like beer, then to guzzle it. Tracey took me to my first X-rated movie and my first adult bookstore, all within my first week in Austin. Later, she wound up dropping out of school.

On the night of the Longhorn Band party, I floated into Scholz Beer Garten, proud of my first college accomplishment. There, standing near the gate, were some of the other tuba players, holding pitchers of beer in both fists. One of the guys offered me a pitcher. I told him not to do that because he wouldn't get so much as a sip. I was just making stuff up as I went along. I didn't really mean it. But he challenged me to try to drink a whole pitcher. I took it, decided not to waste time looking stupid, turned it up and drank it in one gulp. Tracey had taught me well. My stunt drew applause from people I didn't even know. Later in the evening, the same guy bought another pitcher of beer and I did it again. Was I drunk, or were people friendlier? Before I lost complete control of myself, I marveled at how easy it was to make friends.

Later that evening I was hungry, so I left Scholz and walked up to the drive-through at a Wendy's near campus. I had to jump up and down on the tire-activated buzzer, trying to make the bell ring inside so they would take my order. I was jumping and laughing. I placed my order, then threw up next to the pick-up window. Another band member was with me but I don't remember who it was. On the way back I was loud and obnoxious and two policemen approached me. I cursed at them. I don't know where that came from; I never cursed at home. My bandmate convinced the policemen not to take me in. I made it to my dorm room and slept it off.

Playing in the Longhorn Band was a great experience for me. I learned that people love someone who does something special. There was a big article about me in my hometown newspaper with a picture of me sitting in my parents' living room at the piano wearing my Longhorn sweatshirt. People would call my parents and tell them they saw me on national television during a halftime show. My high school band director introduced me to the band when I went home for Friday night football games. Each year, the Longhorns played the Aggies on Thanksgiving Day. For two years, my parents packed up the entire Thanksgiving dinner and brought it to either Austin or College Station, home of the Aggies. I had to buy at least fifteen tickets to the football games because the family wanted to see me march. All of this over something I had no idea was so important. But it gave everybody else pleasure, so I continued. I lettered four years in Longhorn Band with more than four hundred other band members each year. After it was all over, to this day, there is not a single person I keep in contact with.

The next night after the Scholz party, there was a party at my dorm. I lived in Jester East, third floor. Our dorm was connected to the athletic dorm and the athletes sometimes used our floor as a passageway to their side. I heard the music and the loud voices, but I wasn't invited. Then there was a knock at my door. It was a guy going around and inviting us homebodies out to the party. The beer was flowing and I was drinking and meeting more and more people. Someone called the police and when they arrived, I felt it was my obligation to stand up for the hosts of the party since they were gracious enough to invite me. My behavior was out of character, but of course I was drunk. The policemen told them to keep me quiet or they would arrest me. Someone wrestled me down on the bed and covered up my mouth. The next day, not even the stench of beer, pizza and vomit kept me from doing it all over again.

Yet another party the next night. This one was thrown by Jester East *and* Jester West. I lost control again and met even more people. The first few days of classes, people I didn't even remember were speaking to me and calling me by my name. I just spoke back and tried to figure out who they were and how they knew me. It was difficult to establish real friendships with people I met while I was drinking. I began to feel more and more unreal.

Anna, one of the girls I met at one of the dorm parties, invited me to go to church with her. On Sunday, we met outside of Jester and walked to The Drag. The Drag, actually named Guadalupe Street, borders the westernmost part of campus. The church, University Baptist Church, was on Guadalupe. The X-rated movie theater and the adult bookstore Tracey took me to were both on the same street, one north of the church, the other south. I guess the church was in the middle of sin. University Baptist Church was nice, but much quieter than the church I attended back in Marlin. Obviously, Anna was raised in a church like mine. During the service, a lady sang a beautiful solo. Then Anna did a solo of her own. She said "Amen!" really loud. It seemed to bounce back and forth across the sanctuary over everyone's heads. I was slightly embarrassed, but Anna was confident in her worship. I went to church several times with her because I was raised that way: Sunday was for church. One Sunday, I was dressed and leaving Jester by myself to walk over to University Baptist. I saw a group of students who were dressed as though they were going to church but they were all standing on the steps of Jester West. I didn't know any of them but I walked over to see what was up.

A van from Higher Ground Missionary Baptist Church pulled up. I figured there couldn't be much harm in getting in the van. So as they moved toward the van, I did too. I stood at the end of the line wondering if they had called and reserved a seat and if so, how I was going to explain my presence. The bus was full but I made it on. It took us to the church and once we arrived and filed in, an usher guided us all to one side of the sanctuary. I found a seat and began to look around to get my bearings. That's when I saw him. My father! But it wasn't my father. My father was back in Marlin. It was a man who looked exactly like my father. I took it as a sign that this was the place I was supposed to be. I joined Higher Ground Missionary Baptist Church and spent the next thirteen years there. On the Sundays I attended, I sat in the very same pew as I did the first time.

Stop. I'm having a hard time with this part of my life.

Why?

Because during my first semester in college I really started giving up on my life.

What?

It's the truth. There was so little of me left. There was no way I could be the person my family wanted. The friends I had before I went to college became unfamiliar to me. The friendships I made in college were following the same pattern. They weren't real. I wasn't real. I didn't know how to be me, and I didn't know who I was. A lot of great things happened while I was in college, but it was like they were happening to someone else. The other me.

So what do you recommend we do here? Stop the meeting? Terminate the session? Forget about the new and improved you? Stop and just stare at the silver box then walk away? Again?

What do *you* suggest we do?

It is all up to you.

Me?

You.

Me?

You! IT'S YOUR LIFE!

But it's boring, depressing and full of failures. I know the way the story ends. Can't I just skip to the next part?

No. Whatever happened here you need to put it on the label. She needs to know exactly what she's getting, remember?

Alright . . . Damn . . .

It was just like my childhood. I kept trying to make sense of things and the way they were supposed to be, but it just didn't make any sense. I had no clue what I wanted to be in life. I had no idea of what I expected of myself. I went to college because that was the unspoken rule in our house. Somewhere in the back of my mind, I kept thinking that when I left Marlin, things would all make sense and the outside world would be much different. But college was surreal. I even ended up with a bully for a section leader in band. It was my childhood all over again. Expecting the grown-ups to stop this guy from bullying us, from bullying me. But no one did anything. They just let him terrorize us. I remember the same rumbling I had felt when I was a kid, building up inside. I tried to control it, but I couldn't anymore. Before I knew what I was doing, I lost control. I felt my hands clenched around the bully's throat, squeezing hard. I thought I was going to kill him, but I didn't. I saw his face turn fire torch red. His eyes reminded me of the burning rabbit. He choked and gasped for air. He was luckier than the rabbit; I spared his life.

There was too much anger, confusion and pressure inside of me. I needed to get rid of that side of myself. So, in my freshman year, I buried myself so deep inside that I went through five years of college not present.

So what did you do?

I remembered my vow not to burden my parents the way my brothers and sisters had done. I only wanted to do things that made them happy. I tried to make other people's lives better. Mine was so bad.

Okay, that's three things you listed; maybe you can explain how you accomplished each.

I'm too drunk. I don't know if I can even remember what I just said.

Just try.

But I'm so tired. And I really want to spend a little time on the side of the house.

Don't go there. Literally. Now, go on. Talk about what you did to prevent yourself from being a burden on your parents.

I tried to do the right things. I didn't complain. I didn't ask for money or help or advice; I tried to figure life out for myself. I had saved enough money to pay for my first year of college over and above the scholarships. But I knew the money wouldn't last forever. I decided to continue playing for the church in Marlin at least two Sundays a month. My friend Laura had a little hoopty, a red Maverick with a white top. She and I rode back and forth to Marlin together; I paid for the gas. It was tough, especially during football season. Sometimes I wouldn't get in from a football game until one or two o'clock in the morning. But if I was supposed to be in Marlin for Sunday morning service, I was there. When football season was over, I started going home on Fridays as soon as I could after class to work at the Snack Center. I'd work until two o'clock in the morning. My parents let me sleep through the eleven o'clock shift at the Snack Center. I conducted choir rehearsal on Saturday afternoon, worked again at the Snack Center on Saturday night until two o'clock Sunday morning, played for Sunday school, eleven o'clock worship, the three o'clock service if there was one, and the six o'clock service if Laura could wait for me. Then I'd return to Austin and try to study for the next week. My parents were happy. The church was happy. But my grades went downhill fast.

The first semester, I majored in music, with tuba as my principle instrument, piano my secondary. I learned very quickly that I couldn't compete on the college level. My private instructor told me I had learned a lot of techniques wrong and that I would have to work very hard to re-train myself. The music was difficult and I would get physically ill each week before my private sessions. Piano was about the same. I had stopped reading music when I had to take over the choir in the seventh grade. Back then, I had to learn so much so fast that my instructor taught me to play by ear, more like the church wanted me to play. So in college I had a hard time reading music. But there was one good thing that they taught me as a music major. The music professors told us we should be able to walk anywhere on campus and sing middle C without hearing it first. I learned how to do that. But I only stayed in the music depart-ment for one semester. By the second semester, I decided I wasn't going to go very far in music and I switched to the business department to major in accounting.

In my second year, I started work-study. That gave me a total of three jobs while carrying a fifteen-hour course load. That's the way the next four-and-a-half years went. I always had at least three jobs. I hardly had time to study. In my first accounting course, at the end of the second semester, the bell curve caught me. So the beginning of my second year I changed to general business. I still struggled with statistics, pre-calculus, history . . . . You name it, I struggled. But I was determined not to be a financial burden on my parents and I was determined to graduate. The only courses I didn't struggle with were English, especially creative writing. During my senior year in high school, my English teacher had really prepared me for college-level English courses. She was tough. For our term paper, there were no A's and only two B's in the entire senior class. I was one of the B's. I breezed through those courses in college but didn't have the common sense to pursue English or writing as a major. I was lost. And nobody was there to help.

My scholarship provided tutoring and I tried to utilize that resource. The first time I tried was in accounting. The graduate student I was assigned to didn't speak English well, was impatient, and had very poor teaching skills. He also made it clear that he had his own workload and didn't have time to teach me things I should have learned in class. I wondered about his definition of tutoring. After several tries, I gave up on him. I tried the tutoring again when I took my first computer course. Back then we had to write programs on punch cards and it was Greek to me. It was the same story. I just kept moving. In a daze.

The semester before my fourth year, I knew I had to find some way to get out of college or my parents were going to be disappointed in me. And I really, really didn't want that. I got the course book and looked for degree plans that would count the classes I had already taken. That's when I found sociology. I had never heard of it before. I had heard of social work, but not sociology. I matched up my credits, looked to see what I could petition to count toward the degree plan and struck out to be a sociologist. Sociology stirred the ashes of the dead side of me while adding a ton of confusion to the recreated me. Dr. Susan Marshall taught "Sex Roles" and I couldn't believe what was happening in the world. There was so much I hadn't been exposed to. That class raised more questions than anybody could answer. Issues between the sexes. Studies being done on sex-related issues. Things I wasn't taught. Who were these people who would even study something like this? What had I gotten myself into? This was not the world I was brought up in. There was even a sociology professor who had hyphenated his last name, adding his wife's last name as part of his own. Dr. Sheldon Eckland-Olson. That was interesting to me. But I didn't have time to ponder it. I had tuition to pay. I graduated with a degree in sociology and a minor in English. When people ask me what my major was, I ask them, "which year"?

Where are you going?

To the side of the house.

Again?!

Yes, again.

Well hurry back. And don't even think about doing what I think you're going to do.

Whateva!

Aaahhh! There's nothing like pissing out a bladder full of beer! But even better, I would just love a little Onan activity right about now. But I won't. At least not right now. On the other hand, how wicked would it be to do a little Onan dance right here on the side of the house. Outside the very room where it is possible I was conceived. It would be like my parents were watching me and I wouldn't care.

Sigh . . . .

CHAPTER TWENTY-EIGHT

My attitude about money has always been that you make it to spend it because there's never enough of it to start with. And if by chance you manage to save a little bit, it is not to live on in the far future, but to buy something in the near future. Daddy took each one of us—me, Harrell and Darrell—to the bank and opened up a savings account. When we were very young, he encouraged us to save, and we each learned how to do that. We saved for things: birthdays, anniversaries, Mother's Day, Father's Day, Christmas and school clothes. Each time I saved enough money, I made a purchase and the passbook account dwindled down and I started saving for the next thing.

I also learned that if you create debt, you pay it off. My father didn't buy much on credit, at least not as far as I could tell. But I saw people come into our restaurant and ask for food on credit. A man or a woman would come into the restaurant with their head hanging down to ask Daddy if they could have some food on credit until the first of the month. My father rarely said no. Even worse, some parents sent their kid in to ask for food on credit. Each time, I would stand back and watch to see if I could tell whether the husband was just trying to give his family a little variety in life or if the mother really didn't have enough food in the house to feed the family. Or if they were just trying to run a game on my father. Either way, I cringed each time Daddy said yes. Then the poor pitiful soul would play king and act as though he had killed the fatted calf for the entire family and even a few of their friends.

There were times I felt Momma and Daddy were going through financial hardships because one of the kids away from home needed money for something. I would add up the credit accounts, show Daddy how much was outstanding and encourage him to collect. But he didn't want to hear that from me. It seemed like he didn't care if we needed it or not. Daddy seemed more kind-hearted toward his customers than to us. Some would pay, some would not, but I never liked the food-for-credit deals Daddy made. Especially when I thought it hurt us as a family. That's another reason why I really didn't want to be a financial burden on my father. I didn't want to use him like that. So I made it a point to try and pay for as much college as I could and to only ask him for what I really needed.

Until now, I never realized how much of a "guy" my father is. Remembering my financial struggles through college reminds me of phone calls home. When I was at home, I assumed my father's lack of attention was due to the fact that there were so many of us; he didn't have time for me. Not with all the responsibilities he had. But when I left for college, he still didn't take time for conversation when I called home. My mother would call me and ask me if I needed money. She must have felt how determined I was not to ask for anything more than I needed. Somehow, she would know that I was buying macaroni and cheese, three packages for one dollar, and a half-pound of ground beef and stretching it out for a week. I left my old passbook account as well as a checking account open in Marlin so I could get money from my parents quickly if I needed it. But I was determined to show them I was responsible.

During my second semester in college, the apartment bug bit me. Life in the dormitory was okay, but the cool people had apartments with their own showers. I had also grown weary of cafeteria food. I cooked more and more in my room, which was against dorm rules. I tried to obey the rules, but ended up breaking some rule either way I went. I decided that I wouldn't cook in the room, I would just make tuna fish. But I liked boiled eggs in my tuna fish salad. The only place I could get boiled eggs, without boiling them myself, was the cafeteria. So I would wear long white tube socks to the cafeteria and put three boiled eggs on each leg then take them back to my room. It worked, but eating tuna every day got old too. Then I started bringing more and more food from home on my regular visits. Potato salad, barbequed chicken, pot roast, green beans; whatever we had for Sunday dinner. This was before everybody had a microwave oven. A hot plate and a toaster oven were my cooking contraband. People loved to come to my room to eat. Packing food for me made Daddy happy too. I couldn't understand it. But he genuinely loved loading me down with food. He baked cookies, pies and cakes. He bought food for me that he found on sale, food he thought would be delightful for college dorm students. He even thought of Laura while squirreling away food for me, and sent the same for her. I didn't understand it, but it seemed to make him truly happy to do this for me. So I began to look forward to Sunday before returning to school. But I really didn't appreciate it. I wanted something else from him.

Before the second semester ended, I prepared an analysis for my parents showing my scholarship money, what I expected to earn from the work-study program, the church, and what my tuition, books, room and board were going to cost. I compared those costs with what it would cost to live in an apartment with two roommates (I had already picked them out and found an apartment). It was a good analysis. The costs were, in fact, cheaper than living in the dorm and my money would go a long way toward paying for everything. So they agreed to let me live off campus the fall of my second year. I didn't know how much added pressure I was taking on, trying to be grown. I wanted to make more money to put in the bank before the fall semester, so after my first year at UT, I returned to Marlin to work for the summer. But there were a couple of hitches. I had experienced a taste of freedom living as an adult and making my own decisions. I remembered the fiasco with Vern after she tried to come home and live like an adult. I didn't know if I could live by my parents' rules. I was the good son, so that shouldn't be a problem. The other hitch I encountered was one I hadn't planned on. I didn't want to work for my father. I had never worked anywhere else, except for my father and the church. I was approved for the work-study program at UT, but that wouldn't begin until the next fall.

Both my parents smirked when I announced I was going to try to find a job in Marlin. I had already justified in my mind that since they had hired Windsor, a kid who would later become like a brother to me, there should be no problem in my working somewhere else in town. So I set out to find a job in Marlin. I applied and applied and applied, but no one would hire me. There were jobs, but no one would hire me. I felt cursed. And I couldn't help but feel Daddy enjoyed seeing me unable to find a job. His attitude made me so mad. Again, I had given up on trying to talk to him and ask for his direction and advice and he didn't offer any. My mother finally came out and said it didn't make sense for me to work for somebody else when my father had a job for me. But the image in my head wouldn't let me do that. In my mind, I could see him sitting behind the junky desk in his office at the restaurant, leaning back in his used, third-hand chair with his fingers clasped together over his protruding stomach, that smug look on his face. I couldn't deal with that. But the weeks were ticking away on my summer and so was my need to earn money and not be like my siblings.

Then my answer came. Harrell left college after his first year and against my parents' wishes moved in with a girl who lived in Bryan, Texas. He worked for a computer manufacturing company in College Station (home of the Texas A&M Aggies, the sworn arch rivals of the UT Longhorns) and they needed help for the summer. I couldn't believe he even called me. This was my brother who had tortured me as a child. Our relationship had grown close, but from my perspective, it was twisted so I wasn't sure how it would play out. Over time, me, Harrell and Darrell continued our warped relationship and had great times as adults. This would be one of them. Harrell described the job and it sounded great. The company wanted Harrell to drive a thirty-foot truck filled with computers to Chicago for a trade show but they couldn't spare one of the regular guys to go with him, so he called me. It paid more money than I had ever made in my life. We would be on the clock for almost twenty-four hours a day for over a week. Overtime! Once the Chicago trip was over, the company wanted me to stay for the rest of the summer to go on short trips in Texas delivering computers. I don't remember telling my parents or how they reacted. I just remember getting the job and being one of the guys in the warehouse, getting paid and banking the money.

The summer was fun and profitable. But then, the car bug bit me. I had money in my pocket and money on the way. Both added up to more than I expected my bills to be for the next year. So why not? I talked about it with Harrell endlessly. Our discussions about buying a car, with or without my parents' consent, was the first time I discovered Harrell's concern about Momma and Daddy's opinion. He refused to help me find a car until Momma and Daddy said it was okay for me to have one. Period. There it was again, my parents' control over my life. I didn't want it, and Harrell was *giving* it to them. It was a form of torture all over again. I tried to look for a car on my own, but I didn't know how to judge whether a used car was any good or not. Harrell had taken auto mechanics in high school and had restored the car he was still driving. I looked and looked until I found a white Chevrolet Chevette with a blue top. It was definitely used. I could pay cash for it, but then I had to pay the monthly insurance. I figured I could play for another church for the two Sundays a month I wasn't in Marlin. Two churches had already approached me. I even got an offer to play in a bar on 6th Street in Austin. Something, I don't know what, but something deep down inside told me the bar scene wasn't a place I needed to be. I considered it for a minute, maybe a week, then turned it down. But another church I could handle. I crunched the numbers. It would be hard, real hard, especially with all of the other commitments I had. But I wanted a car and I wanted to do it without getting my parents involved. And now, I had something to prove to Harrell too. My God!

I was at a car lot in Bryan, Texas, ready to do the deal, when I came to my senses. I couldn't do it. I couldn't go that far yet. My parents, Harrell . . . my life seemed like it was under a microscope. Buying a car would definitely increase my chances of failure. Maybe that's what the others had done. Maybe they had made decisions like the one I was about to make and Daddy ended up paying for them. I decided not to buy the car. I returned to college, to another Hell Week in Longhorn Band, another job and more struggles in school. But I couldn't shake the car bug.

I needed a car. I wanted a car. But I couldn't or didn't want to do it on my own. I was only nineteen years old and my life was dangling somewhere between being a walking-dead adult with independence and a scared, uninformed child with leg irons attached to his parents. I couldn't free myself of either. My mind couldn't formulate a plan that would change my future. I felt like I was headed down the same road as the others. I remember being at home with my parents one weekend and out came the words. I had thought about it and tried hard not to ask them. But the words just came out by themselves. I asked them about me getting a car. When I asked, I felt like I didn't even know my own name. Was I John or Randy? Linda or Vern or Stine? I felt so out of control of my own destiny. How was I going to be different if I followed the same path they did? But the words were already out there. My father had that smirk again and it made me really mad. Each visit home after the question still produced a bounty of food for me, but I needed more than just food. Especially from my father. But the look on his face told me he didn't see Winston. He saw another one of his children. He wasn't in favor of me having a car, but never really told me no. I knew what he was thinking. My mother, on the other hand, seemed to be the one working behind the scenes to make it happen, and it did. They gave me the 1977 canary yellow Ford LTD with the brown top. The same car that had caught fire. The same car my father seemed so much more concerned about than me. I took it with great pleasure.

The first test of responsibility with my new car came during the summer after my second year in college. As usual, I was struggling financially, but was determined to stay in Austin for summer school to retake a few courses I had bombed during the first two years. My boss at the work-study job converted me to a regular position and allowed me to work extra hours over the summer. I was a good and dependable employee. My father had beaten that into me. I moved from the apartment into a private dorm that was cheap to reduce my living expenses. Jose, one of my room-mates from the apartment, needed a place to stay for the summer. He had graduated from Marlin High at the same time and was on the same scholarship as me. I let him move into the private dorm illegally. He was supposed to pay me for living there, but he never did. He bought an expensive Pioneer stereo instead.

The car helped, as I continued to go to Marlin on the weekends to work at my parents' restaurant. I also picked up more Sundays playing for the church. I knew that cars needed regular maintenance and I didn't know how to do it myself, so I made sure I saved enough money to get an oil change and a tune-up. I took the car to Tune-Up Masters. I felt grown as I drove the car onto the service lot but scared because I didn't know what a tune-up really entailed. I just knew a car needed one from time to time. One of the guys behind the counter filled out the service ticket and took the keys. I sat in the lounge area with the other grown folk and waited for my car to get its first tune-up under new ownership.

I happened to glance up from the magazine I was pretending to read and saw when they drove my car into the bay to do the work. After a while, one of the guys came into the lounge and asked for me. I met him at the desk and listened as he explained that the car hadn't had a tune-up in a long time and the spark plugs hadn't been changed. He told me that one of the spark plugs was stuck in the head. I thought to myself they ought to just get it out. Why did he have to come and tell me that? He went on to explain that they were going to have to try hard to get it out but . . . . But what? Just do it! I thought to myself. I continued to listen. But there was a chance that the grooves on the spark plug could get stripped. That would be a problem. If that happened, then it would take a machine shop to re-groove and repair the head. I asked him what my options were. He told me they could leave the car alone and not change the plugs or they could try to get the one plug out. I asked him about the chances of them stripping the plug. He said there was a one-in-a-million chance it could happen. It took me only a split second to see my future pass before my eyes. If they didn't fix it, I would have to go home and tell my father that not only could I not tune the car up myself, I couldn't even pay someone to do it. Once again, I was determined to show my father that my name was Winston.

My desire to go home and report to my father that I had the car tuned up and it was purring like a kitten was the foundation for the decision I made. I told the guy to go ahead and try. One-in-a-million. I could live with that. The guy had me sign a waiver stating he had explained the risk and that they were not responsible if what they thought could happen did happen. The waiver scared me. But I was already committed to my decision. Besides, the other grown-ups in the lounge had heard our conversation. It bothered me to think that they would think I was too scared and immature to take that small of a risk. So, I signed the waiver and watched him as he hurried to continue the work. Briefly, I became angry with my father for giving me a car he had not taken care of himself. Why would he do that? Why would he not get the car tuned up on a regular basis? I tried to remember what I was supposed to know about cars from my days in line behind the others. All I could remember was that if I didn't know how to repair a car myself, I had better make enough money to pay someone to do it. So that's what I was doing.

I returned to my seat and waited. I saw three guys pushing the LTD out into the sunlight. My heart sank. I felt as though I stepped outside my body and stood beside myself to see what was about to happen. The two of me watched and waited for the guy to come into the lounge and tell us what had happened. But we already knew. Then I hovered above my body while my brain remained in my empty shell to receive the news. Yes I was the one-in-a-million catastrophe. I was glad I was absent from my body because being one-in-a-million under these circumstances was bad. The disbelief. The failure. Why was this happening? Was I going to be forced to bring my father into this? What had he done to deserve children who couldn't do things right? I didn't want to be in my body. If that body was so determined to go down the same path as the others, I didn't want to be in there. We both listened as the guy told us the spark plug did in fact get stripped in the head, which rendered the car inoperable. The waiver released Tune-Up Masters of any liability. They could refer me to a machine shop and call a tow truck for me. Myself and I listened and we both heard money, money, money. Money we didn't have. The guy paused and looked at my body for a response but there was none. My body and my brain needed me back in order take action. Besides, I couldn't hover forever, even though that's what I wanted to do. So I slipped back into my body. The tightness in my chest, the pressure behind my eyes, the blurred vision, all scared me. But I didn't have time to think about all of that. I had a car to get fixed.

I needed help. I needed someone to help me through this problem so I could learn how to handle it next time. But as usual, there was no one. As usual, I just did the best I could. The guy called the machine shop and explained what had happened. I spoke with them and confirmed that I wanted them to fix it. It was going to cost a fortune. I didn't explain to them that I didn't have any money. The machine shop sent a tow truck and added it to my bill. I stood at the busy intersection of Lamar and Koenig Lane and watched as the tow truck took the 1977 canary yellow Ford LTD with a brown top away. My dorm room was in the same direction as my car was going and I knew I needed a taxi. But standing there on the corner, alone, among all the people and traffic, I wondered if my life would change if I just turned and walked in the other direction. But what would I be leaving? My parents? My brothers and sisters? My life? And where would I be going? Life anew? I called the taxi and followed my car.

Later I applied for a credit card but didn't get it before I had to have the car in order to go to Marlin, so I used all my available cash. When I finally got the credit card, I lived on it. I even had to use credit to eat. I was one of those people who had to get food on credit just like the ones at my father's restaurant that I didn't want to be like. That was the beginning of credit card debt that lasted for more than twelve years. I never told my parents about the car.

Why?

Because I was out of line. I wasn't marching in step. I couldn't tell my parents that. So I just continued living without them knowing that I was just stumbling through life.

The LTD continued to transport me to and from Marlin on the weekends and helped me make money to pay for my education and living expenses. It was on one of those weekends that hope poked a tiny hole into my life. There was light on the other side of the darkness. The tiny opening only allowed a threadlike stream of light into my world but it was light just the same. I grabbed hold of that thread and pulled, hoping my weight wouldn't break it.

My father hired a fourteen-year-old kid named Windsor to work at the Snack Center. I had known Windsor for a long time before that, but only by name and family. His family went to our church and their small wood-frame house was outside the city limits near our church. Actually, you could see their house from the steps of the pastor's study. It seemed to sit in the middle of a field, all by itself. There were several children in his family. All of them were being raised by their mother; their father wasn't around. One of Windsor's sisters could stand up in church on command

and recite all of the books of the Bible. And in order too! Like me, Windsor was the youngest of the bunch. He was noticeably different than the rest of them in a lot of ways. And his thumbs were made funny. But he always seemed to be happily going about his business. Windsor had been working for my father for several months. He worked at night during the week and on the weekends. I thought he was learning his way around the kitchen pretty well. Funny thumbs and all.

One weekend, I didn't go home on Friday night. On Saturday, I arrived in Marlin just in time for choir rehearsal. The men in my church had a crazy notion to create a men's group to sing on Mother's Day. I doubted that the men came up with that idea of their own accord. More than likely a few of the women whispered it in their men's ears during the night. The women wanted to wear their best dresses and hats and be entertained on their special day instead of donning old robes and singing in the choir. The men had rehearsed for weeks and we actually had a good time. Like I said, my father was not a singer, he was a hummer. It was strange to experience another side of him. I had no idea my father was such a cut-up. I had a hard time keeping the men under control because my father kept them laughing. Sometimes I wanted to stop rehearsal just to see what my father would do or say next; I wanted to know that side of him. I thought we might be able to connect. But I didn't have time to observe. We had songs to learn.

Windsor couldn't carry a tune in a backpack. But he didn't seem to mind. He was always at rehearsal, singing off-key, loud and strong. But on this day, he wasn't there. He finally came in near the end of the rehearsal and sat quietly in the back corner at the top of the choir stand away from the other men. I knew something was wrong, but I didn't know it had to do with my father. After rehearsal, I heard him ask my father if he should come to work that night. My father said no, like he was telling one of his own kids to get on 'cross the tracks. Windsor had been fired. I didn't want to get involved. I felt sorry for Windsor because he probably needed the money and I could tell that he really liked my father and liked being around him. But I recognized the look in my father's eyes as he talked to Windsor. I also recognized the look in Windsor's eyes. I had seen it in my own. I had nothing to offer him. He was on his own. I left the church and went home. Windsor came looking for me and asked me what should he do. I couldn't help Windsor because I'd never really learned to help myself. But he was persistent.

That's when I did the adult thing and told him things I really didn't believe myself, but it was better than the truth. I told him to go back to work. That's what my mother would tell us when my father fired us and sent us across the track every other week. I told him that Daddy liked him but just didn't know how to show it. I didn't believe it myself, but it all sounded so good. I was proud of myself, but I shouldn't have been. Windsor came back to the restaurant that night but didn't work. He just hung around. I was so proud of him for doing that. I couldn't have done that. I had been humiliated enough. The atmosphere was tense, but my father agreed to give him another chance. That night, when we closed the restaurant around two o'clock in the morning, I took Windsor home down past the city limits sign, near the church. We sat in the car and talked for hours.

He told me things about his life that I didn't know. He told me about how hard it really was. We laughed a lot. He was a funny kid. He told me how he really didn't have anyone else to talk to. He said I was like a brother to him. But then he told me he had been on the verge of killing himself. The weight of hearing that made me forget about my own problems for a minute. What was I supposed to do with that information? Tell him that he would probably be better off if he did? That's what I really felt, but I couldn't say that. This time *I* was the older brother. Here was my chance to be for somebody what others had not been for me. I told him that killing himself wasn't the answer. I told Windsor he could always depend on me. And I really meant it. We continued to talk and I found out he really looked up to me. It made me feel so good to know that I mattered in someone's life. That night, Windsor was the hope that poked a little tiny hole into my life and that hope was light in my world of darkness. There is a song we used to sing in church:

> *If I can help somebody*
> *As I travel along*
> *Then my living shall not be in vain*

Maybe if I repeated the message of hope enough, I would start to believe it myself. I wanted to make other people's lives better than mine had been. Maybe if I helped somebody, somebody would help me.

Windsor became like a little brother to me and the rest of my siblings. He also became a son to my parents.

CHAPTER TWENTY-NINE

I met Mike while working at the General Store in the Texas Union on campus. We were both in the work-study program. Mike and I were the same age, about the same height, but he was thinner than I was. He had a long face and a distinctive nose; not a bad nose, just distinctive. He walked with an old man's shuffle. It was kind of funny, at least to me. We had the same work schedule the entire semester. We became friends and remained so long after we both left that job. Mike was from Miami Beach, Florida, and loved to windsurf. He opened a windsurfing business in Austin. I never went windsurfing with him nor did I ever see him surf. I just heard a lot about it. He also owned a motorcycle and we used to ride up and down 6th Street being cool. Without helmets. Wow! Youth. Mike was a lot smarter than me, but that didn't bother me. A lot of people were. He studied hard and it paid off for him. But he wasn't very social. I, on the other hand, seemed to be the life of the party, but it was all a façade. My friendship with my new little brother Windsor helped me explore the possibility that maybe I had a gift for helping people. After Windsor, people came my way with problems that I helped them with. Mike was one of those people.

College exposed me to a new side of guys and how we react to women, especially breaking up with them. I was cold and callous when it came to women, because I just didn't care. I didn't feel. But some guys would lose their minds. That's kind of what happened to Mike. He had a girlfriend at another college. When they broke up it seemed to add to all of life's other pressures and he crumbled. I can't remember whether he told me he was thinking about ending it all or whether I felt it from him. I just knew he was in trouble.

183

Finals were coming up and we both needed to study, but I promised him we would go out and have a good time after we finished studying. He had his favorite spot in the Perry Castaneda Library and I had mine, even though I preferred the smaller Undergraduate Library. We had been studying separately for hours when I packed up my books and notes and went to meet him downstairs at the designated meeting place. I walked down the stairs instead of taking the elevator. In the stairwell, I had a strange feeling of death. I thought it was about me. I kept walking. I reached the second level and decided to look down over the atrium to see if Mike was waiting for me, but he wasn't there. Then, the feeling nearly brought me to my knees. I hated that feeling. I had felt it before, but I wouldn't let myself get worried. I knew where his study place was but I didn't want to go there to look for him. My heart, slow down, my heart, slow down. No need to get worried. Was this the gift again? I didn't know. My mind, be still, my mind, be still. Did I remember someone telling me that there was an open window near Mike's study spot? Did the PCL have windows that opened? Was my mind playing tricks on me or did I actually remember someone saying that? Was this the gift again? I didn't want to be Mike's friend right then. I didn't want to know.

I caught an elevator and went up to Mike's study spot and he wasn't there. I looked out a window near where he sat but couldn't see over the ledge. I ran down the stairs with death taking each step with me. I hated that feeling. Dear God! What was I going to do? I reached the ground floor and went toward our designated meeting place. I was so mad at myself. Mike was waiting for me. I didn't dare tell him what had gone through my mind. He had a way of bringing up the past and making fun of me just to piss me off and this would go right to the top of his list. We got in my car and went to a convenience store to buy a six-pack of beer. We finished three beers each before we got to the Filling Station. At the Filling Station, we drank the house limit of Tune-Ups. Patrons are only allowed two Tune-Ups; the drinks are just that potent. We left the Filling Station and went to Mike's apartment near the Colorado River off Riverside Drive. There we did multiple tequila shots. Drinking really helps guys talk about what's happening inside our heads.

Mike and I laughed and talked in our drunken state. But then it got ugly. Mike was really hurting over the breakup. He started crying because he couldn't figure out why she didn't want to be with him. He wanted to kill himself. I tried to talk him through it. But he wasn't listening. He wanted to leave his apartment and go walking by the river. I thought it was a good idea until he crossed Lakeshore Drive and started walking toward the water. Instinctively, I knew what he was going to try to do. I ran to catch up with him. I grabbed him and tried to steer him back to his apartment but he was determined. We struggled but kept getting closer and closer to the water. Then I got tough with him. He was thinner than me but his determination made him strong. We reached the water. I tried to stop him. We had a knock-down drag-out fight. He wanted to die. And I couldn't let that happen.

We were shin high in the water, fighting, when he finally collapsed. I picked him up and laid him on the bank of the river. He continued to sob uncontrollably. I sat next to him and tried to be for him what others had not been for me, comforting him and reassuring him that everything was going to be all right. I got him back to his apartment and stayed with him until he went to sleep. I left him and drove back across town to my apartment. Near my apartment at a red light, I vomited on myself behind the wheel of my parents' 1977 canary yellow Ford LTD with the brown top.

If I can help somebody
As I travel along
Then my living shall not be in vain

Mike and I remained friends after graduation. A few years after graduation he had another bout with suicidal thoughts. He was traveling for his job from city to city over a two-day period. At each city, he would call me and tell me he wanted to kill himself. He was very depressed. I was too far away to be with him. I knew I couldn't stop him. During our last conversation, I told him that suicide might be the best thing for him to do. I hung up knowing that I had done all that I could do. Knowing I would be envious of him if he succeeded. He didn't do it. Several years later, I was the best man in his wedding.

Hey Windsor, would you? Tell her how you know me?

Well, I guess the first time we met was back in 1984, I believe he was about to graduate college. He had come down to choir rehearsal at the Upper Zion Missionary Baptist Church, in Marlin, Texas. I was trying to sing in the youth choir. Thanks be to God He called me to the ministry . . . . Ha! Ha! Ha!

It was after choir rehearsal that we really began our relationship. Because of my childishness, I was playing around and I hit him in his chest, and immediately he grabbed me and said, "Little ol' boy, what you hit me for?" with that little laugh he always does. And that's where the sperm met the egg in our friendship.

After months had passed and he would drive from Austin to play for church, I began to look forward to seeing him and talking to him on the weekends. I admired him for his dedication and goals. I really had a great amount of respect for him, not only because he took time out to talk to me, but I wanted to be just like him: a business-minded man with a twist of wildness. I had a friend named Russell, and Russell use to hate when Winston came to town, because if Winston was not around, Russell and I would hang out or talk on the phone like a couple of girls. But when Winston came to town, I didn't talk to Russell. Winston and I would sit in the restaurant or in the front of my house and talk all night. Words could never tell how much I appreciate all the information he gave and questions he answered. I hate that we don't communicate more often. It hurts me to my heart, because I feel like we are not even brothers anymore.

I can remember those days as if it was last year . . . I grew close to him because I felt like he was my older brother. I didn't have anyone at home with me during those years, and I didn't want to be like the other kids. Winston helped me understand a lot of things. He gave me a new and different insight on life, both spiritual and carnal.

Throughout high school, I could appreciate all the work and discipline I had to endure at school and at the Williams Snack Center, because he gave me an understanding of the root of growing up. Struggle makes the tree stronger. I believe that if he had not been there for me the tree probably would have toppled over a long time ago.

Even though he was a college student, he still took time out of his schedule to check on me and made sure that I was doing o.k. and that Dad wasn't being too hard on me like he is known to do, to all of us . . . but that was also part of making the tree stronger.

Then there was my vacation to Austin during the summer before I joined the military. Oh, how much fun! I'll never forget running in and out of the street in front of the Capitol trying to take pictures.

That was the best summer trip I ever had during my high school years. Thanks to him . . .

After I joined the military, Winston's advice and letters during basic training helped so much. I guess you can come to the conclusion that "HE IS A VERY GOOD BROTHER TO ME."

The thing I did not like is that he wanted me to be all that he wanted to be. I couldn't be Winston: I don't think like Winston, I don't act like Winston, I just loved Winston. I loved him then and I love him now. Even though he never calls nor writes . . . LOL! But other than that, I can find no fault in him, other than he needs to get married . . . .

Rev. Windsor L. Archie
Texarkana, Texas

Introducing
Winston Gordon Williams
W. G. W.
W. W.
Work. Women.
The G. was the Me
I Could Bury

CHAPTER THIRTY

A woman once told me she thought I got more excited about work than about having sex with her. She said it while she was yelling at me and poking her finger in my chest. Go figure. Work. Women. That's it. It's time. I still have beer left but I'm only drinking it when I get thirsty. Now I want something else, and it's not a cigarette. I'll have a smoke afterwards.

I return from the side of the house the same way I went, stumbling, but feeling a little better.

You did it anyway.

Yup!

Even after I told you not to.

Yup!

Satisfied?

Yup!

I think you should work on not planting those types of seeds.

I don't understand why God slew Onan for spilling his seed or why people in the church would interpret that to mean that masturbation is evil and sinful. Is that really what Onan did?

Are you asking me?

Who else is here?

Please don't ask me questions like that.

Why not?

We'll get to that later. Right now, let me ask the questions and you give the answers.

You haven't changed.

And probably never will. You were talking about Onan and masturbation. Continue . . .

Anyway . . . I like a little Onan activity. And who came up with the stuff about it making you blind? I'm thirty-six years old and it is the best pleasure I know how to give myself. I can do it when I want, how long I want, how slow I want, how fast I want. And when I'm done, I am satisfied.

Go back and read your Bible. Onan's story is not even about masturbation.

Oh . . . was that an answer?

Now that you've satisfied yourself, let's go on.

I've searched for satisfaction all my life. When I graduated from college I found it in work. Work was what I knew. That's how I was raised. That's what we did. As a young kid, when I visited my older brothers and sisters, I admired them when they went off to work each day and couldn't wait for the day when I could have my own real full-time job. Sadly enough though, I didn't make the connection between what you learned in college and the job you would later get. I just figured something would happen. No one taught me there was a connection. I was also influenced by a couple of movies that depicted what I wanted to have when I got my real job. It wasn't the job that caught my attention, it was the lifestyle. Remember Richard Gere in *American Gigolo*? I wanted to be able to go to my closet and pick out shirts, ties, slacks and jackets. Later, it was Eddie Murphy in *Boomerang*. The clean apartment, the grand piano with the lilies on it, women and friends. I had to live like them. But I didn't know how to make the money. I just figured it would come.

The last year or so of college I worked as a runner for a law firm: Argless, Badlands & Beamers. I remember walking down the hall with Debbie Beamers when she told me she had heard I was graduating from UT. She asked me what my plans were. I told her I didn't have any and asked if I could stay with the firm. She said sure. Wow . . . I had a job when I graduated! They were very good to me and I worked hard for them. Evenings, weekends, holidays. Whatever they needed, I was up for it. I wanted to be the best runner I could be. After I graduated, they promoted me to a paralegal trainee position. It wasn't a big raise, but I got a desk and vacation days. I worked hard but couldn't see how the legal pieces I worked on fit into the bigger puzzle. It was different from being a runner. As a runner, I knew what part I played. But I didn't need to know any more; I was still part of the team and being a needed part of something was very important to me.

The September after I graduated from college, I took my first adult vacation. Darrell and I went to Oakland, California, to see Vern. A week off with pay. This was unreal! And to top it off, when I got back to work, the firm offered me another promotion. The firm was growing and needed to implement a new billing system. They wanted me to become the billing coordinator. Wow! What a title! But it was using a computer to do accounting. I sat in Angie Preston's office and listened to the offer and I couldn't believe it. Here was my chance to have responsibility and a title, but it would be doing two of the things I damn near flunked in college. Life is so unfair. What was I going to do? I was sure to fail. Who could I call on? Where could I run to get away from this conversation? Computers and accounting. My God, why?

Right there in Angie Preston's office I created another me. A me who was confident, assured and determined. And it was all fake. I had no idea how I was going to succeed at this new job. I knew I would fail. But the new me would have a damn good time until failure came. Looking back, it's amazing how the new me just took over. How quickly I came to the decision to go for it. And how quickly I developed a backup plan for when I failed. But there was a closet full of shirts, ties, jackets and a grand piano in my sights.

The firm sent me to Nashville for training. I received software manuals and read them cover to cover. I paid close attention in class. I liked this type of learning. It was like the accounting class in high school, hands on, for a purpose; not abstract learning. I returned and faced one last challenge before I started to live my new life. The firm's controller, who was responsible for training me, seemed to hate me. I had to share her office with her until the firm moved into its new and larger space where I would have my own office on a separate floor than hers. She seemed so mean and nasty. I hadn't done anything to make her treat me badly. I was trying hard to learn something and I needed her to help me. I was doing well enough on my own, but there were things I needed her to explain. Things not found in books that only she knew. The way she treated me made me rumble inside, and that scared me. I was at work. I couldn't start out like this. I couldn't become my father in the workplace. This was not the way I was going to fail. Why couldn't she see my potential and help me? I didn't want to be left alone to do this. I wanted to be a part of the team. I wanted to be a part of something that wanted me. I thought I would fail because I failed computers and accounting in college, not because another adult wouldn't give me the information I needed to succeed.

The day I was about to explode I decided to try one last thing. On our floor, in the back corner of the offices, there was a closet where they stored the sodas. As a runner, I was in and out of there everyday re-stocking the refrigerator. But I didn't have to go in that closet much since I graduated. That day I went into the closet and talked to God. I asked Him to help me with this woman because I was about to hurt her. It wasn't a long talk. As a matter of fact, it was a very short one. But my prayer was answered instantly. I walked back into her office, sat at my computer and the flood-gates of information opened up and flowed until the day she left the firm. She taught me so much about law firm accounting. It was unbelievable. Why had God chosen to answer that prayer? I had prayed so many other prayers that seemed to go unanswered.

God! I remember that day like it was yesterday. God? What do you think of me when I talk to you when I'm drunk? What do you think about me when I jack off and enjoy it? What do you think of me when I smoke, knowing it damages my body? Why do you answer prayers and we still get led into destruction? Hey. Coach. What do you think of me?

Does it matter what I think of you?

Honestly?

Honestly.

It's hard to be honest about this.

But that's why we're here.

I know, it's just hard.

But no one is here but us. Why can't you be honest when no one is even listening?

Strange you should ask that question. I have come to understand something about myself.

And what is that?

If I acknowledge it, that makes "it" all the more real. Writing "it" down is even worse. In my mind, I can control what you think of me. It's like I think you have no independent thought, no life experience that lets you know when you're being told a lie. It's like I think you don't have your own connection to God and that He won't show you what I don't want you to see. That's the way my mind works. And to be honest, yes, it matters what you think of me. Because I think nothing of myself.

And who do you think I . . .

Wait . . . . Damn . . . don't respond to what I just said. It's a little too much to deal with right now. I need to save my energy for the big finale. But the visit to the side of the house must have given me my third wind because I feel good. Even the beer tastes fresh and new.

We'll come back to that. Tell me more about your relationships.

God's answer to my prayer ignited a twelve-year-long fuse inside of me. I became a workaholic. The explosive itself had been planted during my childhood. Nothing came before work. Not family, not friends, not fun, not me, not church, not women, not sex. Nothing. Work gave me something to do. Even my hobbies were work related; volunteer "work." Windsor was the hope that had poked a tiny hole in my life. I wanted to help people. It made me feel needed. Helping people was "work." Work made me feel wanted. I spent many hours there. It also allowed me to hide from emotional bonds. I worked with a lot of people because I coordinated many variables that came together to produce the end result. But I didn't have to work with anybody in close proximity. I isolated myself with self-made rules. For instance, I wouldn't date anyone I worked with. I wouldn't even date anyone who worked in the same building. This was a good rule because my relationships always went badly. Always.

Then tell me about them, the bad relationships.

Let's see. Who shall I tell you about? Which bad relationship shall I rant and rave about? Let's start in college. There was Donna. Donna and I never really dated but she taught me a lesson I took with me forever. Donna was older than me. I was only nineteen years old and she was close to graduating. She was very down-to-earth and very outspoken. We were in her apartment one evening, lying in bed. Of course I thought we were headed toward the natural thing when she started talking to me about her feelings. Talk. Aaarrrrggghhh!!!!!!!!! Talk. Com-mu-ni-ca-tion. It's a good thing when the other person really wants to hear and accept what you have to say. Don't ask me a question you really don't want to know the answer to. The evening with Donna is a blur, but the lesson is as clear today as it was then.

Donna was telling me that if I married her, I would never have to work again. She would take care of me. She must have thought that would make me happy. When I got up and out of the bed, she seemed confused. She asked me what was wrong and I said, "You intimidate the HELL out of me!" She got really upset and asked me why men say that about her. I couldn't speak for any other man, but as for me, I hadn't dealt with a woman who was that strong and had the potential to make more money than me. What was sex with her going to be like? Oh no! I wasn't ready. I left Donna's apartment that night pondering the possibility that a woman could make more money than me. My view of a home, husband and wife, changed. It didn't take long to get used to the idea that I could be a househusband. My wife, whoever she was, could have the babies and I would raise them. That's what Donna taught me.

Then there was Marie. I don't know if we ever called each other boy-friend and girlfriend, but we spent a lot of time together. She was a smart girl who, even though we were the same age, had graduated from high school at sixteen. So by the time I got to UT, she had already been there two years. Marie was my first experience with a woman who was "saving" herself for marriage. She was really into God. So was I, but I didn't get her approach. Marie was, and still is, a talker. I didn't have to say much when I was with her, which was good. I avoided meaningful conversations; I just needed companionship. She never asked me any questions about what I did when I wasn't with her. I think that's what made our relationship last so long. But it still surprised me when we had "the conversation." She had graduated from UT and moved back home to Fort Worth with her par-ents while she got established in her job as a teacher. We continued to talk and visit each other. She told me she had prayed to God for me and He had answered her prayer. We were supposed to get married. Huh? This conversation confused me. How could God tell her one thing and not tell me? I prayed too but I didn't get the same confirmation she did. What length would people go to in order to get what they wanted? Marie was so serious. She couldn't listen to reason. Seems like I've learned a lot from women and none of it has been about love.

Marie taught me that women would look at me and see right through me to the future they wanted. I knew she didn't know me. She is still a good friend today, but was always so busy talking. She never learned who I was. She was too holy to see life's realities the way I saw them. Her relationship with God was different than mine. We made it through the difficult time, acknowledging we were not going to get married. She is one of the few women I dated who is still a friend. She got engaged, got married. I went to the wedding and was introduced by Marie's sister as the guy Marie should have married. I didn't want to make any trouble for Marie and her new husband. I met him and liked him, but I could see down the road, so I kept my mouth shut. Two children later, they got divorced. I'm glad it wasn't me.

Then came Rachel, a native Austinite. Some Austin women had problems with guys who attended UT. The stereotype was that we thought we were better than Austin girls. That wasn't true for me. By the time I met Rachel, my wardrobe had slid down a slippery fashion slope to basic brown and blue: work clothes. Gone were the days of flying out to California and spending my money on the new styles. Gone were the days of taking scholarship money and going to the mall, trying to fit in with the rich kids on campus. Rachel worked at Foley's and got a great discount. She bought a red cotton shirt for me and told me to send it to the cleaners and get it starched. I didn't want to wear that shirt, but I didn't want to hurt her feelings either. So I did as I was told. I couldn't believe the attention I got from simply wearing a red shirt. Rachel was tall and slender with a nice body. And she wasn't saving herself for marriage. We had a lot of fun. But I was in college and had three jobs. That was a problem for Rachel. I couldn't understand why she didn't support me in what I was trying to accomplish. She said all I cared about was my career. My career? I was just trying to survive. Why would a woman want a man not to be successful? It ended.

Then came Paula. Paula was a graduate business student at UT. I had already graduated and gotten my promotion at the law firm. I was already taking work home, working late and on weekends. I was a workaholic and I didn't know how I was going to fit a woman into my life. But, there is something instinctual about the pursuit of a woman as beautiful as Paula. She had everything. A warm smile, a great voice, brains, nice down-to-earth parents. I thought she really liked me. Paula and I hadn't really started to date yet but we were talking. Wilbert, another friend from my high school class, had moved to Austin and he had introduced me to Paula. He invited me to a party where I planned to see Paula and make a stronger move toward her. I was getting ready for the party when my phone rang. It was my brother Darrell.

He had news about Stine. I don't remember how long we had known about Stine's breast cancer. At least a couple of years. I had received the news in the midst of my own funk and don't know if I had ever processed it. I think I filed it back there in my brain with so many other things. I had grown weary of being mad at God for not letting it be me who got cancer. Stine was married with four children. She needed to live. I was already dead. God. . . . Go figure.

But on this night, a night that held so much promise for me, Darrell told me Stine wasn't expected to live through the night. A yell exploded from somewhere deep inside me. Pain, deep unendurable pain clutched my heart, my bones, my belly. Oh, the pain. It is still indescribable but fresh in my body, even now. It has been years since that day and it is still so fresh. Will it ever go away? My mother was in Houston with Stine and her family. My father was in Marlin, alone. My job was get to Marlin as quickly as I could and pick up my father and take him to Houston to see his daughter before her final hour. I put my car's flashers on and floated up I-H 35 toward Waco. It was the same route I had taken so many times but this was so different. The pain. The tears spilled, but somehow I made it home.

I walked into the house and found Daddy standing by himself in the kitchen. It was the first time my father hugged me so tightly. He . . . we . . . cried. I held him and felt his body shake. For that moment I was his strength. I had longed to connect with my father on a deeper level and hated how it seemed to be finally becoming a reality only through Stine's dying. But it was as though he felt me taking comfort in the hope of a greater and deeper relationship. He took a deep breath and withdrew. I don't remember the ride to Houston. But do I remember walking onto the hospital floor where my sister's body was shutting down organ by organ. The doctors were allowing family members to go into the room and say our good-byes.

The three desperados, me, Harrell and Darrell, went in together. She was leaving us and was going out in her natural beauty. She opened her eyes and looked up and around at the three of us and told us we were as tall as trees. I remember those words. I thought if I were a tree, even a tall one, I was a dead one. And with her gone, so was my support. Soon I would fall in the middle of the lonely forest and no one would be there to hear. Most of us left the hospital so her husband and children could say good-bye.

Back at Stine's house, I helped my mother as she busied herself in the kitchen preparing food for the people who would soon fill the house. That day, I learned how to prepare my mother's okra gumbo. Harrell came to me in the kitchen and asked where certain parts were located in the human body. I knew he was trying to pray to God for the body parts that were shutting down. I thought about praying for that too but I don't think I did. Anyway, God said no to Harrell's prayers. Stine died.

The pain. The pain. The pain. Work. I had to keep going, no time to grieve. I made my work so important to me. Pursuing a woman wasn't as important as work. But I continued to engage in the pursuit half-heartedly. Paula and I started seeing each other. I wanted her so badly, maybe to replace my loss. Maybe for the wrong reasons, but I wanted her. But in the end, she didn't want me. She reached a point, not through arguments or disagreements or anything negative that I could see, where she didn't even want to see me. I needed her to explain what was wrong. I needed her to explain why. She wouldn't tell me. She had the information I needed to understand what was happening between us, but she wouldn't talk to me. One night I sat outside of her apartment door. I knew she was there. I knocked and knocked, then wrote her a letter and waited until the sun came up for her to just open the door and talk to me. But she didn't. Soon after that, she left Austin for North Carolina to take a position with IBM. For weeks, I contemplated quitting my job and moving to North Carolina with nothing. No job, no place to live, nothing. I wanted to pursue whatever she sparked within me. But I talked myself out of it and stored away another incident of a person withholding pertinent information no matter how much I desired and begged for it.

CHAPTER THIRTY-ONE

I focused even more on work, if that was possible. I felt I was an integral part of something, the team, the family. The company was still relatively small and there were people there who had been there from the beginning. Ollie was one of them. Ollie was short, bubbly and fun. I'd met her at UT, and she was the person who told me about the runner position at Argless, Badlands & Beamers. One Sunday at the mall I saw Ollie with another friend of mine. We all chatted for a moment and as I was walking away, I off-handedly mentioned I was looking for a job. Ollie said the firm she worked for was looking for a runner. I wrote down the information and was there at the office with my resume on Monday morning. I interviewed and got the job! That job would lead to a promotion and lay the foundation for everything I have today. Ollie also introduced me to Rachel.

Having been with the firm almost since it opened, Ollie had developed personal relationships with all of the attorneys and their families and everybody else in the office. She even babysat for them. Everyone loved her because she was a genuine person. We became instant friends. She was from a large family; her father was a minister. I met several members of her family and liked each one. Her boyfriend Victor was a strong, personable construction worker with a bright smile. I became friends with him and his family. Ollie possessed many of the things that were missing in my life. She seemed to balance work, family, love and life so well. I don't think she ever knew how much I appreciated how she included me in her world. I admired Ollie's work ethic. She pulled more than her share of responsibility in the office and she did it with a unique, motherly type of caring. She was a true nurturer. I emulated Ollie and it helped make me successful. I also admired her honesty about her life and relationship with Victor and her determination to be with him. This is where I got lost in more confusion about life, love and relationships.

Ollie and Victor seemed to have been dating forever. But she endured so much to be with him. In a short period of time I grew to care about each of them individually and as a couple. But I struggled to understand what was going on. Victor had been unfaithful to Ollie and the seed of unfaithfulness produced fruit, a child. Daily, Ollie spent hours talking about what transpired between them. I listened and let her talk. The story was really twisted. One of Victor's sisters was friendly with this girl who visited Victor's parents' house often. This girl, according to Ollie, was not all that attractive but managed to seduce Victor right there in his parents' house, even when other people were in the house! Ollie and Victor survived and continued to date. Ollie supported Victor's relationship with his child. She bought clothes and toys and did all sorts of things for the child. The child's mother would take the items Ollie and Victor bought and refused to send them back for the baby's visits with her father. Victor's family considered the girl a friend and she was often at his parent's house when Ollie and Victor were there! Ollie was in so much pain, but she stayed with Victor. Then it happened again. Victor and the girl had another child. Ollie's life with Victor continued to be tumultuous. I continued to listen.

The one time Victor and I talked about what was going on, he basically summed it up as "it just happened." What chilled me the most about that explanation was that deep down, I understood Victor better than I understood Ollie. If a person causes me pain, I leave them, but for the pain that I cause, it just happens. I kept that admission buried deep inside of me. I was taking the high road to my pedestal. I was going to be different. Ollie and Victor got married and started a family of their own. I still admire her determination. But I couldn't do that. There had to be something I could do to keep that kind of drama to a minimum. But in the meantime I emulated Ollie's hard work.

I believe that's what led to my promotion. The Friday that I received the news about my promotion to billing coordinator, the firm bought me a huge flower arrangement. The flowers were beautiful; I didn't even wonder whether it was customary for a man to receive flowers for a promotion. I just beamed. That evening I drove to Marlin and told my parents about my promotion. They beamed. I gave the flowers to my mother. It was like I was trying to present my bride to my mother for her approval. But she wanted a human daughter-in-law.

CHAPTER THIRTY-TWO

My role in the law firm was a rewarding one. My job gave me instant gratification because I could see the results of my labor. If an attorney worked hard to get a new client, they sent me the setup information and boom, it appeared in the computer system for them. Each month all of their data came to me for processing and I would work my magic, no matter how long it took, to produce invoices to be sent to clients. The most rewarding part was when clients paid the bills and money came into the firm for all of us to get paid, take our paychecks home, and provide for our lives. I understood that it didn't matter how hard an attorney worked for a client; if the client didn't receive an invoice, the client couldn't pay the firm and none of us could get paid. I finally mattered to someone. They needed me. But the professional community was telling me to say that my job didn't define me. I learned to repeat that phrase with conviction. I actually had to make myself believe it, but now I know differently. My job did define me.

There was really no time to develop a relationship that would eventually replace the flowers I gave to my mother, but I kept trying. I had become very process-oriented. So I started developing a plan for marriage. I worked on it like I worked on anything else. I wrote it down and then executed it. One of the first things I told myself was a take on something I had heard: "if you want to be successful, surround yourself with successful people." I figured if I wanted to be married, I should surround myself with married people. So I did. I knew I wanted a Christian marriage and household, so I decided to surround myself with Christian married people.

There were people in my life who were Christians whom I knew outside of church, but I thought it would be easier to get to know people at church. I consciously excluded my own family because I knew them too well. By that time, out of the seven of my siblings, there were already seven marriages and five divorces. The ones who weren't divorced seemed to always be on shaky ground.

Darrell had married someone I didn't think he should have married, but he did it anyway. Their wedding was at her mother's house in San Antonio. I was his best man. Darrell and I sat in a bedroom in the house waiting for the ceremony to start. I didn't think he wanted to do it. We admired ourselves in the mirror, all decked out in our navy blue tuxedoes. The bedroom had a door that led to the front porch. I could see his blue and white Monte Carlo sitting on the street with the streamers I had hung on it and witty sayings written in shoe polish all over the windows. I told him all he had to do was say the word and we would burst through that door and never look back. He actually thought about it but went through with the wedding anyway. A few years later, I drove from Austin to Houston late at night and slept in my car in the parking lot of his apartment waiting for his wife to get up and leave so I could help move him out. They got divorced.

I wanted to start attending Wednesday night service. Life was still confusing and hectic and I needed a boost in the middle of the week. Besides, I needed to become more active at church so that I could meet more married Christians. My life had been filled with strange supernatural experiences, and my first trip to Wednesday night service fell in that same category. I took my usual route to church even though I had left from work instead of from my apartment. I like familiar routes. I made the right turn onto the street where my church was located. When I reached the entrance to the parking lot, I tried to turn the wheel of my car to make another right turn. My car wouldn't turn. I tried to turn the wheel and couldn't. The car simply would not go into the parking lot. I tugged at the steering wheel as the car passed the church. I looked back at the church behind me. Then I looked at the church through the rear view mirror. It was barely dusk, evening. I could see the church leaving me. I didn't understand what had just happened. Before I put the entire incident out of my mind, I noticed how the world looked better from my rear view mirror.

I was still determined to get involved with church. One Sunday, I sat in church waiting for service to end so I could go to work. I looked in the bulletin and saw that there was a Brotherhood meeting that coming Thursday. I decided right then I would attend. I would actually leave work to attend. It made it a lot easier to think of this as a mission or a process than as leisure time. So on Thursday night, I was there. With a purpose. It was strange to finally introduce myself to people that I had seen for almost six years but didn't know. Two guys befriended me immediately. My paranoia slapped me on the back of the head when these two guys recounted my life for me. One told me how he knew my face, where I sat in church, and strangest of all, commented that I had lost a lot of weight within the last year. I hit my paranoia squarely in the jaw with my Christian fist and made myself believe this was good.

Here were two guys who were good and kind and each was married. They introduced me around and made me feel very welcome, a part of the Christian family. In Brotherhood, we had Bible study and I quickly found that I talked too much. I seemed to raise more questions than any member of the Brotherhood had answers to. I knew that wasn't my purpose, so I shut up. I joined the men's chorus and met even more men. The first two guys I had met were close friends and invited me to their houses for Sunday dinner. Sometimes we had lunch during the week. We even went to UT football and basketball games together. They looked to be very successful. They had professional jobs, drove nice cars, had nice houses and beautiful wives. Things were going well.

When Stine died, my two church brothers took off work and came to Marlin for the services. At the funeral service I was hurting and confused. I didn't know they were there until after the service. I embraced each of them and tried not to cry, but I did. Their being there meant a lot to me. I had not befriended them to be friends with them, but to learn from them. I made a mental note that this was a lesson in support and continued to watch them when I returned to my life after the funeral.

Over time, I continued my mission. I met more and more married people at church. I didn't become close to them all but was around enough to watch them. I resolved in my own mind that my style of worship was not ever going to be as charismatic as some of theirs and I was okay with that. I also resolved that I was not going to have an opportunity to discuss my views on religion with them because that seemed to make many of them uncomfortable. So as long as I was on my mission to learn from them, I continued to hang around.

Then all at once . . . was it all at once or did it just happen over time? I don't know. I started noticing things. The men's chorus accepted a singing engagement out of town. We were actually pretty good. On the bus ride, the drummer and one of the two guys I was hanging out with got into an argument. It really shocked me that they were about to go to blows. I was sitting next to one of the deacons, a married man, when it became obvious to me, as oblivious as I can be at times, that something wasn't right. If I noticed it, I knew everyone else must have noticed and no one was doing anything about it. I whispered to the deacon that maybe he should say something Godly and Christian-like to calm the situation down. He refused. I asked him if he really understood his role in the church. He told me their problem was none of his business. Then the arguing back and forth became filled with cursing and my mind just shut down as I watched them lunge toward each other with clenched fists. That's when the deacon jumped in to do something, when it was out of control. That night we sang praises to God. Looking back, I know now that I started believing less in the words we sang.

Another Sunday afternoon, one of the ministers invited me home with his family. I was friends with his sister-in-law, who was a fun-loving, beautiful and voluptuous woman who had attended UT when I did, but I only got to know her after college. The minister and his wife had two beautiful children and a nice house. That day, the house was filled with the aroma of home cooking. The women worked in the kitchen while he and I talked. He wanted to take me for a ride in his new truck. I chuckled to myself. He was a short man, his wife was a little taller than him, so he had to sort of leap up into his truck. Given his vertical challenge, I marveled at his confidence and positive outlook on life. He talked to me about God's goodness. He told me that he had prayed for children and God had blessed him. He told me how he had prayed for a nice house and God had blessed him. He told me how he had prayed to have ten thousand dollars in the bank and God had blessed him. I wanted to lie down in the radiance he exuded and soak up his God-given goodness for myself. So God *was* the answer. I had been praying but my prayers were not being answered like his were. I enjoyed that day so much and wanted more lessons like that. Time passed; then I found out he had been arrested for drugs and went to jail. He and his wife divorced. She married another minister in the pulpit. His children were definitely affected. So was I.

Something happened between me and the two guys from church. I noticed the three of us weren't hanging out together anymore. I thought it was just scheduling. I always believed that wife and family come before friends. So I really didn't pay much attention to it. One night one of them called to see if he could come by my apartment. Of course I said he could. In the middle of a nondescript conversation, he asked to borrow money. I didn't have any money to loan him, and I really didn't want to put that weight on my relationship with him. I couldn't understand why he needed to borrow money when he was looking and living so well. He explained his need for a loan and that he would pay me back quickly.

Then he, to put it bluntly, made a pass at me. When I realized what he had done, I didn't hesitate. I walked to the door of my apartment, opened it and told him to leave. He asked why I wanted him to leave, as if he hadn't done anything. I simply said I wasn't stupid and he needed to go. I wanted to cry but I didn't. I was used to shutting off thoughts and feelings, so I just blocked it out of my mind. I couldn't figure it out so I just kept moving toward my goal. What did I learn from that? I don't know. It was too confusing. It didn't make sense. I didn't allow myself to wonder why he had chosen to hit on me. I just didn't want to deal with him ever again.

For days my phone rang and I was afraid to answer it. I didn't have an answering machine so I was missing other phone calls as well. In a fit of desperation, I used my cassette tape recorder to tape a message as though I had an answering machine but I didn't have anything for the beep at the end. The phone was ringing while I was contemplating how to pull this off. I had it! I knew what I would do. I taped a message on the cassette recorder and at the end, I simply whistled. I played the message back and lay in the floor of my apartment and laughed until I cried. I got it set up for the next time the phone rang. Was it him? I pressed the play button then the pause button and picked up the phone. It was him. My rigged recorder worked beautifully. The first thing he said was, "When did you get an answering machine?" He left a message about the loan and nothing about what he had done. I didn't want to think about why he thought I would be receptive to his advances, so I just lay on the floor and laughed about my makeshift answering machine. The dumb-ass called right back before I had a chance to rewind the cassette recorder. It didn't work as well and he was suspicious. Then I began to care more about being dishonest than why I was doing all that. I continued to attend church but it was hard difficult, especially since he was one of the ministers.

His friend, the other guy, noticed I wasn't too interested in hanging out with the two of them anymore. He was concerned. I didn't want to tell him about what had happened, but he seemed genuinely concerned. I decided to deal with the issue by getting someone else's opinion on what to do. I invited him to my apartment one evening to explain what had happened and get advice on how to handle his friend. But instead, when he arrived at my apartment, he started another conversation. He said he needed *my* help. The look on his face concerned me. The nurturer in me, the one who wants everybody to have a better life than mine, took over. I listened while he told me that his friendship with the other guy was more than I knew. They were lovers. I tuned him out and retreated to my child-hood coma. I don't even remember him leaving my apartment. But I do remember calling Darrell after he left and crying on the phone for almost twenty minutes. Darrell kept asking me why I was crying and I couldn't stop long enough to tell him. And when I was able to stop long enough to speak, I just told Darrell thanks and good-bye. I continued to go to church, but my relationships there deteriorated. I began sitting closer to the front of the church so I didn't have to look at too many people sitting in the pews. But I still had to look in the pulpit. That's where the one who had made a pass at me sat. I tried to focus on the pastor and the message, but I was on a slippery slope and I couldn't stop sliding. No matter how much I clawed at the earth passing beneath me, I couldn't get a grip.

As I continued to surround myself with married people, I learned that Christians didn't fare much better than the rest of the world. My informal survey revealed that in eight out of ten married couples, one of the spouses was cheating. Cheating was added to a long list of other things like being addicted to work, drugs, alcohol and pornography, having children from other relationships, not paying child support and all kinds of confusion. What I was learning had no place in the "me" I had created and wanted to be. The lessons I was learning must have been a part of the God in me that was getting buried. I didn't want to be like them. I had to be better, so I tried to take care of myself.

After graduating from college, I went on the Rotation Diet and started jogging five miles three times a week. It was the first time in my life I felt like I was in control. I lost weight. Eventually, I bought a Soloflex. My body was in good shape and I thought that would make me more balanced. Maybe even more happy. But it didn't. I was self-destructive. I would jog five miles after working all day and into the night, then go out drinking until the bars closed down and in the morning still be at work before anybody else. I was still trying to find something to hold onto, something that made me feel wanted, something to give my life meaning. Work didn't do it for me.

College was over and so were the football games that made my parents beam. I graduated without incident, or at least without my parents knowing about any of them. I had only borrowed a little over three thousand dollars for the entire five years I was in school. I bought my dream car as my graduation present to myself. A 1986 caramel-colored Cutlass Supreme with an eight-cylinder engine. Power! Style! It had enough room for my parents to ride with me if I needed to drive them somewhere. Before I graduated, I envisioned living in an apartment that had a view of the downtown skyline. It wasn't until I was moving furniture into my post-graduation apartment that I realized it had the view that I had seen in my vision. It was also big enough for me to put a queen-sized bed in it for when my parents came to visit. I seemed to always plan around my parents, as though I was still living at home but just visiting another city. I was home so often; my life still revolved around theirs. But I didn't feel like they wanted me there.

One day, while visiting my parents, my mother sat me down in the living room, the special room where we had company and Christmas, although we didn't have plastic on the furniture like some other folks we knew. She told me that she was leaving my father. Again, my funk was so deep that I hardly processed the information. I didn't say much to her about it. I wondered why she was telling me that. To this day, my mother will tell you about how I used to get so upset because they weren't paying attention to me. I exploded once because I was trying to talk to my parents about the serious issues I was facing in college and they were tuning me out and I yelled, "Why don't ya'll pay attention to me?" I regained my composure before I let everything out that day. But it would be years later when, in my presence, she recounted the incident to someone else, that I knew that I had gotten her attention. At the time, I hardly knew either one of them were listening. So when she told me she was leaving my father, I drifted off in thought. My body language must have conveyed, "So?" I filed that day away in the back of my brain with so many other things and continued my own search. She didn't leave him.

I invited my parents to visit me at my post-graduation apartment, the apartment where I would receive the news of my sister's limited time on earth. I needed them to be proud of me. They agreed to visit, but not to stay overnight. My father brought a complete dinner. I invited a few friends over. When my parents arrived they walked into my apartment and I basked in their glow. Mission accomplished. My friends arrived, ate and raved about my father's cooking. He beamed some more. After dinner was over and my friends were gone, before it was time for my parents to return to Marlin, they decided to take a rest. They both took off their shoes before kicking their feet up. I remember automatically taking their shoes and putting them in the coat closet at the entryway of the apartment. I felt my mother watching me before I heard her speak. She told me I had better hurry up and get a wife before I reached a point where a woman couldn't do anything for me. What in the hell did that mean? She said that I had my own place, my own system of doing things and I was neat and orderly, I could cook and clean for myself, etc. I let her continue, but I didn't really respond, at least not the way I wanted to. I laughed and said, "Well, I want to want a woman, not to need one." Which, after I said it, I found, was a profound statement. But what I really wanted to say was, "Aren't you the same woman who beat my ass to make me learn how to be neat, orderly, cook and clean for myself? Why in the hell did you teach me

all of that if you were going to complain when I learned how to do it?"
But I never cursed, at least not in front of my parents.

By 1989, I was getting a little full of myself. I had learned so much and
come so far, further than I had expected to. I had blocked out my academic
failures at UT and found a new way of learning. I could read books as long
as I obtained information that I could apply to what was relevant in my life:
work. I felt like I was about to wake up for the first time in my entire life. I
was doing my job well and working more and more hours.

The firm moved into a newly built office building. Since it was new,
the building had brownouts and blackouts. My computer system had a
power supply backup on it, which sounded an alarm that allowed me to
shut the system down within fifteen minutes of a blackout. I didn't know
the power supply wasn't working when we had a few brownouts. I continued to work on my data and back up every night. It was weeks that later I
discovered a brownout had caused some corrupted files in my data. Then
I found out that all of my backups had the same corrupted files in them.
We had to restore to a prior month's accounting and recreate an entire
month of processing. Neither the brownout, the failed power supply, nor
the bad backups were my responsibility, but I volunteered to fix the problem so we would stay on schedule. The firm set me up in a hotel conference room with a computer and mounds of paper while the building's
power was stabilized. I stayed up for three solid days working to recreate
the data accurately. It was tough, but I did it. We were up and running
again and the money kept coming in. I did it for the team, for the family,
and it made me feel good.

But I discovered that in the work family, not everybody took
responsibility for their mistakes. Sometimes I would get in trouble for
things I didn't do. Many times, I wouldn't acknowledge any guilt or
innocence, I would simply move the focus to the solution. I didn't care if
they thought I caused the problem, I was used to that from Harrell and
Darrell. I just wanted them to know I fixed it. This seemed to work well
for me until people found out I didn't fight back, that I would just smile,
take the verbal lashing and then fix the problem. More and more of the
problems I faced weren't fixable. Many of those problems revolved around
adult personalities I had neither created nor could I fix. I worked with

procrastinators, narcissists, paranoid schizophrenics, manic-depressives and just plain fragile children housed in adult bodies.

The firm kept adding more and more people to the family and trying to house us all under one roof. Even though we had moved to a bigger house, we still had to work together and try to get along with each other. My job became more and more difficult. I faced problems that working more hours in a day couldn't fix and I didn't cause these problems. I couldn't make attorneys log more hours on the books. I couldn't make them turn in their time daily. I couldn't make them review their invoices and get them back to me on time. I had no control over them, and that meant there were areas of my own work I couldn't control. But I did what I could, as well as I could.

I was shocked when one of the partners called me into a meeting to discuss the large amount of overtime I had been paid the previous year. She must have thought I was very arrogant. And why not? Even my mother had taken to calling me arrogant since I graduated from college. I asked the partner why she called a meeting with me when my boss could explain the amount of overtime. I had established a time schedule. I kept a log of who turned in what and when. If my boss wanted me to meet the deadline, I showed her why I was late, which usually meant the people at fault were people I had no control over. I always asked her to approve my overtime and she would. I told the partner to wait while I fetched my "CYA" (cover your ass) file. I returned and showed her the documentation I kept. The culprits were very obvious. The tone of my meeting with the partner changed from accusatory to informative. I made it a point to defend myself and inform the partner that my boss knew all of this. I still wondered to myself why my boss hadn't explained this. Why didn't she protect me from this? Didn't she know I kept all of this stuff? I was hurt. Will I ever do enough? Will anyone ever protect me? My attitude toward my work family changed that day. I decided to quit, start my own business and go back to school.

So I did. I quit the billing coordinator position and took a contract position with the same firm under my own company name, WGW Consulting. The G. was back. I contracted with them to build a huge research database. I also got a part-time job at Foley's and a part-time billing job at a much smaller law firm. At the same time I enrolled at Austin Community College and Southwest Texas State University to take some business classes I needed before applying to graduate school. I also started looking around for volunteer opportunities. Maybe I could devote time to people who really needed it. Maybe I could make somebody's life better. I was still trying to find something to hold onto in life.

Then came Grace. At the wrong time. Imagine almost two hundred, mostly single, young black professionals ages twenty-five to forty, joined together in community service two to three times a week. Then throw in networking on top of that and you have the formula for instant fun. That's what I found in Texas Organized Professionals, or TOPs. It was a great organization in which to meet people and hopefully, eventually, get married. Numerous relationships were produced as a result of our hard work in the community. There were people from different companies with a wide variety of professional skills. I learned a lot from them. I tried to limit my participation, but ended up taking on a lot of responsibility in my new volunteer family. I later found out I didn't experience nearly the number of relationship opportunities as others in the group had. I was a workaholic and that trait transferred into my volunteer work as well. I became overwhelmed.

The smaller firm wanted me full time so I wrapped up my client work and let WGW Consulting go into a coma-like existence. Was the G. gone again? Anyway, I found being self-employed created a lot of problems for me. But soon I mastered the accounting position with the smaller law firm and became bored with it. So I struck back out on my own full time. January 16, 1991, was my first full day of self-employment. It was also the day that the Gulf War went full-scale. I had done my homework, obtained a client base and outlined potential work with solid commitments from prospective clients. I had a good business idea and good connections. I had no idea the war would cause the economy to go south and that I would be affected by it.

Around the same time I was preparing to start my own company and applying for graduate school, I met Grace purely by accident. About twenty of us from TOPs decided to go out to eat after a meeting. We went to Catfish Station on 6th Street. Legend has it that actor Matthew McConaughey was our waiter, but I really don't remember. The table was full of excitement. We were a volunteer group doing good things in the community and we were all single and "available." You were considered available whether you were dating someone or not, as long as you weren't married. I was there at the table, but not there. I often drifted off while I was in the midst of a crowd of people. I often thought of work when I was out trying to have fun. It was good mind filler for me.

On that night Darlene was sitting next to me. She brought it to my attention that people were sitting around the table hookin' up and she was being left out. Sure enough she was right. I hadn't noticed it. She asked me who she could hook up with. She inquired about Maurice. I remember telling her I thought he was a little strange, but she could at least get a date with him. We worked it out and got them set for a date later that week. Incidentally, they got married some years later. Then Darlene started working on someone for me. I didn't have the heart to say that I wasn't really interested. But before I knew it, I had a date with Grace. Our first date was at the restaurant at the Hyatt Hotel on the lake, famous for their margaritas and fajitas. We had a good time and agreed to see each other again.

So I started another relationship in the midst of my self-employment struggle. In my first month of business, potential clients were obviously affected by the war and economy and didn't come through as I had planned. By June, my savings were gone and I was back on the pavement looking for a job. Grace and I were hanging out, but I knew I wasn't in love. I wasn't interested in carving up my deadness and trying to graft it onto a woman's life. I was feeling like a failure in my business venture and I was broke. I had fourteen hundred dollars in past-due bills, no clients, no money and my car was about to be repossessed. I was severely depressed about it all. Grace knew of my financial situation and offered to loan me about eight hundred dollars and my mother loaned me six hundred dollars. To top it all off, Grace was pressing me for a statement about the direction of our relationship.

I've always been a little stupid when it comes to wanting to tell the truth—not always accomplishing it, but definitely wanting to. I've heard many married men say, "Lie! Lie! Lie! Never admit to anything!" I didn't and still don't understand that. I managed to put Grace off without an official statement while I found a job. One of my clients needed a bookkeeper and I thought it would be ideal for me, even though my actual skills and knowledge fell way below what they actually needed. I figured I could get books, read and ask some of the other folks in TOPs to help me get up to speed. I knew it would be hard work but I needed the job and the money.

After interviewing with the firm and separately with their CPA, I got the job. Of course, I threw myself 147 percent into my new position and didn't have much time for Grace. But she focused on her agenda. So when pressed for a statement about our relationship, I was stupidly honest in saying that I didn't have the same feeling for her as she had for me. Why in the hell did I do that? Even though I wasn't in love, I still wanted to hang out when I had time. But after I told her the truth, she was so angry with me. She's the one who told me that I liked working more than I liked having sex with her. She didn't know that I was struggling with my religious beliefs. I wasn't supposed to give in to every sexual desire, only when I absolutely had to. She didn't know I was really struggling with trying to have some discipline when it came to sex.

One night when I was about to leave her place, she asked me to stay over and I told her I needed to get back to my own apartment. She got upset and started yelling at me. When was I going to be the man? When was I going to wear the pants? Why did she always have to initiate sex? She came at me, poking me in the chest with her finger. I thought she was going to hit me. I began to rumble like I had never rumbled toward a woman before. I knew I had to get out of that apartment and away from her. I couldn't understand how she could say such hurtful things to me when she said she loved me. I tried to understand it, but it didn't make sense. If I knew how to love and felt love for someone, I don't think I would say things like that to her. I definitely wouldn't be showing such violence and anger toward them. I felt my father in me rumbling to come out. I never saw my father raise a hand to my mother, only his voice. But I felt that what was inside me was a more dangerous mutation of my father's temper. Did my mother treat him like this? Is this what made him rumble at her like he did? Surely not. Maybe other women before my mother treated him in a way that made him rumble toward her just like my siblings made him rumble at me, even when I didn't deserve it.

That night, Grace did more damage to any "us" that was, could have, or would have been. Here was another relationship that could not, would not support me, hold me up and help me be strong. Things got worse with Grace.

My parents raised us with certain rules that I took into my adult life. One of them was that we couldn't just drop by a person's house. We always had to call first. It was okay to run into someone on the street and then accompany them to their house, but we couldn't go to someone's house unannounced. Even if you were out and had a notion to visit someone, doing so unannounced was unacceptable. All of my friends knew not to drop by my house without calling first. Didn't matter who you were. Grace ignored the rule. She showed up at my apartment one night unannounced, and angry. When I heard the irate knock, I tiptoed to the door to look through the peephole and saw it was Grace. I returned to my sofa and continued to watch television. She yelled at me through the door and I didn't answer. So she went to a pay phone and called and I answered. She was obviously very upset and I was cold and heartless. I couldn't care because if I cared I would start to rumble inside and I would rather not rumble. I explained to her that I wouldn't open the door because she came by unannounced and furthermore, I refused to deal with her when she was that mad. I had to let her go. I didn't love her and what she was showing me wasn't love. No one in the world really loved anyone else. The world just uses the word without knowing what it really means. She wanted to know why I didn't feel for her what she felt for me. She wanted to know why I was treating her badly. She had a lot of questions that I didn't have the answers to.

I listened to her and thought, "It just is what it is." That seemed very logical to me. I couldn't understand what she wanted me to say besides a lie like "I love you with all my heart, my darling." I refused to do that. Then the money she loaned me became an issue. I had promised to return the money to her in a certain amount of time and that time had not come yet, so I was well within the agreement regarding the money. But she wanted to be sure she would get it back, and the forceful, vulgar language she used to convey that to me showed me yet another side of her. She told me she was stronger than me and I really didn't want to mess with her and

I should really think about making sure I paid her back. The situation was insane. I paid her back on time.

We had several more heated conversations before our time apart increased and helped settle things down between us. A year or more later, we were talking again, but nothing more. She made advances in her job at Dell Computers, and I heard a rumor that company stock was being doled out generously. I had become the administrator of Short, DeFreeze, Goers & Close, another accomplishment I really wanted, but which had a huge learning curve and I needed to devote even more time at the job. I was working six and seven days a week. During the week, it was common for me to arrive at the office at seven o'clock in the morning and not leave until sometime between eleven o'clock that night or two o'clock the next morning. This lasted for a long time. But it was what I had to do. Since Grace and I were not as closely involved, the hours at work didn't matter. We were getting along on the phone and occasional outings. Nothing more.

Then, Grace won a trip to Hawaii from her sales accomplishments at Dell and invited me to go. I thought it was a strange invitation. We had been through a volatile time and I asked her if she really thought it was a wise thing to even consider. She used the words I needed to hear to assure me she had no expectations and that it would just be a fun trip. But there would be sex on the trip. Commitment-free sex? No problem. I would be her date; I would play the role and that would be it. I thought I understood what I was getting into.

The corporate world was foreign to me. I had never worked for a company as large as Dell. It was an amazing experience. Flying on a plane full of Dell employees made it easy to get caught up in the trip. It was such a charge to be around so much energy and fun. The company had made extravagant arrangements for all of us. We stayed at the Four Seasons Resort. Our room had a lagoon with a gondola in front and a dolphin pool in back right outside the window. It was amazing.

My role of hand holding, hugging, smiles and taking pictures with Grace was right on cue. But . . . the first night we were there, we were getting ready to attend a dinner with some of her friends and co-workers. The mood was right. She made her move. I engaged gladly, I knew my role. We started at the vanity in front of the wide mirror. I could see my reflection and realized that mirrors don't lie. Both Grace and I knew I was playing a role . . . for her. We moved to the bed. The window was open with a soft and gentle breeze blowing through the window sheers. The sun was sinking toward the horizon. It was perfect. I liked my role. After our usual foreplay, I excused myself to follow the rules I had developed about sex. I needed a condom. Grace got very upset. But I was confused, because we always used a condom! I didn't understand what was wrong. She pouted, she fussed, she yelled! I thought she was going to try to hit me again. She said she didn't understand why I had to use a condom every time we had sex. She said my using a condom made her feel unclean. What? Unclean? Where in the hell was she getting that from?

Stupid me. After hearing that, I thought I had the perfect explanation, which was the truth. I thought that this moment was going to be classic. I would get a chance to truthfully explain myself and it was perfectly reasonable, logical and most of all, considerate of her. I talked about *my* responsibility in our sexual relationship. I explained to her it didn't matter whether she was on the pill or not, *I* needed to do this in order to prevent a pregnancy. I explained that I had *always* lived up to my responsibilities. And preventing an unwanted pregnancy was *my* responsibility. Then to cap off the conversation (and I really thought this would be a moment for the violins to swell), I told her that the only sex education my parents had ever given me came from my mother, which was, "if you get a girl pregnant, you're gonna marry her." It didn't help.

She gave me the silent treatment. I hate the silent treatment. You don't know what the other person is thinking. We got dressed, in silence, and left the room to meet the others. Grace struck out at a fast pace in front of me. I was already tired of fighting but I was not about to go through the first night with her acting like this. I stopped walking. I stood there on the walkway that went over the lagoon, underneath a canopy of tropical wandering flowers. I called her name. She had her nose in the air and continued at her determined pace to the meeting place. I called her name again. She kept walking. I stood firm with my legs square with my shoulders, my slacks flapping in the evening breeze. I called her name yet again. She stopped. I told her to come to me. She turned and looked at me. I repeated myself. I fully expected her to tell me that she was neither a dog nor a child. She dropped her head and walked toward me. When she arrived at my planted location, she looked up at me. I put my face close to hers and told her that she could choose to go do dinner with her friends and make a scene, but I would follow her lead and make it an even bigger scene than she could even imagine. I explained to her that if I was going to be with her, she was going to have to be with me. And that meant she was not allowed to walk in front of me. And if she did, we were both going to be miserable for the duration of the trip. She dropped her head again and walked beside me to dinner. I had a great evening. I was proud of myself, but I hated myself at the same time. I hated women and the things they made me do.

The trip and the struggles with Grace didn't end that night. There was so much beauty on the island, but Grace wouldn't let me enjoy it. She had a revised script for me that I hadn't agreed to. The script I had received said my role was that of a date: caring, together and physical. The revised script that she sprung on me had several scenes added, one of which included us looking out at the ocean in the tropical breeze. This was the scene where I was supposed to propose marriage to her. I hadn't received that version of the script, so I didn't follow along very well and we had yet another fight. The bottom line was that I had to get off of that island and back to Austin. This trip was getting to be insane. I contacted the hotel concierge and explained my situation and desires. The real bottom line was my bank account. It was very expensive to leave ahead of schedule. So I endured the last two days of the trip.

I don't understand how married people can walk around the same house for weeks at a time and not speak to each other. It was so difficult for me to be around Grace when I knew how angry she was with me and how her anger made me feel. I tried to make peace. But she wasn't having any of that. Love? She says that she *loves* me? More like loathes me. I . . . we . . . made it through the final days of the trip. I was so glad to board the plane for home. But . . . the drama continued. It invited a whole bunch of other people into my private space. I have a thing about my privacy. I'll say it again: I have a thing about my privacy. What happens between me and a woman should stay between me and her. If I wanted the entire world to know, I would take out a full-page ad and tell the world. Or even better, write a book about it! Everyone on the plane knew that we were having problems. Grace's friends had already reassigned me to another seat away from Grace for the eight-hour-plus flight from Hawaii to Dallas. I took the new seat assignment happily. It gave me time to devise my action plan. I determined that she was insane and wanted nothing else to do with her. I had eight peaceful hours on the plane. When the plane landed in Dallas, I called Harrell and told him not to ask any questions, just meet me in the airport in Austin. When we landed in Austin I never even looked for Grace. I didn't talk to anyone. I just walked down the long corridor. I exited the gate area through the double doors and saw Harrell sitting outside waiting for me. Wow, he was there. I wouldn't be embarrassed. I made a bold statement that day. Grace couldn't control me or my emotions and she couldn't buy them either.

She called the next day and wanted to meet to discuss what had happened. I agreed and we met at Luby's. We got our trays and sat down. She seemed to be at a loss for words and just kept looking at me. I was hungry and wanted to finish my food, so I waited until I was nearly finished eating before I asked her why we were there. She had hardly touched her food. When she started to speak, her voice was loud and I asked her to lower it. She refused. I explained to her again that if she wanted to have a scene, I was perfectly willing to make one. She continued to talk loudly. So, I went completely crazy! I don't know what I said, but I made a huge scene. I got up from the table, walked to the front of the restaurant, paid our check and left. I knew that type of behavior was inside me, but I never intended for it to come out. I was really afraid of what else she would push me to do. I never wanted to see her again. And I haven't seen her to this day. Shortly after our Luby's incident, she took a leave of absence from her job at Dell and went to Europe for six months and came back with a husband. That's her style, melodramatic movie stuff. She had a baby and got divorced.

CHAPTER THIRTY-THREE

Remembering all of this stuff is . . .

Is what?

I don't know. It's sad.

Sad?

Yeah, sad, but I don't want to stop now, even if it is sad. I want to continue. The next part is more important to how I got here.

That sounds good.

Well, hold off on that verdict until I'm finished.

Okay.

When I met Zanovia, it was a strange time in my life. I admit, my entire life has been strange. I had been through a lot, and despite everything, I was still trying to execute the plan that I had devised for my life. I was still riding the wave despite feeling betrayed by everyone. Every problem that came up, I just blocked it out and tried to keep going. I was working on the plan. And the plan still included getting married. I was more and more into selling myself as a product. And I was working on making that product look good. I knew I had time to be rough around the edges. I was still relatively young, so I let some things go, but I still worked on it. I was five years into my employment with Short, DeFreeze, Goers & Close, the law firm I worked for after my brief stint of self-employment. I had actually tried to leave the firm shortly after getting the bookkeeper position because I realized my duties included a lot more than just bookkeeping. All I wanted to do was close my door and count the pennies and not deal with any people. But the first day on the job I read the employee handbook and found that the bookkeeper had a lot of human resource responsibilities. I didn't want to do that. I didn't want to deal with people. I didn't like people at that point in my life. But I kept my mouth shut and collected the paycheck I needed, especially to pay back my mother and Grace. After a few months of doing a lot of work that I hadn't agreed to and trying to clean up huge messes the person before me had created, I drafted a long memo outlining how they should reorganize, including hiring an administrator for more effective management. I included an organizational chart with responsibilities and how the changes could increase revenues and pay the salaries of the new management and administrative positions that were added. I knew I didn't have the skills for the position, so I said if the reorganization was approved, I would leave once the administrator's position was filled. They offered the job to me.

Donnie DeFreeze put a lot of confidence in me. I had found a new family and my nurturing nature took over again. Long hours and a huge learning curve. I was facing tough issues. I was in charge of the entire firm and dealing with things I had no idea how to handle. I needed a mentor to help me cope with this new challenge in life. I asked several older professional men if they would mentor me both professionally and personally. I needed help badly. They each, individually, politely declined. Not by giving me an emphatic no, but by either ignoring the request or throwing the question back at me; "Why do you think you need a mentor? You're doing just fine." I finally found Mary Smith, who answered questions for me about law firm management and listened to me vent. But as for the larger issues of profession and life, I was alone, again. I was still in the "new me" I had created and I charged ahead. I had the same failsafe backup plan I had when I was promoted to billing coordinator. I have to admit I thought my product was looking pretty good. I continued to work hard in TOPs and that took up a lot of my time. But I had added another dimension to my crazed and hard working world. I was working on projects with my brother Harrell.

Harrell and I worked on several ventures together. We co-wrote a sitcom, "Real Money," and co-owned a production company. All in all, Harrell had become something else for me to try to latch onto for hope. He had so much potential in areas where I didn't have talent, and vice versa. Together, I thought we could conquer the world. My every waking moment was filled with work. I wasn't dating anyone, just working at my job, working in TOPs, and working with Harrell. Even though it was much less than a relationship with a person, work gave me something to do and a sense of value. At around two o'clock on a Monday morning, after taping the fourth episode of our sitcom, "Real Money," Harrell yelled, "It's a wrap!" We all hurried and broke down the set because we were over our scheduled time slot and the next show was waiting for us to clear out. Once the U-Haul was loaded and all of the stuff was out of the studio, I remember telling Harrell that the sitcom was my last adventure with him and I was going to find me a woman, build me a house, get married and have some babies. That was in June of 1996. I met Zanovia in July. In August I put earnest money down on the lot where I wanted to build my house. And that was it. The plan was finally being executed.

I first saw Zanovia at a Sunday evening jazz concert at the Oasis. Asking someone for her number was a big move for me. She was so beautiful. She was tall with shoulder-length hair, long pretty legs, great bone structure, a perfect smile and an inviting personality. She didn't even know my name and she was giving me a hard time. I liked her instantly. I got her number from my friend Sharon, the one who said I needed a starter house and a starter wife. You remember Sharon, she's the one who said I was the common denominator. I called Zanovia and we made plans to go out that same week. We met across the street from the Filling Station and loaded my car with blankets she brought and a picnic basket that she had prepared. We drove to Zilker Park to see a play, *A Midsummer Night's Dream*, at the amphitheater. The evening was perfect. I didn't even mind all the bad-ass little kids surrounding us. I drove her back to her car and re-loaded it with the stuff she had brought. I couldn't believe how much I enjoyed just watching her lean over and put stuff in her car. We shared a very gentle hug good-bye and went our separate ways. On the way home, I was overcome with fear. I tried to block it out but it shook me deeply. What was I afraid of? Not now, not when my plan was about to be executed. I could do it with this one! I knew I could! And if I did, I would be right on schedule with the plan. Married by age thirty-five, first child by age thirty-seven, the same age my father was when he had me. I was already building the house, and if we didn't like it, we could sell it and get another one. I was finally making the salary I wanted and I had a career that would take me to retirement. Here was my chance for my plan to be executed, and I was shaking with fear. Why?

I decided I would take it slow and do something I had never done. I wanted to approach a relationship with Zanovia carefully, and in doing so, try to give her an in-depth view of me. By this time in my life, I was getting pretty good at burying things inside of me. I was pretty much numb all over, but the "me" I had created for work and women knew how to feel when called upon to do so.

I was so excited to discover Zanovia was interested and that she wanted to see more of me. Our schedules worked out well since she worked full time and was going to graduate school for an MBA. My new work family seemed to be getting crazier and crazier. I developed a daily outlook for work that helped me function better. Each day I would wake up and say to myself it was going to be a horrible day, so that when it happened, I wouldn't be disappointed. I was the first administrator for the firm and a lot of things had to be implemented from the ground up. We all had a lot to learn about my role, responsibilities and authority. Among the attorneys, legal assistants and secretaries, I was the youngest. No one knew how insecure I was in that position and I never let it show. I couldn't. There were too many people waiting to attack me if I let my guard down. I took everything so personally. I really wanted to create an environment where people where happy, yet I wanted to put the attainment of happiness in their own control. Meaning, if they played by the rules and did their work, they would be treated fairly and rewarded accordingly. That was hard to accomplish in an environment where people were used to working in small teams (a.k.a. fiefdoms). As I began to interview and hire people, I developed a speech that reflected my role in the firm. I would tell interviewees that as the administrator of the firm, I wore two hats; one was as their protector, I would protect and defend them to the ends of the earth if they played by the rules and did their work. But the other was to reprimand them when I had to. And, when I did, they would not have to question whether I was right or wrong because the rules were clear. That speech really helped when I had to fire people. While it was still hard to do, I never felt I did it unjustly. As a matter of fact, I'm still friends with a few people I fired.

There were constant stressors on the job and I hadn't learned how to deal with stress, I just internalized it. One attorney, in particular, gave me a hard time. She could be so mean and nasty and she cursed like a sailor. She stressed me out so bad, I was having paralyzing chest pains. That year on Valentine's weekend TOPs had its annual Valentine's party. Instead of going to the party, I lay on my back on the floor in my apartment, with my arms stretched out on either side of me trying to relieve the chest pains. I had to lie like that for a day and a half. But on Monday morning, I was right back at work.

One weekend, I was at the firm moving furniture around when I felt a pull in my groin. Of course I ignored it and the bulge that ensued for months. The doctor told me I needed hernia surgery. Surgery? I had never been in the hospital for anything. I didn't want to do it because I thought that my health would end up on a slippery slope if I let them cut me. But it became increasingly uncomfortable. If it was going to kill me, I would have left it alone, but instead it would have just made me miserable so I decided to have the surgery. I was afraid to tell the shareholders of the firm I needed to be off for a week. They weren't the kindest people when it came to folks being sick. I had defended too many employees behind closed doors, but now it was my turn and I didn't know who would be in my corner. But I had to tell them and I did.

Then I had to figure out how to take care of myself. I had just met Zanovia and didn't want to impose on her or make her feel obligated to help me. I didn't want or need that from her. I didn't want any help from anybody. For some reason, I had to do it on my own. I felt like things in my life had added up to a point where I couldn't depend on people. Based on past experiences, I never really asked people for a lot. I mostly helped other people. And if I got to a point where I needed something, I would carefully assess who *could* best help me before I asked. And when I determined who *could* help, I decided whether or not they *would* help. I would go through all of that before I would even ask for any help. What surprised me time and time again was that the people that I had helped in the past simply walked away from me when

I needed them. Even if they had what I needed, they just walked away. So, I tried hard not to need anybody.

I made arrangements for my nephew, Brennan, Stine's oldest son, to take me to the hospital and drop me off. He had moved in with me after he graduated from high school and I helped him get started in life. At the time I needed surgery he had moved into his own apartment. He agreed to keep my car for a week, which he thought was great. He hated the bus. I figured I could take a taxi from the hospital once the surgery was over and I was released. For information purposes only, I told Harrell I was going to have surgery and what my plans were. He blew a gasket! He thought I was crazy! I told him I could take care of myself. He called my mother and told her to come and take care of me. She called me and said Harrell was very upset and that she would come to Austin. But I didn't want her to come, not for that. I told her not to worry and that I was going to be fine. I would call them every day if I had to. But most of all, I couldn't figure out Harrell.

I hadn't asked him to do a thing but . . . anyway, he volunteered to pick me up from the hospital and check on me. Before I left for the hospital, I bought groceries and cooked a week's worth of food. Brennan dropped me off at the hospital and I went into surgery. I woke up three times during surgery and could feel the doctor cutting and pulling on me. I even talked to the doctor and nurses but each time I woke up, they put me back under again. I woke up in the recovery room, called Harrell and told him I was ready. He picked me up, took me to get my drugs and took me home. He sat with me for a couple of hours but I was fine. I rested for three days, and only took one or two painkillers, which had a strange effect on me. The doctor told me that they were strong. They had codeine in them. They made me hallucinate like crazy. After taking the first one, I lay on the sofa and I thought I was asleep but I could see a man standing outside my sliding glass doors trying to break in. But I couldn't get up to run or chase him off or anything. He just kept trying to break in and I lay there helpless. I didn't like taking those pills but I got the refill anyway. Just in case.

CHAPTER THIRTY-FOUR

While I was an administrator, I grew to hate December. I grew to hate the holidays. I grew to hate the end of the year. I said that already.

Yes you did. But say what you need to say. Say what you feel.

The tax planning, the annual shareholder meeting, the Christmas bonuses people thought were a guarantee. The year-end shareholder distributions, the Christmas party somebody was bound to hate no matter how much work I put into it. And most of all, I hated sending out the firm's Christmas cards. Have I already said this?

Yes, but that's okay.

Every year, we had the same problems with the Christmas card list and the same people yelled and screamed about the same thing but wouldn't take their hands out of it so I could fix it for the next year. That frustrated me to no end! But I had to endure it. Zanovia let me vent about this stuff and for the first time it seemed like a woman didn't criticize me for working so much and so hard. We had only met in July and were getting along really well. We made plans to spend Christmas with her father and his new lady friend's family in San Antonio. Zanovia's mother was deceased. I decided not to have my annual New Year's Day party because I was packing to move into my new house. It was looking good. Kent, a friend who worked in commercial construction, helped me monitor the building of the house. I worked with a decorator to select paint, carpet, tile, backsplashes, wallpaper, trim; all the things I dreaded but had to do and did well once I got into it. But it was December, the month I hated.

Damn I'm drunk.

I can't really tell, keep going.

One day, I was on my way out to the house to deal with a brick issue. I had taken a friend out to see my house under construction. She pointed down the street and said she liked the brick on another house. I said I did too and that's why I had chosen that brick for my house. She said that the brick on my house was different. I argued with her until I realized that my brick, in fact, was different. My house was completely bricked but the brick was the wrong color. Damn! My life was so busy I hadn't even noticed. So on this day I was on my way to discuss the brick issue with my salesman. I was on MoPac heading south toward my subdivision when I got a real bad pain in my chest and my left arm went numb. I ignored it and kept driving. It continued. I kept going. I met with the salesman and a representative from the brick company, who explained that it was the same brick by name but because they had moved to another part of the quarry, the color changed. In a nutshell, I negotiated a credit with the builder that satisfied me. The builder was good about situations like that and I appreciated it. I was on back on MoPac headed to my office worrying about the things waiting for me there and my chest got tight again. The numb tingling in my left arm intensified, but of course I returned to work and ignored it. After five-thirty, when most of the staff was gone, I doubled over in pain. Again, I asked myself, is this something that will kill me or just make me miserable? Right then, I was just miserable. I couldn't depend on death to relieve the pain. So, I went to my car and drove myself to the emergency room.

They ran tests and admitted me. I called Harrell, and he came to the hospital. He sneaked a burger and fries in for me. After he left, I checked my messages. Zanovia had left several. I waited until late that night to call her back. I didn't want her to come to the hospital. She was so upset with me for not calling sooner. I didn't know how to take that. No one really cared about me. The next day, I was sitting in a wheelchair outside the physical therapy room where they were going to give me a stress test. I was still wearing what I had on the day before. I remember thinking I was going to have to walk on a treadmill in my Ferragamos. I sat in the wheelchair facing the entrance to the therapy room. I let my mind wander down the empty hall to my right. I heard footsteps approaching from my left but I didn't turn to look. The footsteps walked behind me and passed me. I saw the back of a tall, shapely woman in a flowing royal blue dress with a belt that accentuated her waist and royal blue high heels that clicked against the floor as she walked down the hallway. I thought to myself, who is that woman? They wheeled me into the physical therapy room for the stress test, then wheeled me back to my room. There, in a chair in the corner, was the woman in the blue dress. It was Zanovia. I couldn't believe a woman that beautiful was with me.

I called the office to let them know I was in the hospital, but I didn't want it to be public information and that I was fine and would be in the office the next day. I looked at Zanovia and the fear jumped up and down on top of the stress in my chest.

CHAPTER THIRTY-FIVE

By the time I went into the hospital for chest pains, Zanovia and I had gotten to know each other pretty well. I knew she didn't have a strong connection with God. I knew she'd had a bout with Grave's disease. I knew her mother had passed away and her attitude toward caring for her father was different from mine. I believed she loved her father, but if he needed help around the house, she would prefer to hire somebody, while I would prefer to go home periodically and help out. I liked being able to get to spend time with my parents and do something useful for them. I told her about my mother and father each being the designated caregiver for their parents until their deaths. I showed her the letter my mother wrote to me a few years earlier.

June 23, 1993

2:00 a.m.

Dear Son,

In each family there is one child that is the one to take care of the parents. As you know, I was that child in my family and your father was that child in his. In our family, you are that child. I know that it is a big responsibility but don't fight it. Just accept it as I did and it will all be alright.

Love,

Mother

Zanovia looked at me strangely when I explained that I was "the one," and if I had to, I would move back to Marlin to care for my parents. I felt like I owed that to the woman who carried me for nine months and the man who worked to put food in my mouth. She didn't agree. I also explained to Zanovia about my relationship with my nephew Brennan. He was Stine's oldest child but wasn't my brother-in-law's biological son. My brother-in-law, Carl, whom I think of as my own brother, had adopted Brennan and raised him as his own. I told Zanovia about how Stine used to call Brennan by my name because she had raised me as well. I liked that. But after Stine died, Carl raised the four kids on his own. I told Zanovia about how, after her death, Stine would visit me on a regular basis. The dream was always the same. I would drive up in front of a hospital and she would be waiting for me dressed in her hospital gown. She would get into the car and her drab blue-green gown would transform into something fashionable. We would ride and laugh and she would comfort me with her presence. Those dreams helped me through many sorrow-filled nights.

After Stine died, Brennan visited me on his spring breaks and we would go to arcades, talk, go out to eat and do the movie thing. He loved to go to the movies. When he graduated from high school, I felt compelled to call him one day. I didn't fight the feeling. I called him. I asked him what his plans were and he told me that he might go to the military. I asked him why and he said the military was his "only option." I explained to him that the military was a fine choice, but I was concerned because he thought it was his only option. He said he wanted to go to college but had not applied and didn't have the money. I told him I would help him. He came to live with me and enrolled in Austin Community College. I don't know why I expected a grown man to show up at my doorstep, but he was a child and I wasn't prepared. I paid tuition, bought clothes and food and dealt with the foulest odor coming from his room. I forced him to learn the bus route so I wouldn't have to transport him back and forth. I made him find a job.

Finally, one day I was through with him. He hated riding the bus. He had gotten lost several times. Each time he got lost, he called me to pick him up, but I wouldn't. I told him to learn the bus routes. One morning it was raining and I heard the front door of my apartment open and close after I knew he had already left. He was back. Why? He knocked on my bedroom door and told me he had missed his bus and it was raining and he was getting soaked and could I take him to work. He was working at the State Capitol during the legislative session. He had to be at work at some ungodly hour early in the morning. I didn't sign on for all that. I dressed for work and we got into my car. I couldn't help preaching to him about his dislike for riding the bus. He looked so pitiful. I told him I was sorry he turned eighteen; I was sorry he graduated from high school; I was sorry that he had to grow up, but that he did have to grow up. I told him that I wished I could let him be a kid forever but I couldn't stop time. But what I really wished was that I could tell *myself* that and understand it. Out of the corner of my eye, I could see his fist clenching. I rumbled hard inside and I didn't hold it in. I stopped the car and asked him if he wanted to hit me? And before he could answer, I reached over and slapped him hard on his head. I was through with him. We rode in silence.

That same afternoon, he called me at work and told me he was lost again and would I come and get him. He didn't even know where he was. He had just gotten off the bus after he noticed he was back at an HEB he had already passed once on the bus route. I told him to ask someone where he was. He did and he told me. He was on the opposite end of town from where we lived but he had started out trying to get home. I wondered how he couldn't have known he was going in the opposite direction. I hung up the phone and went to find him. I saw him standing in front of HEB at Hancock Center, where the buses dropped off and picked up riders. He started walking toward the car and I passed by him. I parked my car and walked over to him. I told him I wasn't taking him anywhere. I took him to the pay phones. I made him pick up one and I picked up the other. I showed him the free number to call for bus routes and schedules. I did the same thing at the same time to be sure we both got the same information. He told me what he had found out and I pointed to the bus that was sitting right there in front of us. He pleaded with me, but I refused to take him with me. I told him he had to learn how to do this.

That evening I walked into the front door of my apartment and he was sitting on the sofa watching television. We looked at each other and I couldn't help but laugh and I did. Real hard. Earlier that day I was mad as hell at him but when I got home, it was over and it was funny. He said it wasn't funny. I said it was. Then he told me the rest of the story.

He told me he was determined to show me that he could make it but he got lost again, he figured he missed a transfer somewhere. He recognized the street name, Ben White, and knew that was a street that led to my apartment. He decided to get off and walk the rest of the way. He was miles from the apartment. I laughed harder. He kept talking. It started to rain so he decided to run to make better time but he was getting soaked. It was painful to run because that morning, while waiting for the bus he missed, he had stood in a bed of fire ants and been bitten all over his feet. He's allergic to ants. His feet were swollen. I looked at his feet and sure enough they were huge. I still laughed but I did start to feel sorry for him. He told me to wait because that wasn't the end. It was raining, he was trying to run on swollen feet, he was in pain and getting soaked, then a dog chased him. That was it; I let it go and we both had a good laugh. But the next week we had another blowup and I told him he had to go home at the end of the semester. He didn't seem like he wanted what I was offering him in life. That must have done something to him, because one night he came into my room and told me he was willing to learn. So I taught him all I knew. I bought him a car, taught him how to use a spreadsheet to budget money, opened an account for him at my credit union, introduced him to the loan officers, helped him get an apartment, gave him furniture, a television, a computer and even dishes that had belonged to his mother. But most of all, I gave him support and love. Unconditional love.

Zanovia seemed to admire my relationship with Brennan. I told her more stories about my other nieces and nephews and how I tried to help them because I wanted so much for them. I never told her that I was trying to be for them what no one was for me. I told Zanovia about my gift and that freaked her out. She didn't really understand it. One night, while I lay in my bed in my own apartment and she was across town in her condo, I visited Zanovia. I don't know how I do that, but I can. She felt me; she told me so the next day. She said it was freaky. I had never told a woman I could do that. I told her about how I could think about her and make her call me. My mother and I do that with each other. My mother calls it "zapping" me up. The whole dream/mental telepathy thing really made Zanovia uncomfortable but she enjoyed it when it helped us connect in other ways.

One Saturday, Zanovia and I attended a wedding of a couple from TOPs. Zanovia knew the groom from high school. That night I was leaving for Dallas with one of my married buddies to go to a Cowboys game the next day. Zanovia and I were at the reception, sitting at a round table with a lot of our friends when I told Zanovia we needed to get some cake, then leave. I needed to pick up my buddy and get to his mother's house in Dallas before she went to sleep. Zanovia looked at me lovingly and I leaned close to her face. She asked me if she could trust me. I calmly and honestly replied, "No." She changed. She got up from the table and walked out with one of those walks that let the entire room know I was in trouble. I followed her. We reached the parking lot and she was already crying.

I didn't want to deal with it, not there, not then. It was a deep subject for me. She started in on me. My concern was whether or not I needed to call a taxi, because we had gone to the wedding in her car. She agreed to take me to my apartment. We rode in silence. When we reached my apartment, I was so proud of her and how she approached the subject. She wanted to talk about it before I left. I agreed. She asked me why I said that. I explained that I never wanted to agree to blanket questions like that. I explained if she asked me if she could trust me to make dinner for her every Monday night at seven o'clock in the evening, then I could consider the variables of my life and determine whether or not I could do that. But if she asked me to answer a general question like that and I said yes, then the moment I did something to cause her a lack of trust in me, I would be a liar in her eyes. And from my experience, I was bound to do something that would betray her trust, so why should I lie about it? She pondered what I had said and agreed to let it go and I agreed to discuss it further whenever she wanted to. Wow! That went really well. I went to Dallas and had a great time; just football, beer and fun. But that awkward question at the wedding reception opened another door for Zanovia and me.

Zanovia was divorced. I started asking about her first marriage. What happened? He cheated and I left. Why did you leave? Because he cheated. So cheating is the deal breaker? Basically yes. I didn't like that answer. I asked her what she had learned from the marriage. She said, "Nothing." I probed and she didn't add anything else. That bothered me. I told her that a person couldn't just walk down the aisle, say "I do," and then get divorced and not learn anything. She still didn't add anything to her answer. So I presented a hypothetical to her. I told her if we were married, and she came home and told me she had slept with another man, my first question for her would be whether or not she was coming back home to me. If the answer was yes, the next question would be if she planned to continue the relationship with him. If the answer was yes, then the next question would be the same as the first, was she planning to come home to me? If the answer was yes, then we would continue to be married and deal with the situation. The next part of the hypothetical scenario was if I came home and she had changed all of the locks on the doors. Then I would leave and never return. She thought the hypothetical scenarios were odd. I explained it was all about motivation and intent. If she slept with another man because she wanted to, it wasn't about me, it was about her and I couldn't control what she did. But if she changed the locks to keep me out of my own house, then her motivation was to intentionally hurt me and I didn't want to be with anyone who wanted to hurt me. Not anymore. She pondered that and we had a great conversation about it.

Then I presented another scenario about parenting. If we were married and our sixteen-year-old daughter, Simone Hibu (e-boo), came home past her curfew, the first time she would get a talking-to. If it happened a second time, she would get an ass-beating. If it happened a third time, I would put her out and be sure to go to each one of her friends' houses and tell the parents not to let her stay with them. Because, if she could not follow the rules of my house, then she deserved to support herself without any help from anybody, family included. The childless mother in Zanovia spoke out on that subject, but I stood my ground in needing to establish rules in the house that children needed to follow. And how parents needed to support each other when trying to parent. Zanovia and I shared many conversations like that. We didn't argue, we just discussed issues. We put the issues on the table. I really enjoyed her.

On Christmas Eve we went to LaGrange to spend the night with her father. He was a nice man with a large farm. He was also a barber. We all sat around and talked before going to bed. Spending Christmas Eve with the both of them warmed me. The next morning, Zanovia and I sat around in our pajamas and exchanged gifts. Her father made himself scarce. We were rolling around on the floor in our pajamas when she looked at me and said, "Will you marry me?" I looked in her eyes and said, "Yes." We stayed in that position looking into each other's eyes. She said, "I'm just joking." I said, "Me too." She jumped up from the floor and slapped me on the head and told me I was silly. I told her that she was silly too. There was no fear in me. Wow! We discussed that exchange a few times but never committed to talking about it seriously. I did learn she wanted to have a baby by December 1998. That was a little less than two years away. When she told me that, in the back of my mind I knew Zanovia had a plan that she was executing just like me. If I was crazy, then she was too. Wow!

In January of 1997, I moved into my house, and what a house it was! It was my dream house, the one I had seen in the vision. I had bought and paid for all of the furniture two years before I moved in. My aunt in Waco had given me some antique furniture. I had put a used baby grand piano on layaway long before I knew I would even buy a house. The husband of the one of the secretaries in the firm worked for the piano company. He called one Saturday, embarrassed to tell me that the piano company had been renting my piano out without my knowledge. I called to confirm it, and it was true. They were very apologetic and decided to give me brand new piano for the price of the used one. I had it delivered the day I moved into my house. It was so beautiful sitting in the window of *my* house. I was in my first house. I couldn't believe it. It was so expensive and I could afford it. The day I moved in, Zanovia brought me a gift basket complete with a six-pack of Coronas, a gift certificate for two garage door openers, and a cast-iron skillet. She knew me too well. But I had to convince her that the two garage door openers were too much. I only took one and I paid for the other one myself.

I never told Zanovia, but when I left my apartment, I gathered everything that women I dated had given me over the years and gave it all to Goodwill, except the dining room chairs that Grace had bought for me. Years before, when I first moved into my apartment, I bought one dining chair for my birthday and put the other three on layaway. Grace pulled into the furniture store parking lot one day when I was riding with her. She took me inside and surprised me with the other three. I kept them and I still have them. Unlike our relationship, they have a lifetime warranty.

I didn't want to start accumulating things from women again and going through break-ups and having to deal with looking at all the stuff they gave me. Not in my new house. I told Zanovia all she had to do was sit down somewhere and look pretty. I had coordinated movers and furniture deliveries for the entire day. I had a system and it was working. She sat in the window seat of my kitchen reading a book. I couldn't believe all of this was happening, for me, in my horrible life. Was it changing? I remember how much she was into her book. She kept screaming and saying, "What? Noooo!!!!!" She finally told me what she was reading. It was a book by E. Lynn Harris about gay guys. I hadn't heard of him or his books. I asked her why she was reading it. She said there were a lot of guys living a double life and that's what the book was about. I didn't admit that I knew any.

She told me about some of her married girlfriends and how she knew where I was more than her girlfriends knew where their husbands were. She told me that one woman had gone to her husband's job early in the morning before he got off of the third shift. The woman followed her husband but all he did was go and park at a rest stop on the way home. I thought that it was sad that a man doesn't want to go home after getting off of work. How horrible was home? But I think Zanovia meant something else. She laughed and said that I had better not be like the guys in the book. I looked at her and said, "Yeah right." But I thought to myself, "what kind of shit is that?" I kept moving into my new house. That night after Zanovia left, I slept in the closet in the master bedroom because I didn't have anything to cover my windows. It was around two o'clock in the morning and I wanted to sleep late before starting to unpack the next day. The back of the house caught the rising sun and I knew it would wake me up in the morning. But before I lay down on the floor in the closet, I got on my knees and thanked God for my house.

The house was together in no time. The only piece of furniture missing was a dining table. I had chairs, but no table. The speaker system was great. Me, Harrell and my friend Lee had gone into the house late one night while it was in the framing stage and ran speaker wires to every room. Harrell walked up in the rafters while Lee held the flashlight and I fed the wire to Harrell and looked at the blueprints marking where I wanted the wire to go. I bought a central control system for the speakers. The house was a great party house.

After the big move I was back at work and working hard when things started to happen. I started having horrible headaches. I never got headaches. Never. Was it something that would kill me or just make me miserable? I was miserable. I went to a neurologist. He talked to me about stuff other than the pain in my head. He asked me how my life was going. About my daily routine and habits. He recommended an MRI and I agreed, but then he said two other things that caught me off guard. He told me that he wanted to inject cortisone into my head to relieve the pressure. Ouch! I didn't want a needle in my head. He showed me the needle and it was long! I was in pain so I let him do it. Then he sat down and told me I was depressed and he wanted to put me on medication. What? Depressed? What? I asked him how he came up with that. He told me it was because I couldn't sleep at night. I would go to bed at midnight, one o'clock in the morning, then get up at two or three o'clock in the morning and go jogging. He said it was a sign I was depressed. I just thought I had a lot on my mind and couldn't let it all go at the end of the day. But what I really didn't like was him throwing medication at me without more tests or something to confirm the diagnosis. I became indignant with him. I told him I questioned his diagnosis and I had already agreed he could stick a long needle in my head, but I was offended he would want to put me on medication in such a flippant way.

I left his office pissed off. I took the MRI and went for a follow-up visit. His female associate met with me to give me the results. The problem wouldn't kill me. Damn! I had an infection in the sphenoid cavity in my head and I needed strong antibiotics. I took the medication but my sleeping patterns got worse. I had always had nightmares, but now they intensified with much more detail. I dreamed that there was a dangerous tornado. In the dream I was in my little Honda Prelude. I thought I was in Marlin but I really couldn't tell. The tornado was coming and destroying everything in sight. It took my car with me in it swirling and sucking the air out of my body. I died in the dream. I woke up crying so hard I couldn't stop.

The next week, on May 27, 1997, I was sitting at a computer in the accounting department at work when my assistant came and told me a tornado had landed in Jarrell and then hit Cedar Park, both near Austin. The building wanted us to evacuate. I was a fire warden and responsible for making sure everyone on my end of the hall was evacuated before walking down the stairs myself. I didn't do my fire warden duties. Without thinking, I got my keys and went down the elevator to the garage, got in my car and headed for home. If I was going to be killed I didn't want my co-workers to be hurt. I really thought it was my time and I was okay with it. I had no thoughts of calling anybody or saying anything or writing anything. All I needed to say and do was said and done. I lay on the sofa in my new house and waited to die. The weather got real bad but no tornado came for me. But in Jarrell, many people died. It was horrific.

The dreams continued. I saw things about people that I didn't want to know were true. I saw things about people in my family that were true that I didn't want to know. I tried to talk to Zanovia about it but it made her nervous. I thought I was losing my mind. Work was simply going crazy. I thought I couldn't hold on anymore. The sitcom Harrell and I created aired on a local access channel and there was a write-up about us in the *Austin American-Statesman*. We later heard rumors from the access channel staff that it had been sent to Oprah's production company, but no one would confirm that. I wanted to hop on a plane and go to Chicago and find out for myself. But Harrell seemed afraid. Harrell and I had started writing a book the September after the sitcom was finished. I had promised myself I wasn't going to do anymore projects with him because they weren't going anywhere, and they were too emotionally and financially draining for me. But there I was, involved with him again. Darrell had moved to California with Vern after Stine died. But he and I kept in close contact via e-mail and Sunday morning phone calls. We made sure to talk to each other every Sunday morning and still do to this day. I talked to him about all that was going on in my life. It made his head swim. He started telling me I needed to see a counselor. That really pissed me off. My life got worse.

Zanovia and I weren't spending much time together because she was trying to graduate. I was devoting time to one of the legal departments at the firm, trying to help them address low productivity issues. I got so frustrated in a meeting one day, I asked them why they continued to send me to seminars and conferences to learn how to do my job better if they weren't going to listen to me? I asked how I could get them to hear me? One of the partners in that meeting said something that finally made sense. He told me he would never follow me. His words finally met up with his actions. I knew he was powerful enough to keep things hard for me and I was wearing down. I decided I was going to leave, but I didn't know what I was going to do. I had a new house, I wanted to get married, I was having these dreams, I wasn't sleeping. I was a mess. In early June of 1997, I asked the firm to pay the fee for me to attend the national conference for legal administrators. I would take care of my airfare and hotel. I needed to get away and relax and think about what I was going to do.

I spent ten days in Seattle, Washington, mapping out a business plan that would allow me and Harrell to quit our jobs and pursue our artistic abilities. I felt like the firm was going to crumble and I wouldn't have a job anyway. They didn't want to grow to support what I felt like were ever-increasing salaries and other expenses. I wanted to be ahead of the game. Especially since I knew there was trouble for me in the upper ranks. I continued to talk to Darrell about my plans and he had a lot of concerns. He kept telling me I needed to talk to a counselor. I knew my drinking and my caffeine intake had increased. I was pumping up with caffeine in the morning and trying to crash with alcohol at night. But the drinking didn't stop the dreams. Nothing stopped the dreams.

Zanovia graduated and while we were on the dance floor at her graduation party, she talked of marriage again. I tried to move it to the front of my mind.

One Sunday Zanovia and I attended the church she frequented. I don't think she was an official member, she just went there from time to time. It was a Methodist church. That mattered because I was Baptist. So I figured I wouldn't want to pay much attention to the message when I started to worry about being at church with the woman I was sleeping with. After service, we went back to my house to change and go out to eat.

It was a sunny day and my den was lit with the rays that came in through the arched windows at the back of the house. We stood by the bar that separated the kitchen from the den. I kissed her and she kissed me back, hard. We were standing there being very passionate. I could see the front door with the oval etched glass. I hadn't hung shears in the long, skinny, rectangular window next to the door. I let myself go and didn't care if it was Girl Scout cookie season or if those magazine salespeople had invaded our neighborhood. We undressed right there before my neighbors and God. Sex was very satisfying with Zanovia. She was comfortable with her body and sexuality. Sometimes when I climaxed, I liked to just lie inside of her while she pulsated my very being. We stumbled toward the sofa in front of the fireplace, but we didn't need its heat. I lay on my back looking up at her beautiful body. She smiled down at me and went for the core, the center of my being, and I looked at the ceiling feeling the warmth of her mouth. Then something happened. It was like the flash of a camera kept going off in my head. The fear returned. I shriveled up between her lips. I wanted to run. I wanted to hide. But I just pulled her to me and held her and told her that we shouldn't be doing that, not on a Sunday, not right after church.

She knew how I struggled with my faith and my sexual desires. She didn't question me. But something was very wrong. I tried to explain it to Darrell and I think he understood. But he just kept telling me I needed to see a counselor to help me deal with all of the changes taking place in my life. That was an insult to the "me" I had created. Besides, if everything crashed and burned and I failed, I had a backup plan that was perfect. It was a win-win deal for me. I kept going.

Early in July of 1997, I announced to the firm I was leaving and I was giving them six months' notice. That would give them time to think about how to approach replacing me and allow me to help the new person through the most difficult part of the job, year end. July 25, 1997, I was home alone drinking rum and coke and thinking about marriage. I walked around the house talking to myself. I played songs on the piano and thought about what I was about to do. I took off my shoes and walked in the backyard barefoot while I thought about what to do. I looked up at the heavens and asked God what I should do. I took a small yellow Post-It and wrote down the words, *I want to marry her. But can I?* I called Darrell and left him a message about my wanting to marry Zanovia. That night I went to bed and asked God if I should marry Zanovia. I didn't expect an answer so quickly.

The next morning, I was going about my normal routine. I was about to step into the shower when I heard the answer to my prayer as audible as any human has ever spoke to me. The answer was, "No." It was clear and unquestionable. I looked up at the ceiling. I asked God why. But there was no answer to that. For days, I asked, "Why?" And still no answer. Did I really hear no? Or was it just my fear speaking through my own mind? Was I losing my mind? I decided to ignore God's answer. I wanted to get married and have children. During one of our usual Sunday morning phone calls, Darrell listened to me whine about Zanovia and how I wanted to marry her and how I was even more confused because of the supposed answer from God. He surprised me with a new approach to his old recommendation. He suggested I consider seeing a professional coach. A what? A professional coach. He explained that a friend of his was doing it and it was the new rage for professionals like me. Darrell explained that a coach could really help me. I bought into it. I bought into it so well, I thought if I could find a person with coaching skills, marriage counseling skills and a perspective on God, I could kill three birds with one stone. As long as he knew that the coaching was the priority and the other things were just gravy. I took out my health insurance provider booklet and of course didn't see a list of professional coaches. So I decided to look under general counseling. I found someone and called him. I left a message and he called me back. I talked about wanting a coach and the other things I needed. I was so amazed when he told me that not only did he provide coaching, he also did marriage counseling. Then I nearly fell out of my chair when he told me his next qualification; he had a Master's of Divinity with a specialization in the Baptist faith. Wow! I made an appointment.

I was surprised he could see me so quickly. I was in his office the next day, Tuesday. Before I went, I made myself promise to follow his lead and to be brutally honest about what he wanted to know about me. It was expensive and I shouldn't waste my money. I had never done anything like that before and really didn't know what to expect other than what I had seen on "The Bob Newhart Show." I didn't even know people who had been to counseling. I told Zanovia I was going, and I even told her I was thinking about marriage and I needed to talk it out with somebody. She understood. I thought a woman would ridicule me and I fully expected her to do that. Another bonus point for Zanovia.

I arrived at the coach's office feeling weird, trying to act brave and nonchalant. A tall man in his late fifties opened the door. I remember thinking how uncool he was because he wore slacks and sandals with socks. He invited me to take the sofa or one of three chairs in the office. Sofa? Not me. I sat in a puffy chair and swung my leg over the arm. He pointed out things in the room like a plastic blow up bat, a bear and other stuff he used to help people in the sessions. I thought all of it was stupid. I didn't need any of that stuff. I just wanted him to fix me so that I could start my own company, get married, have babies and get rich. He told me about himself and his background. He was a recovering alcoholic. Then how in the hell could he help me? But I listened. He asked me what I expected from the sessions, and I told him about quitting my job, wanting to get married, the dreams and my relationship with God. He told me we would do some basic work in the beginning but we would start with me telling him about me, about my life.

I didn't know where to start so I just dove right in. I didn't get three sentences out before I started crying. I didn't know why, but I cried and I couldn't stop. I cried for almost forty minutes. Our time was up and I hadn't gotten a chance to say much and what I did say was muffled by the tears and snot. It was awful. What had he done to me? He told me that I needed another session and soon because there was something wrong. I agreed to go back that same week.

It happened all over again. I cried and cried for thirty or forty minutes. He closed the second session by saying that he thought that I shouldn't ask Zanovia to marry me until I had dealt with what was making me so sad. Deep down, I knew he was right and I agreed with him but I didn't want to. I wanted to get married and have babies. I wanted Zanovia.

I was avoiding Zanovia and trying to focus on work. I had a lot to do in six months. I was already getting calls about my new business. Zanovia knew something was wrong. She knew I was pulling away from her. She wanted to see me. One day, I went to her condo. She was distant. We sat on her sofa quietly. No music, no television. She had made a list of questions for me. She read them off and I answered them. I told her that I, that we, needed to take a break until I figured out what was going on inside my head. She started to cry. Her tears fell on the deadness of my life. She asked why. I didn't want to see her cry. She asked me how I could be so much for so many other people and not be what she needed me to be. If I could feel, that question would have hurt. She recounted my relationships with my family and especially with Brennan. I told her I needed to figure out what was going on inside my head. I asked her to wait for me. She said she didn't want to wait. I looked at her. I was confused and empty. I stood up. I wanted a hug from her. She stood and put distance between us. I walked toward the door, opened it and stepped out onto the sidewalk. She held the door and looked at me, then told me to be sure the next time I said I loved somebody. She closed the door, and since that day, I have only seen her once. She met another guy, and a year later, on the schedule she had set for herself, she had a baby by him. They didn't get married.

Hey Robert, would you? Tell her how you know me?

Winston was my supervisor at Short, DeFreeze, Goers & Close from '94 to '96. He and I stayed late at the office one night to set up for Christmas and had a few beers. To make a long story short, I drank one too many and got myself in trouble. This is the event I believe that drew us closer. Winston and I began hanging out primarily at bars and just talking about everything from work to our personal lives. He has given me advice throughout a number of hardships in my life, and he has confided in me regarding his own troubles. How would I summarize Winston? That's a bit tough, but let me use some descriptive words:

- *Spiritual*

- *Brutally Honest*

- *Distant*

- *Result-oriented*

- *Ambitious*

You see, Winston is primarily driven by his spiritual beliefs. If you are not a God-fearing Christian, then you might as well move on. His belief in God is very important to him, and he requires this in a soul mate. Secondly, he is very honest. He will tell you what he's feeling if you ask him. Winston is very good at holding back how he feels about someone if it will be confrontational. I think he doesn't really like to get into confrontational situations unless he has to. This is where the "distant" characteristic comes from. I couldn't really think of a better word, but you'll find that sometimes you have to probe to get certain feelings/opinions out of him. You see, that's why we're here right now. He wants to just lay it all on the line and see how you feel. He feels that his lifetime mate MUST know everything about him, but it's almost impossible for him to do that himself. So he's just running you by people he knows. Winston definitely has a past, but he's not an evil person by any means. In fact, he's probably the most kind and sincere person you'll ever meet. Being kind and sincere doesn't mean he won't dislike certain things about you or others. He'd just rather be honest than act like something doesn't bother him. He wants someone who can accept him despite his faults and love him unconditionally. He will definitely return the favor. Another thing about Winston is he is very methodical in his approach to problems. You need to have the ability to discuss problems, lay out an action plan and execute that plan. That is the way he approaches all his problems. He will drive you crazy if you can't do that. This is typically a good characteristic, but it can be tough if you tend to avoid problems in relationships. If you can communicate effectively with Winston and be able to confront emotions/problems head on then you will be fine. A relationship with Winston is very rewarding, but people sometimes get offended because they can't face the uglier truths in life. Winston likes the truth, the whole truth and nothing but the truth. You have to be that way too.

Robert Lafleur
Austin, Texas

And last but not least, my brother, Darrell, would you? Tell her how you know me?

Hi Lee Lee, nice to meet you. Just joking.

Let me tell you about the man you may be planning to spend the rest of your life with. I first met Winston when my dad brought him home in a cigar box. He lowered the box for me and my other brother to get a peek at the latest arrival. . . . There is no point to this at all . . . just wanted to share.

Winston is very sensitive . . . he puts up a hard front in the company of others only to impress them and give them a sense of his confidence . . . but when alone, he seeks every opportunity to pour out his soul if he feels close to you. . . . Don't crowd him, or tell him what to do or not to do . . . he's a control freak and he must be in charge or feel that he is in charge at all times. When you threaten his control, he feels challenged and backed into a corner and may fire back with anything, regardless if it makes sense or not. He tends to over-analyze and over-rationalize everything . . . and is confused about his spirituality and sexuality. He doesn't want to disappoint God, but refuses to let himself live life to the fullest because in a way, he feels guilty if he's indulging in himself too much and he will start flogging himself. Don't be afraid, just listen and embrace him in his fears and sorrows until he comes out of it. This may take a few days but he will resurface . . . and start the cycle all over again.

Welcome to Winston's cycle of hell. He is very moody, especially when things are not going according to his universal plan—college, good job, money, wife, two kids and a dog, nice car and family— when he jumps on that track, get off at the next station and come back in a few days.

We love our brother . . . so treat him with kindness, don't let him have the upper hand always because he is used to having it and will try to dominate every minute all the time. Show him you have a spine . . . bite when he barks. . . growl when he frowns . . . don't let him see the fear in your eyes.

And love him . . . please love him. He needs you more than you will ever know.

Aubrey Darrell Williams
Kansas City, Missouri

The End,
So I Thought . . .
I Executed the Backup Plan

Chapter Thirty-six

Whew! I sit here on this cement sofa, working with the counselor in my head, trying to repackage myself, trying to touch the silver box, trying to go all the way. Back here in the place where the storm started brewing years and years ago. The storm that took everything I had. I knew it was brewing out there, in the back of my mind, but I didn't pay attention. I just let it go on. I thought I could outrun it or outlive it or outsmart it. I never thought I would ever have to weather it. And now, I don't think I am weathering it very well. The foundation that I had built on was weak, unsteady and unable to withstand the storm. I am sitting here in the darkness of my life. The sun fell out of the sky a long time ago. And now, there is no bright moon on the horizon. No stars. No little holes poked in the darkness to let the rays of light through. No hope. I am back in this dark place.

There is one good thing about being here now. I know how to move on. I know how to be free. Free to learn. Free to love. I just have to tell the truth. I may be drunk. I may be tired. I may stink of beer and cigarettes. I may be damp from the tears and the snot of my life. But even with all of that, I am still me. Nothing more. Nothing less. Just me. And any woman will have to take me just as I am. For better. For worse. For richer. For poorer. Until she can't stand me anymore and files for divorce. Yes, I have also come to know that I can never be married unless I know that divorce is an option. What kind of psychology is that? I have to embrace the very things I ran away from. I have to embrace the very things I tried to prevent from happening in my life. Trying to avoid divorce didn't allow me to get married. It kept me from it. Sorry, that's just the way my brain works. I can't fight it. This has been an excellent session. I have made a lot of progress in repackaging me. The label is just about complete with all the necessary information that the buyer needs.

Chapter Thirty-seven

You just made some good observations.

Yeah, I did, didn't I? So? What next?

Are you finished?

I kind of thought *you* would tell *me* when it is finished.

Well, knowing what I know about you so far, I don't think you are.

I didn't think you would. So what should I say next?

Tell me more about your counseling sessions.

I had hoped that seeing the counselor would give me a quick fix so I could move on with life, but he wasn't giving me the answers that I needed or wanted. All in all, it was sort of like talking to you.

Me?

Yeah, you.

How so?

He would say a few things or ask a few questions, then, I would talk a lot. Just like you, he was a counselor.

Is that who you say I am?

Yeah, who do you say that you are?

Me? I just am, who I am.

Whateva . . .

Go on.

I couldn't believe I was seeing the counselor. Not the professional coach. Not the theologian. But the counselor. And not even for marriage. But for me. For my life. I couldn't believe how much I had bought into the purpose of seeing the counselor before I even made the first appointment.

I remember thinking of the money. It was so expensive, it would have been a waste of time and money not to get the most out of it. I convinced myself of that when I thought I was going to be coached. I've always wanted a "coach" in life and never found one no matter where I looked. So now that I was going to pay for one, I had better utilize him to the fullest.

I was embarrassed to have to pay someone to be a father, a brother, a minister, a friend . . . to listen to me, to care about me. What kind of psychology is that? I knew there was stuff I shoved way in the back of my brain. The flashes in my head when I lay on the sofa with Zanovia were proof of that. But I didn't know how it affected me. Before my first meeting with the coach, I struggled with how much to tell him. What would he think of me? Would he give me that disapproving look? I could tell him things to make him beam, but that would only be half the story. I bought into the truth wholeheartedly. That's why I cried the first two times I saw him. I hadn't cried for myself in a long time. I am a man. Men are strong. We don't let water come from our eyes. We fight it. Hold back the tears. But I couldn't hold them back this time. They had to come out.

The third time I met with the counselor, he opened the door just like the first two times. He was so uncool. He invited me in and we exchanged pleasantries. I sat in the same chair and again I put on my confident act. I sat in the same position with my leg over one arm of the chair. A masochistic part of me wanted to recreate the first two visits, to re-feel the feelings so I could explore them further. Even though the first two visits were in the same week as the third, I didn't take time to think about what had happened inside that office after I had left with tissue in hand. I filed the first two visits away in the back of my brain until the third visit. It worked. He talked to me. Asked me questions. And I did it again. I began to cry. This time I told him why.

Through the tears, I looked at his large socked and sandaled feet. I shifted my position and moved my leg from over the arm of the chair. I planted both feet on the floor, but they seem to dangle in the air as the chair swallowed me. No more pretending. I was not confident. I didn't know what I was. But I was going to try and find out. I hadn't figured out I should bring my own handkerchief, so I continued to empty the box of tissues he provided.

My chest heaved up and down, in and out. The tears poured from my eyes. I fell backwards inside my brain. I kept falling until I was eight years old. I needed to speak but I couldn't find my voice. I found comfort in the socks and sandals. That combination was a cardinal sin to an eight-year-old. A major fashion boo-boo. Kids who did that were nerds and geeks. I was better than them. I didn't wear socks with sandals. I began to speak.

I told him about the summer day when me, Harrell and Darrell went to spend the day at the old Booker T. Washington Wildcat gymnasium. We had all gone to that school before it was closed. I only went there for first grade before transferring to a different school. So I followed in their footsteps in that respect too. By the time I was eight, it was used for after-school and summer programs and some other stuff too. Having a day to just play instead of fitting in play around work was a treat for us. We set out to have a great time. On one side of the gym, there were concrete bleachers high above the basketball court. On the other side there was a huge stage with heavy, thick, gold curtains that were controlled by a heavy rope. You could get lost in those curtains. The stage also had thinner curtains that ran parallel to the side and back walls of the stage. On each side of the stage, there was room behind the thinner curtains big enough for a lot of people to stand and not be seen from the stage area. Each side also had doors that led to a flight of concrete stairs down into large rooms. These rooms had windows near the ceiling of the gym. The rooms also had doors that led to the gym floor where you would find yourself standing at either end of the basketball court. It was a beautiful old place. I loved being there. For the summer programs, they would put a trampoline on the stage of the gym. The more dangerous kids would bounce high into the rafters and do all kinds of acrobatic tricks. Others of us would play it safe and do simple flips and enjoy our ability to soar.

On this particular day, there were a lot of kids around. I made my rounds, playing in the curtains while I waited for my turn on the trampoline. Harrell and Darrell stood with a bunch of other kids at the side of trampoline along the back wall facing the concrete bleachers across the basketball court. The screams of all the kids created an amazing echo throughout the gym. Fun! Fun! Fun! Then . . .

I didn't even see him coming. He came out of nowhere like a thief. He grabbed me, threw me across his shoulders and carried me across the stage with everybody watching, even Harrell and Darrell. He held my legs as I kicked. I pounded his back as he walked. I yelled for him to leave me alone. No one did anything. It was like they didn't even care what was happening to me. He took me behind the thin curtains. No one was there. It was not where all the fun was happening. He threw me on my back on the floor. I looked into the horrible face of Male Cow. What did he want with me? Why was he doing this to me? My insides told me my life would change forever at that very moment. His sinister smile told me nothing. I looked into the rafters. The water poured down both sides of my face. I heard the screams of the other kids having fun. They couldn't hear my screams. Or could they? Did anyone care? No. I didn't matter to anyone. No one paid attention to me. I was just another kid at the end of the line. Marching. Left-right. Left-right. So why even fight? I don't know what Male Cow was doing, but even as an eight-year-old kid, my body responded. I turned my head to the left, toward the curtain with the trampoline on the other side of it. I could see the feet of the other kids and hear their voices. I closed my eyes and died.

Are you okay?

I'm dizzy. This is too much. I can't take it.

But you need to go on. This is why you are here.

I'm sick.

The pain. The searing, horrifying pain. Remembering it now, here in the darkness, on this cement sofa, remembering it then as I looked at the socks and sandals. And being there when it happened. The counselor told me to go ahead and continue to let the tears flow. He told me that there was a little eight-year-old boy who needed to let the tears flow. He told me the eight-year-old boy had never grieved for himself. Psychobabble! I guess I didn't expect the counselor to have such a generic statement for me. The socks and sandals fit him. But I was determined to plunge forward. I had never told anyone that story. I told him that I died that day and hadn't lived since. I told him I know I had faked my entire life trying to endure the pain of that day. I told him that ever since that day, I wanted my physical body to be where the emotional me was. Dead. Every day since that day, I had contemplated suicide. He asked me if I had ever acted on those thoughts. Truth. I had to tell the truth. I had bought into this process and it would not work without the truth. The answer was yes.

I told the counselor that since I was eight years old, all I ever wanted to be was dead, physically. I never made plans for life because I knew I wouldn't be around to live it. I wished for some catastrophic illness to take my body away. And all the time, I knew that if I didn't die of an illness, I would do it myself. It was just a matter of time and courage. I told the counselor about being ten years old and trying to run away from home. Miz Minnie saw me and took me inside her house. She talked to me and told me to go home. I don't know if she ever told my mother or father. They never said anything to me about it. But after I returned home, I went into the kitchen and took out my mother's favorite butcher knife. The same knife Darrell used to terrorize me. She still has it and uses it to this day. First I held the black handle with both hands and pointed the long sharp blade toward my naval. Then I thought for a second and moved it toward my heart. That would be more effective. I pressed real hard but couldn't make the knife break through my white t-shirt. Then I put the butt of the handle against the kitchen counter cabinet and steadied it with both hands. I thought I could throw myself against it. But I couldn't. I just couldn't do it. But I wanted to, so bad. The pain of life was just too great.

Male Cow started coming into my parents' restaurant more. He would wait for me to take his order. That fucking sinister smile of his. Fooling my parents. Give the customers what they want. Couldn't they see what was happening? Male Cow would pay for his order, then slyly grab my hands when I gave him his change. Over time, Harrell and Darrell saw what was going on. They even saw when he blew kisses at me. That's when they added the "moooo" to my regimen of daily torture. I was already dead. I just hadn't been buried yet. But every time Harrell and Darrell said "moooo" to me, they heaped a shovel full of dirt on top of me. These were my brothers, my family, and they were helping to bury me alive. They told me Male Cow was going to get my booty.

I told the counselor about the time Stine took me, Harrell and Darrell swimming. I was slow putting on my trunks in the changing room. Male

Cow came in and cornered me. I don't even remember what he did or said. I blanked it all out. The next thing I remember is being in the pool, but I didn't want to swim anymore. Life wasn't about me. I had to get in the water. I splashed around trying to act normal. Doing the few strokes I had learned. Holding my breath underwater. Trying to have fun. But at the same time trying to keep an eye out for Male Cow. He appeared out of nowhere, he always appeared out of nowhere. He grabbed me and I started to fight in the water. Stine, Harrell and Darrell saw him with me. They watched as he forced me to go to the deeper end of the pool. The end where my feet had no chance of touching the bottom. The end where I couldn't stand on my own. He kept saying he was just going to teach me how to swim. He said it aloud so that Stine, Harrell and Darrell could hear him. He kept rubbing his hard body against mine. I had nowhere to go but inside my head and even there I was left with the darkness of death, left in place from the first time he had grabbed me. Again, even at the age of ten years old, my body responded. I didn't know what was happening to me. He pinned me against the side of the pool in the deep end. He pressed his body against mine. I cried aloud. I cried for help inside my head. But no one did anything. I felt like the other kids in the pool, including my own family, thought I was being a sissy. He told me he would drown me if I didn't stop crying and if I told anybody what he was doing. He was going to kill me. I told the counselor how at that time, my life had even less meaning. To me or to anyone else. I didn't matter. That was my life. Things went that way for two more years after that. Harrell and Darrell were relentless in their teasing. I walked through life dead.

I told the counselor that by the time I was twelve I was so tired. I was so alone. One weekend my sister Vern came home to visit from Houston. She had dealt with her big blowup with my father and had settled into her own life. She brought my mother's brother, Uncle Jack, home with her. She had bought a beautiful little blue Camaro. I wanted to be big and take care of myself. I would sit in her car and pretend I was grown and on my own. I sat on the passenger side of her car marveling at its beauty and wishing for a life I didn't have. I opened the glove compartment and there it was. A .38-caliber pistol. I knew this was my chance. My chance to end it all. I took the gun out of the glove compartment and held it in my right hand. I placed the gun to my temple. I don't remember what happened but my physical body was still walking around. That's when I found myself sitting in church listening to Rev. Sanders talk about Jesus raising Lazarus from the dead. I wanted Jesus to raise me from the dead. But he didn't.

I told the counselor about Windsor and how I helped him at a time when I myself was contemplating killing myself. Windsor didn't know, but my words to him helped me stay alive a little while longer. Then there was Mike. The night I helped him through his bout with suicide, I had actually planned to fill my parents' 1977 canary yellow Ford LTD with the brown top with gasoline, drive real fast toward a brick wall and light a match just before impact. I was sure that would do the trick. But then Mike needed me to help him stay alive.

Then, there was June 1993. I was at the end of my rope again. I was so miserable. I couldn't feel. I couldn't love. I relived my childhood each and every day. And each and every day, I would think of how I could kill myself. All I could do right was work. Grace and I were over. I had made it through an almost devastating attempt at self-employment. I had rebounded financially. But I just couldn't take it any more. My parents' wedding anniversary was June 17th. As a gift, I gave them round trip airfare and hotel in Las Vegas. The news spread through the family quickly. Someone had the bright idea we should meet them in Las Vegas. It was a welcome diversion for me.

We began to plan the trip. Harrell, his wife and two kids and I would rent a van and drive to Arizona. Darrell would fly from San Jose and Linda's son would fly from Los Angeles. We would all go to the Grand Canyon, then drive to Las Vegas. And we did. In all, there were twelve family members who met in Las Vegas for our parents' anniversary.

We saw the jousting tournament at Excalibur. We saw an Andrew Lloyd Webber musical. We had a great time. No one knew I had deemed that trip as my farewell tour. I would have a chance to say good-bye in style. When the trip was over, me, Harrell and Darrell returned the same way we had come and I made it a point to do all of the driving. I wanted time to get my nerve up to kill myself when I got back to Austin.

The plan was pretty much the same as when I was in college: gasoline in the car, driving toward the wall and lighting the match. But my parents' 1977 canary yellow Ford LTD with the brown top was long gone. That was the year I had prayed for a new car for my thirtieth birthday. At the time I prayed for it, I didn't know how I was going to buy a new car, but I definitely wanted one. One night, after leaving a TOPs event, I sat at a red light waiting for it to turn green. When it did, I proceeded on my way home but a car came out of nowhere and broadsided me. Sent me and my Cutlass Supreme spinning around in the intersection. My head hit the driver's side door window and broke it. When I came to, a young girl was running to my car cursing me for running a red light. I was so dazed, I thought I had actually caused the accident until a passerby came and straightened out the story. The girl was a drunk college student. I was in a neck brace for weeks. It was strange working for a law firm that did defense litigation for insurance companies and having to deal with plaintiff attorneys that they despised. My car was totaled. That's how I got my 1993 Honda Prelude. My second dream car, just a few months before my birthday. But dream car or not, I had no problem using it to kill myself.

We dropped Darrell and our nephew off in Arizona and I continued to drive. Harrell offered to give me a break, but I had a lot of thinking to do. It was late in the night when we reached somewhere outside of El Paso, Texas, along Interstate 10. Everyone in the van was asleep. There was no music. Just me and my thoughts. I was sure I was ready to leave this earth. I was sure I was ready to kill my physical body. I knew I didn't want to hang myself. I knew I didn't want to cut my wrists. I didn't have access to pills strong enough to do the trick. I only had pain pills from the car accident. Yes, gasoline, brick wall and a match was the way I was going to do it. I just had to find a brick wall that wouldn't give way. Would it be a building? Would it be a bridge wall or support beam? Minor details. Would it hurt? Would I feel it for long? A small amount of pain for an eternity of relief. I thought I could deal with that. As I drove along Interstate 10, I played it over and over in my head. Gaining confidence in the idea.

I suddenly noticed the beauty of the night. There was lightning far off in the distance over the mountains on either side of the interstate. I smiled.

Each time the lightning came, I could see the outline of the peaks. It was simply amazing. A tear came from my right eye. My nose began to run. I held back the sadness of my life. I didn't want to disturb Harrell and his family. I returned to my thoughts of death. That's when the Voice spoke to me. I heard it clearly.

"You are not going to kill yourself."

"Yes I am!"

"No, you are not," the Voice said.

"Why not?" I asked.

"Because you have things to do," it proclaimed.

I was more upset about the subject of the conversation rather than the fact that there was no one there. Who was this speaking to me? Had I lost my mind? Was this God? It didn't matter. I had my mind made up and I was not about to change it. And if it was in fact God or even one of His agents, why did He bother to come to me now? Where was He when I needed Him? I rumbled inside. I felt my temperature rise and it dried the water that had gathered in my eyes and the snot that had begun to clot my nostrils.

"What do you mean, I have things to do?" I shouted inside my head. I could see an image of myself standing, looking toward heaven with both hands clenched in a fist and the right one raised up to God.

"You have to care for your parents." The Voice said calmly. It didn't seem fazed by my rumbling.

I had a comeback. "My parents have six other children still living. Why do I have to be the one to care for them?" The discussion was over. I was going to ignore the Voice. The Voice didn't provide an answer. It just made another statement.

"You are not going to kill yourself."

"Yes I am," I responded, stubborn.

"Then I'll prove it to you," the Voice said.

"Prove it to me? How?"

"Your parents are going to be in an accident."

Did I hear the Voice correctly? It said that my parents were going to be in an accident.

"This is between you and me. Why are you messing with my parents?"

The Voice was gone. It didn't answer me. I didn't ask again. The conversation was over. Even though I had the last word, I knew I hadn't won the argument.

I drove beyond the lightning on toward Austin along Interstate 10. I continued planning and tried to forget about the conversation with the Voice. After twenty-three hours of continuous driving, we arrived in Austin around eight o'clock Sunday morning. Harrell helped me return the van and I made it to my apartment with barely enough energy to climb the three flights of stairs. I dropped my bags by the door and didn't bother to unpack. I lay down fully dressed to go to sleep.

The phone rang. It was a friend of mine from high school, Lawrence. Lawrence and I had been friends since the fourth grade. Lawrence was tall with a strong physique and very athletic. In high school we seemed to part ways for a while as he did the athletic thing and I did the academic thing. But after high school when I went to college and he went into the navy, our friendship picked up again. We would hang out when he was on leave. But why was he calling me now? He was on deployment somewhere in Spain. Rota, I think. Lawrence noticed that I sounded groggy but that's not why he asked me how I was doing. He said I was on his mind.

Even though we were friends, I never really let Lawrence into my life. Like everybody else, I kept him away from me for fear of him finding out. But Lawrence had an uncanny ability to call me right at my most desperate moments. Yet at those times, the irony is, his calls were never about me. He would call when he wanted to discuss life. One of my favorite topics, although I wasn't living. I told Lawrence I was okay. He asked me if I was sure. I confirmed. Even though I was tired, I wanted to talk to him. What he told me next made me shiver. He told me that after all the years of me talking to him about God, he had finally decided to read the Bible and had found that God wasn't so bad after all. I wanted to cry. My life! My miserable dead life! How could I tell people about a God that I didn't even like? How could I tell them about a God that had let me down so miserably? Was I that good of a liar? Was I that good of an actor? The enthusiasm in Lawrence's voice angered me. He was still my friend and I wanted to talk to him but just not right then. Not about his revelation. But I let him talk and I encouraged him, never letting on about my life, my death. As was typical with Lawrence, when he was finished talking, the conversation was over. He said a quick good-bye and hung up.

I lay there, on the floor in my apartment, still fully dressed and totally tired. About an hour after I finished talking with Lawrence, the phone rang again. Fortunately I had put it next to my head so it was easy to get to. I answered it. It was Vern. She lived in northern California in small town called Salida. She hadn't been able to meet us in Las Vegas. I thought she was calling to see how the trip went. But she sounded somber. She asked me if I was okay. I said yes. Then she said she had some bad news. I braced myself. She told me Mom and Dad's flight had made it to Austin safely. Uncle Bill, Daddy's brother, had picked them up from the airport. But about twenty-five miles outside of Marlin, Uncle Bill had a wreck. Mom and Dad were both taken to the hospital in Temple, but they were back at home. I was silent. Vern tried to determine if I had gone into shock. She kept asking me if I was okay. I told her I was fine. She asked me what I was going to do. I told her I was going home. I had a job to fulfill. She seemed confused by my reaction. I put my suicide plans out of my head and returned to my pretend life of confidence and added responsibility.

I arrived home to find my father with a huge bump over his right eye and my mother with a sprained wrist and bruised face. I held back the rumbling I felt for the Voice. I had no tears to shed for my parents. But my mother was upset. She told me she felt like God had punished them for going to Las Vegas. I told her no, their accident was a message for me. I could tell she didn't understand and we never discussed it again. The counselor didn't understand my gift.

I told the counselor how strange it was that every human being who had encountered me from the time I was eight years old never knew that when they were looking at me, talking to me, laughing with me, making love to me, inside my head . . . I was dead. In each moment of each day I was trying to figure out how to kill my physical body. My counselor asked me if I still felt that way. Truth? Truth. The answer again, yes. He asked me if I would promise to talk to him before I did anything like that again. I looked at his socks and sandals again. Who was he? Why did he think I would talk to him? For all I knew, he really didn't care either. For all I knew, he was just like the rest of them. Being the honest person I had been beaten into becoming, I told him I wouldn't promise that to him. He pressed the issue, but I resisted by changing the subject. I wanted to talk to the theologian now, not the counselor. I asked him to explain to me why God would let that happen to me, His child. If I could just understand, I knew things would change. I wanted definitive answers about my Creator. He had no answers, at least none that gave me peace. Only psychobabble. I returned to my conversation with the counselor and left the theologian alone for a while. We discussed my future sessions, but I was less committed than when I first called him.

I continued my sessions twice a week for months. We talked a lot. I came to admit out loud that I hated myself. I came to understand that my self-hatred was the reason I couldn't love anyone else. I admitted out loud that I didn't know why my body would respond to Male Cow's sadistic acts. But still, the questions I had for the counselor were not followed by concrete answers. I had been programmed to have faith but that faith wasn't enough. It didn't help me live. I told him about the neurologist and his diagnosis of depression. The counselor agreed with the neurologist. I felt bad for having been so rude to the neurologist. The counselor wanted me to see a psychiatrist and obtain a prescription for anti-depressants. I refused. I didn't want a drug to put me in la-la land. I wanted to deal with the problem head-on. He talked to me about my drinking and defined alcoholism for me. I didn't think I fit into that category, but he suggested I attend AA meetings anyway. He had told me he was a recovering alcoholic and if I attended a particular group meeting he suggested, I would probably see him there. I couldn't believe I was getting counseled by an alcoholic who wore socks and sandals.

One day the counselor gave me a sheet of paper with three long columns of words. He explained that each word represented a feeling. He asked me to look at the words and tell him which ones I could identify with. I tried real hard to pick out words but I made myself tell the truth. The only word I could identify with was sadness. That saddened me more.

The sessions were making me deal with some tough issues, but I still had a mortgage to pay, my own company I was starting, a business venture with my brother Harrell and the entire other life that I had created. Life was too busy to deal with all of that at the same time. I continued, but I really struggled. The sessions brought about an awareness of the many "me's" I had created. There was the social me the professional me, the religious me, the family me, the dating me and the me that I was when I was all alone. They were so distinct and functional in their different environments. The sessions also added a new dimension to the dead me and the created me. Paranoia. I was more paranoid than ever that people were going to find out I was in counseling and worse, that I was in counseling for having been molested, and even worse, that being molested caused me to question my own sexuality. Why did my body respond to such sadistic acts? I was so young. What was wrong with me? I heard a report on television that said sometimes when people experience a trauma like I had, they become schizophrenic. They create different personalities to deal with the trauma. I asked the counselor if he thought that I was schizophrenic. He assured me I was not. I was not confident in his answer.

When did the molestation end?

When I was about twelve.

What happened?

I don't know why children can't talk to their parents. I don't know why I did it the way I did it.

What did you do?

I made up a lie.

A lie?

Yeah, a lie. One day I had had enough, but for some reason, I couldn't tell the truth. I pulled a lot of unconnected information from the back of my brain and made up a lie. I got my parents together and told them that Male Cow had chased me down the tracks behind the Snack Center near Granddaddy's pasture, near Blackie's house. I told them that I ran as fast as I could on the train rocks. I told them that he chased me and kept yelling that he was going to get my booty. In my mind, I can't see my parents' faces. I can't remember them hearing me. But inside my head, as I told that lie, it became a reality for me. It's as though it really did happen. And because the lie became reality, over time, I started to question whether any of it actually happened. And now, I just don't know.

I'm crazy.

You're not crazy.

I am crazy. And I'll never be sane.

Believe what I say to you. You are not crazy. You are human. You are normal!

How can I believe anything anyone says anymore? You were there, you knew what was happening to me and you wait until now to talk to me? Why? Can you please tell me why? Why didn't you love me enough to protect me?

We all love you. You have to believe that. Keep going. Tell me what your father did.

I don't know. But it stopped almost immediately. And to this day, my father and I have not spoken about it. But it has haunted me every day of my life. I thought my Father would help me, but . . . here I sit.

Keep going.

New Year's Eve 1997, I sat alone on the large rocks I had placed underneath two tall trees in the beautiful backyard of my dream house. I have never been one to make New Year's resolutions. Typically, I just reflect on the past year, assess it and make plans for the coming one. I sat on the rocks where Zanovia and I had made love one warm summer night beneath the moon and the stars. I reflected on the many losses and changes of the year gone by. Zanovia was gone. I reflected on my revelations and admissions in counseling. I asked God to bring all of the "me's" together and make me whole. One me, who could face the world and tell the truth. One that could say, "Yes, that happened to me" or "Yes, I did that." I knew in just a few days, I would be in business for myself again and I would have to hustle to make it work. I had enough clients already, enough money in the bank and a backup plan if I failed. The New Year came. The sky above the neighborhood lit up with fireworks. I was alone. I cried for myself.

January and February of 1998 were exciting months for me in my new business venture. I had tons of work and I was enjoying it. But at the same time, the last months of 1997 were haunting me. The counseling sessions had not coached me at all. The sessions had made me face things I had buried deep inside of me. I even started to notice how much time my subconscious thought about death. I realized that while reading, watching television, driving down the street, listening to music, during lulls in conversations, I was always thinking about what Male Cow did to me and how I wanted to kill my physical body. It was too much for me to deal with. Several times my new company required me to miss my counseling sessions. I rumbled inside because I had agreed to pay for sessions that I didn't cancel within a certain time frame. Money was too precious to me, being self-employed and all. By March, I was not going to counseling anymore. I tried to forget about my new revelations and simply go back to the "me" I had created. At least until my business was up and running. But I couldn't. I had opened the door to my past and I had to go back. Even though I didn't want to. I had no choice.

I found myself not being able to concentrate. I took days off from work and convinced myself that it was a reward because I was the boss now. My schedule and projects were flexible. So I got away with it. Oddly enough, my business increased very quickly. I was months ahead of my own projections. By April, I knew I needed help. It was time for Harrell to come on board. Harrell didn't know anything about my counseling sessions. But Darrell did. I hadn't told either one of them how the way they treated me had hurt me so bad. I was afraid of losing them if they knew how much they had hurt me. I invited Harrell out for drinks and told him about my progress in business and told him that he should consider coming on board by May. He told me no. What? Did he say no? I think that's what I heard him say. He told me he had been thinking about it and that he just couldn't put that kind of pressure on me to provide for his family. What? I explained to him that I had money in the bank and I was confident the business income was stable for the rest of the year. And if anything happened after that, I had enough money to take care of us both until we found other jobs, if we had to. He said no. He had been in business with Stine before she died and he had suffered too much behind that venture.

I sat with him, thinking, why in the hell didn't he tell me all of this before I quit my job? Why in the hell did he keep sucking me into these ventures if he wasn't going to follow through with them? Why in the hell was he even in my life? I was devastated. I had made major changes in my life to pursue something with my brother. Something I believed in. I believed in his work more than I believed in myself. And he was throwing it all away. His words, facial expressions, everything about him seem to pour out anger toward me. I went home and sat alone, wondering what I had done to turn him against me. Why had he done this to me? He was my last hope for something meaningful in this world and he didn't even know it. I couldn't tell him how much I was banking on his work, his screen-plays, his writing, to help me have a purpose in life. I thought maybe he would change his mind. During April and part of May, I tried to convince Harrell to change his mind and he seemed to become angrier and angrier with me. I left him alone. I was still very busy and needed help, so I hired someone else. My first full-time employee. Then a second, a part-timer.

My new employees were great. I was lucky to have both of them. But by June and July, I was spending more and more time unable to get out of bed in the morning. My work suffered greatly. I knew it, but my clients were not able to tell just yet. I transferred as much work to my new em-ployees as possible while I tried to figure out what to do. I thought about going back to counseling but I chose not to. I knew what was happening. I was headed back to suicide. I called Harrell and told him I needed to talk to him. We went to my favorite Chinese restaurant on South Lamar. Over lunch, I told him that I had been depressed a lot. He immediately told me that I had nothing to be depressed about. He told me how bad his life was and that I had everything. He didn't even let me tell him what I was depressed about. All he kept referring to was all the friends I had, all the traveling I did and all the money I had. He had no idea what I was going through. I rumbled inside so loudly that it exploded out of my mouth. I growled at him and asked him couldn't he at least let me explain myself before he told me how I should feel? He growled back. That day we caused a scene in the restaurant. But I needed my brother to under-stand my pain. I didn't give up on him.

One night in August, I invited Harrell over to my house. We drank beer and stood in my backyard and smoked cigarettes. After we laughed and talked about stuff happening in the world, I told him that I was still having trouble getting out of bed some days. He started in on me. He ridiculed me for being depressed. I told him it didn't matter what he thought, the fact was, I was depressed. I told him I had been in counseling. He ridiculed me more for having paid somebody to tell me what I should already know. I told him it didn't matter, the fact was I had been in counseling. I told him I just needed him to listen to me and not say anything. Just listen. He told me he wasn't going to just listen to me without giving his opinion. He told me that was just like me: I never wanted to hear anybody else's opinion. He left my house that night without hearing me. That was it. It was over. We had been working on writing a book together and it had been a hard thing to continue after all we had been through. But I finished the book and delivered it to his doorstep and walked away, not wanting to deal with my brother any more.

September 4, 1998, I sat in the atrium of the Radisson Hotel in downtown Austin. I was meeting with the owner of a consulting company. He had more work than he could handle and hired me and another consultant to be a part of his team. This was another dream come true, to be a part of a consulting project outside the scope of my own line of business and learn new areas of consulting. When the meeting was over, the other consultant and I stayed to have drinks and talk. Her name was Belinda. Belinda was a beautiful woman I had known for years. She was a singer and poet and was studying for her CPA license. She had been an actor in the sitcom Harrell and I had produced. She was as talented as she was beautiful. We laughed and talked and sipped on our cocktails. The conversation turned to gay men. She told me about a family member who had been close to her before he came out of the closet. I don't know why, but her words made me so paranoid. As if she was telling me the story because she knew I had been molested. The conversation made me very uncomfortable. I wanted to run but had nowhere to go. At that moment the storm in my life was in full force. It had been brewing since I was eight years old. I had seen the warning signs and even tried to take cover, but nothing was sheltering me from being beaten and battered by it each and every day of my life. So I decided to succumb to it. I decided that September 4, 1998, was the day that I would die.

That evening I went to the grocery store and bought two packages of sleeping pills. I went to the liquor store and bought a bottle of rum. I hadn't planned this out very well but I didn't care. I was going to do it. I went home and paced around my beautiful house. I played one last song on my baby-grand piano.

There is a fountain
Filled with blood
Drawn from Emmanuel's veins
And sinners plunge
Beneath that flood
Lose all their guilty stains

In my final hours, I concluded that suicide was just a sin like any other and my friend Jesus would forgive me and finally welcome me home.

Did you try to commit suicide?

You know I did! You were there! You've been there from the very beginning! I know who you are!

What?

Don't play any more games with me. Why do you do me like this? You have all of the answers and you won't just tell me. You brought me back to this god-forsaken place. And I know why!

If you know why, then you know what you have to do.

Yeah, tell the rest of the story.

Then tell it. Say it. Out Loud. Finish it.

I drank and drank and drank. I wanted the alcohol to help me go to sleep forever. I paced outside of my house in the backyard and remembered the parties, the good times. I talked to God and told Him I would see him soon. Then He could tell me what the hell he'd been doing to my life.

When I was good and drunk, I collected all of the pain pills from the car accident, the neurologist and the hernia surgery along with the over forty pills from the packages of sleeping pills. I placed a pot of water on the stove, I brought it to boil and watched it, convincing myself to move forward with the backup plan I had created years ago when I created the new me.

See, all along, I was able to be adventurous in my career and take on the things that I had no idea how to do as long as I knew that when I failed or simply got tired, I could just kill myself. I had an image of me in my head. I was the man on a high wire, dazzling the crowd below performing tricks that no person with my limitations should be able to perform. My trickery didn't scare me because I had a safety net. That net was suicide. My performance had come to an end. I fell. I failed. It was time for my physical body to meet the "me" that died when I was eight years old. I took a yellow Post-It note and wrote on it: *It's not about you, it's all about me. Love, Winston.*

There was no turning back. I moved with comfort and ease. Once the water was boiling, I measured out a glass three-quarters full, poured out the water I didn't need, then poured the glass of water back into the pot over the gas eye. I took all of the pills and put them into the water to melt down. I was just making it up as I went along. I thought if the pills were already dissolved, they would get into my bloodstream quickly and more effectively. All of the pills dissolved. I poured the concoction into the glass. Looked at it. Looked at the note and decided that it said enough. I drank the concoction just like Tracey had taught me years ago, in one gulp. I walked to my master bedroom and lay in bed and waited to go Home.

What's wrong? Why are you stopping?

I can't breath. There's no air here!

There is air. Just breathe.

I can't. I can't do this. I can't keep going through this! I can't tell this story! Who would want me?

But you must! This is why you were born!

Why are you doing this to me? I tried to be everything you wanted me to be! And it wasn't enough for you! . . . I can't breathe . . . I . . . can't . . . breathe.

Lie down. It's going to be okay. Catch your breath.

This cement feels cold. It feels like a morgue. It feels good.

It's not the morgue. You are going to live and live abundantly. Just finish what has been assigned to you, so you can begin life anew.

I fell asleep but could feel I was still alive. It was a strange feeling. I began to feel like I was hovering above my body. I couldn't move, I couldn't speak, I couldn't see. I mentally told my spirit to go Home, it was okay.

I can't do this! It hurts too much! I'd rather die than do this!

You have to do it! I can feel your pain. You want to cry. Let yourself cry. It's okay! Keep going!

After a long, long time, I could feel the warmth of the sun on my paralyzed body and could see the redness of light from behind my closed eyelids. But my soul still hovered. I knew the sun had come up. It was

Saturday. I was still sinking and that was good but my spirit just wouldn't let go. I started mentally pushing my spirit away from my body. Trying as hard as I could to send it Home. I felt something pushing back. Something was pushing my spirit back into my body! This battle continued fiercely until Sunday night. The entire time I was still paralyzed and blind. I lost the battle with suicide. In the wee hours of Labor Day, Monday morning, I regained feeling in my arms. I flipped myself over and drug myself onto the floor. I pulled myself by my elbows to the master bathroom on the ceramic tile. I was sick to my stomach. I'm sick now! I want to throw up!

No, you're not sick. You are in pain. I feel your tears. They are wet, they are salty. I feel your body shaking. Let it all out, this is good for you! But keep on going! Just let it all out.

Once I reached the tiled floor, something came up out of me that was dark, green and plentiful. The bile from my body flooded the bathroom floor. I lay in it for an entire day. By Tuesday evening I was able to walk at a slant. I had managed to call my employees and give them their assignments for the day. I struggled to clean up the mess I made and continued to regain my strength.

That was the storm that led me to losing everything. I lost the beautiful life I had built on a shaky foundation.

That's it. I made it.

Yes you have. It is finished.

Thank you. I understand now.

Sorry for the path, but it was yours alone to travel. Good job.

I have run the good race. I have touched the silver box. The storm that once raged has passed. Now I can sleep. My journey back home has established a strong foundation for the rest of my life. I have finally told the truth. That is what will appear on my new and improved packaging. From now on, I will tell every woman the story, then ask her: Now that I've told you all that, would you marry a man like me, or at least give me a second date?

THE END

EPILOGUE

What if God only created 143 paths of life? What if every soul ever born on this earth was given one of the 143 paths to follow? That's what I feel about this story, about my life. As a child I could see my path and I tried what I could not to follow it. Does that make prophecy true? The path I was given and the results thereof are common. But I didn't know it until . . . until I wrote it . . . until I spoke it.

Is silence the great defeater? Is fear its coach? Are untruths the reality and truth the myth? Is peace forever evasive? Is turmoil our daily bread?

What if we had a love amnesty day? What if February 15th was declared a worldwide day of honesty when all truths could be told without consequence? Could we change our path? Could we find peace? Could we change prophecy? Could we defeat silence?

There is still more to tell . . .